THE
ALL-BREED
DICTIONARY
OF
UNUSUAL
NAMES

Gloria S. Jarrett

1988
Alpine Publications

ISBN 0-931866-32-4

This book is available at special quantity discounts for breeders and for club promotions, premiums, or educational use. Write for details.

Printed in the United States of America.

CONTENTS

To Charlie, Mom, and "the guys"

PART I

DICTIONARY OF UNUSUAL NAMES, WORDS AND PHRASES

UNUSUAL NAMES, WORDS AND PHRASES

Where do registration names come from? Everywhere! The names, words and phrases included in this section can be found amidst a wide diversity of subject matter. They are words of color and magic, heraldry and music, weapons, warriors, fairy tales and folklore; creatures of the heavens, the earth, and the seas; royalty and rogue, food and drink, rules of etiquette and points of honor; the good guys and the bad guys, the pursuits of theater and art, precious gems and fancy ornamentation; sailing jargon and soldier-talk, virtue and vice, occupations nice and nasty, drinking toasts and saloon games, warm greetings and parting curses, famous pirates and pilots and patriots; and the lexicon of Aussies and Englishmen, Germans, Italians, Spaniards, Swedes, Frenchmen, Irishmen, Scots, Greeks, Russians, Rumanians, Czechs, Chinese and inhabitants of the Congo. They are exclamations, expletives, expressions and oaths, biology and botany, astronomy and astrology, science, geology, history, metallurgy, and literature. They are cities and rivers and mountain ranges; trees, flowers, kings, queens, costumes, sailing ships, sea shells, doves, fireworks, outlaws and romance.

Though they differ widely in subject matter, they do share something in common...their uncommonness! The really good names, the unforgettable names, are the unusual names. Remember that, like the best gems, *the brilliance is in the rarity!*

When choosing a registration name, this dictionary allows you to find *one* special word or name that will set your animal's name in cement. Instead of "making-do" with complications of common words, the best registration names come from the simple (but unusual) word, or name, or phrase paired with your kennel name. From the pablum of the show catalogs, every now and then such an extraordinary name appears; and although we all differ in our tastes, there is no doubt that such "unique" names cause us all to pause. Remember that there is always more beauty in *simplicity!*

Dog catalogs list especially interesting names. The silver and black German Shepherd they call WITCHGRASS, the Kerry Blue named CAPE SMOKE, the creme-colored Afghan that floats before her critics is listed as AIRS AND GRACES, and I would like to meet the little Fox Terrier they call PEPPER'S DRAGOONS. Somewhere is the English Setter they list as BRITTANY BLUE, and make room for the Landseer Newfoundland they call SHIVER ME TIMBERS. The little Skye they call SAILOR'S PLEASURE is, indeed, a pleasure to watch, and a Cocker named HONEY SHUCKS is melting the crowd. ESPIRITU is an Italian Greyhound and fine as porcelain, TROLLERI is the sweetheart of an Irish Wolfhound who took group, and LACEWOOD is a Bichon puppy making waves at her first show. There is a beautiful Bull Terrier just waiting his turn, and the catalog calls him BROTHER BLADE. A harlequin Great Dane glides past your chair and you turn the pages until you discover that his name is as head-turning as his presence, for they know him as TEN BONES. There is a commotion over at Ring 6 and flying down the mat is a gorgeous Borzoi, and with a round of applause GIN AND JAGUAR takes breed. The fantasy continues with: SUEDE, HELLKITE, CANNELURE, DEVILSHINE, HUNTAWAY, TRIBESMAN, SHENANIGANS, RIPRAP, LITTLE STEPS, HAGBORN, FEMINIE, GYLLENE, MILLRACE, QUIZAS, WOODS WITCH, TUVALU, FLYING COUNTRY, DAMZEL, BLIXTRA, CHAVI, ERMINE STREET, FALLEN TIMBERS, FALCON-GENTLE, JAMAICA BAY and NO MANS LAND. The names stand alone. Their wearers need no further introduction. The dog...and the name...one-of-a-kinds in the world of duplicate copies. And although someone else may put their kennel name in front of the *good ones*...we retire the *GREAT ONES*!

Read though the DICTIONARY slowly and thoughtfully. Make the correct pronounciations of a new word and study the meanings for those of particular relevance to your situation. The secret of the really great names is *simplicity!*

A

ABACUS *(AB-uh-kiss)*	oriental math reckoning table that uses sliding balls
ABANDONED HABITS	riding clothes worn by young ladies in 1900s Hyde Park
ABBACY *(AHB-us-see)*	an Abbot's office, territory, or term
ABBONDANZA *(ahb-ahn-DAHN-tsah)*	Italian for "abundance"
ABERTILLERY *(AHB-er-TIL-ery)*	a mining town in W. England
ABNAKI *(AHB-nahk-ee)*	a member of the Algonquin Indian Tribe
ABOLITION *(AB-uh-lish-uhn)*	the act of abolishing
ABRACADABRA *(ab-ruh-cuh-DAB-bruh)*	a cabalistic word/spell
ABRAHAM-SHAM	one who pretends to be ill, or poor, etc.; a fake
ABRASAX *(ABRA-sax)*	a man's name; a magic word used to summon spirits
ABRAZAR *(ah-brah-SARH)*	Spanish word meaning "to embrace"
ABSENT WITHOUT LEAVE or AWOL	absent from military duties without permission
ABYSSINIA	the former name for Ethiopia
ACAJOU *(AC-uh-zhoo)*	name of the cashew tree of tropical America
ACCOUNTS RECEIVABLE	monies that are due from one's business customers
ACEY-DEUCY	a variation of the game of Backgammon
ADARA *(uh-DAH-ruh)*	an Arabic girl's name
ADOETTE *(ah-doh-AY-tuh)*	an American Indian girl's name, "tree spirit"
ADMIRAL OF THE BLUE/ ADMIRAL OF THE RED/ ADMIRAL OF THE WHITE	British fleet officers in one of the three, 18th century squadrons
ADMIRAL OF THE FLEET	the highest rank an officer can hold in the US Navy
ADMIRAL'S REGIMENT	the nickname of the British Royal Marines
ADMIRALTY BAY	a harbor in the South Shetland Islands

ADVANCE GUARD	troops sent ahead of a column of soldiers to act as scouts
AEOLIAN *(EE-oh-LEE-uhn)*	Greek, meaning of the wind
AFGHAN TURKISTAN	the old region of Turkistan/NE Afghanistan
AFFAIR OF HONOR	a duel that results in an innocent man's death
AFINA *(ah-FEE-nah)*	the Rumanian for blueberry; also a girl's name
AFLAME	something that is flaming or burning
AFOGNAK *(uh-FOG-nak)*	an island in the Gulf of Alaska (north of Kodiak)
AFREET *(uh-FREET)*	a giant demon found in Arabic folklore
AFRICA SPEAKS	a very strong liquor made in South Africa
AFRIKAANS *(AF-ri-kahnz)*	the language of South Africa
AFRIKIYA *(afra-KEE-yuh)*	the Arabic name for Tunisia
AFTER-DINNER MAN	someone who is an afternoon tippler (drinker)
AFTER IMAGE	a phenomenon where a "visual" remains after the actual image is gone
AFTON *(AHFF-ton)*	the Swedish word for evening; used as a popular girl's name
AGLIMMER	something that glimmers (as in "all aglimmer")
AIDA *(igh-EE-duh)*	the Italian word for happy; a Verdi opera
AIGRET *(AY-gret)*	a tuft of feathers, or gems, worn in a head-dress by royalty (particularly the Indian maharajahs)
AILA *(IGH-luh)*	an Anglo-Irish girl's name, meaning "light bringer"
AIR EXPRESS	sending cargo by airplane or jet
AIRGLOW	the faint lights (aurora) sometimes visible in the atmosphere
AIRS AND GRACES	a colorful slang term for faces (rhyming)
AISHA *(AH-ay-shuh)*	an Arabic girl's name (Mohammed's favorite wife)
AIYANA *(igh-YAH-nah)*	American Indian girl's name meaning flower
ALAMANCE *(allah-MANS)*	headstream of the Cape Fear River in North Carolina

ALAMEA *(ah-luh-MAY-uh)*	a Hawaiian girl's name meaning precious
ALANA *(ah-LAH-nee)*	a Hawaiian girl's name meaning orange
ALAQUA *(ah-LAH-quah)*	an American Indian girl's name; also "sweet gum tree"
ALCANZAR *(ahl-kahn-SAHR)*	the Spanish word for to attain or to reach
ALDEBARAN *(al-DEB-er-ehn)*	a bright red star in the Taurus constellation
ALEUT *(ALL-ee-oot)*	a native of the Aleution Islands in SW Alaska
ALGIERS *(al-JEERZ)*	the capital city of Algeria (on the Mediterranean)
ALHIM *(AHL-heem)*	an occult word that is used for the "pentagrams of fire"
ALICE BLUE	a pale blue color (named after Teddy Roosevelt's daughter)
ALL BRANDY!	something that is wonderful (a 1900s expletive)
ALL CLEAR	a signal (siren) to say that the danger (storm, etc.) is over
ALLEGIANCE *(uh-LEE-jehnce)*	loyalty or devotion to a cause
ALLEANZA *(ahl-leh-ANG-tsah)*	the Italian word for alliance
ALLEGRIA *(ahl-leh-GREE-ah)*	the Italian for fun or mirth
ALL IN THE WIND!	a saying used to describe something puzzling/confusing
ALL-NIGHT MAN	a "body snatcher" (an Old English term)
ALL OF A DOODAH!	World War II British (RAF) usage for trainees who developed a case of mid-air nerves
ALL THAT JAZZ!	an expletive for "all that sort of thing"
ALLELUIA LASS	during World War II the servicemen nick-named Salvation Army canteen girls this
ALLEZ OOP!	an expletive uttered when helping someone up onto something
ALOHA *(ah-LOH-hah)*	Hawaiian word used as both a greeting, and a farewell
ALOHILANI *(ah-LOH-hee-LAH-nee)*	Hawaiian girl's name, "bright sky"

ALSKA *(ELL-skah)*	Swedish for to love
ALSKAD *(ELSK-ahdd)*	Swedish for beloved
ALSKARINNA *(el-skar-IN-nah)*	Swedish for mistress
ALSKLING *(ELSK-ling)*	Swidish for sweetheart
ALZUBRA *(ahl-ZOO-bruh)*	a tiny star in the Leo Constellation
AMAKNAK *(uh-MAK-nak)*	a small island in the Aleutians
AMARELLA *(AHM-uh-rell)*	a type of cherry used in pies (pale-red and sour)
AMATIGNAK *(ah-muh-TIG-nak)*	a small island SW of the Aleutians
AMAUI *(uh-MOW-ee)*	Hawaiian girl's name, "little brown bird"
AMAZONAS	another name for the state of Brazil
AMAZONIA	the regions that border on the Amazon River
AMBERJACK	a feisty game fish found in tropic waters
AMBIANCE *(AHM-bee-ahntz)*	an atmosphere of wealth, grace
AMBLER	one who ambles when they move (a sort of rolling walk)
AMBOISE *(ahM-bwahz)*	town in France that served as home for Valois kings
AMBRIZ *(am-BREEZ)*	a seaport in NW Angola, Africa
AMBSACE *(AMZ-ace)*	lowest throw of dice (double aces, #2, bad luck)
AMBUSCADE *(ahm-bus-kade)*	the one who is in hiding for an ambush
AMEER *(ah-MEER)*	designation for any Arabic prince
AMERICANA	anything that deals with America (antiques, folklore, etc.)
AMERICAN BEAUTY	the famous, purplish-red, American Beauty Rose
AMERICAN ELK	the large, deerlike, Wapiti
AMERICAN ENGLISH	the English language as it is spoken in America (as opposed to British English)

AMERICAN PLAN	when a hotel guest pays his bill on a daily basis
AMERICAN SABLE	term used for the soft, thick brown fur of the Marten
AMERICA'S CUP	famous yachting race between an American yacht and a qualifying yacht from another country
AMERICAN REDSTART	common bird (warbler) of the Eastern US forests (black with salmon/orange patches)
AMERICAN WIDGEON	common wild duck (it has a white crown and apricot chest)
AMERICUS	a city in Sumter County, Georgia
AMICIZIA *(am-mee-CHEE-tsee-ah)*	Italian word for friendship
AMIDSHIPS *(uh-MID-ships)*	halfway between the stem and the stern of a ship
AMOURETTE *(AHM-or-ette)*	French word meaning a trifling affair of love
AMSEL *(UMM-zel)*	German word for blackbird
ANCHOR MAN	a person you depend on to carry the load; dependable leader
ANDROID	a synthetic man (the "humanoid" science fiction creation)
ANFALLA *(AHNN-fahll-ah)*	Swedish word for to attack
ANGEL WING	a lovely, lacey variety of begonia
ANGENI *(ahn-GAY-nee)*	American Indian girl's name, "angel"
ANGUS OG	the mythical Irish god of love
ANICKA *(ah-neesh-kah)*	a common Czech girl's name, "graceful"
ANITRA *(AH-nee-trah)*	the Italian word for duck
ANKA *(uhn-KAH)*	the Turkish word for a "will-O'the-wisp"
ANLACE *(AHN-lis)*	a 2-edged medieval dagger
ANTIOPE *(an-TEE-opie)*	a princess of ancient Thebes
ANZU *(AHn-dsuh)*	the Japanese word for apricot
AOLANI *(ow-LAH-nee)*	a Hawaiian girl's name, "cloud"

APACHE DANCE	the French duet dance where the woman is wildly tossed
APACHE PLUME	a low shrub of the American SW having white, plumed clusters
APE-MAN	another name for the missing link; common term for extinct primates
APERTIF *(uh-PEAR-uh-teef)*	the liquor/wine served before a meal
APOCALYPSE *(uh-POCK-uh-lips)*	Revelations, last book of the New Testament, the end
APONI *(ah-POH-nee)*	American Indian girl's name, "butterfly"
APOLLYON *(uh-POLL-yun)*	an angel of the bottomless pit (Hell)
APOPKA *(uh-POP-kuh)*	a city in central Florida
APOSTLE *(uh-POSS-uhl)*	a person setting out on a special mission
APPALACHIA	refers to the regions of the Appalachian mountains
APPANOOSE *(AHP-uh-noos)*	a county in Iowa
APPARITION *(ahp-uh-RISH-uhn)*	a spector, phantom, or ghost
APPASSIONATO *(ahp-pahs-see-oh-NAH-toh)*	Italian for passionate
APPLADERA *(ah-plo-DAY-rah)*	Swedish for cheering
APPOMATTOX	a town in central Virginia (east of Lynchburg), site of the Confederacy's surrender
APPELLO *(ahp-PELL-lo)*	Italian for appeal
APPLE AMBER	a Scottish apple pudding dessert that has a meringue top
APPLE-JACK	a brandy made from apple cider
APPLE JOHN	a variety of apple that is at its best when allowed to age
APRIL GENTLEMAN	slang for a newly-married man
APRIL FOOLS	April 1st teasing; someone easily duped (an innocent)
APRILI *(ah-PREE-lee)*	African name given a girl born in April
APRIL SHOWERS	the rains of early Spring

AQUAVIT *(AWK-wah-veet)*	a strong Scandinavian liquor
AQUILI *(AK-wee-luh)*	a northern constellation of stars called the eagle
ARABY *(AIR-uh-bee)*	the poetic spelling of Arabia
ARBITRAGE *(AHR-buh-trazh)*	profit from a pricing mistake (usually upon receipt of securities)
ARCADIA *(ar-CAY-dee-uh)*	a region of idealistic contentment
ARCANE *(ar-KANE)*	a secret thing; something shared by only a few
ARCHANGEL	the celestial beings next in rank above the angels
ARCHON *(AR-kahn)*	a heavenly creator, or ruler; subordinate to a god
ARCO IRIS *(ARR-ko EE-reess)*	Spanish for a rainbow
ARCTURUS *(ark-TOOR-us)*	a giant red star in the Bear constellation
ARDILLA *(ahr-DEE-lyh)*	Spanish for squirrel
ARGENT *(AHR-jent)*	anything silver, or silver-colored
ARGOT *(AR-go)*	the language of thieves and rogues
ARGOSY	general term for a medieval merchant ship (or fleet of them)
ARGUS	the mythical Greek giant that Hermes killed (he had 100 eyes)
ARIEL *(ah-ree-AYL)*	the Hebrew word for lioness
ARMADA *(ahr-MAH-dah)*	Spanish for navy
ARRIBA *(ah-RREE-bah)*	Spanish for above
ART NOUVEAU *(ar NEW-vo)*	French for new art; it refers to the 19th and 20th century art direction that used curve, flow, and plants
ASGARD *(AZ-gard)*	in Norse mythology it is the residence of heroes slain in battle
ASHKHABAD *(ahsh-kah-BAHD)*	capital of the Turksmen (on the Russian border with Iran)
ASSAGAI *(ASS-suh-guy)*	the light spear used by African Zulu tribesmen

ASSAULT AND BATTERY	the legal term for commiting physical violence upon another
ASSUMPTION *(uh-SUMP-shun)*	that which can be assumed
ASTRAKHAN *(ASS-truh-kahn)*	down-soft pelts of very young lambs found in Turkish Astrakhan
ASYLUM *(uh-SIGH-lum)*	a place of refuge or retreat (an insane asylum)
ATTABOY!	an expletive for "go it" (from "that's the boy")
ATTORNEY AT LAW	the proper address for a lawyer
AUF WIEDERSEHEN *(owf VEE-dehr-say-hen)*	German for good-bye
AULD LANG SYNE	popular song (sentiment is: "the good old days long past")
AULII *(OW-lee)*	a Hawaiian girl's name meaning dainty
AU SABLE *(OH SAY-b'l)*	a river in North Central Michigan
AUSSIE RULES	in Australian football the game is played with Australian Rules
AUSTRASIA *(ahs-TRAY-zhuh)*	an eastern dominion near the Meuse River in the Bohemian forests of Europe
AVALON *(AHV-uh-lahn)*	literal French is "Island of Apples"; and coming from the Celtic belief that fallen battle heroes were delivered to this island paradise after death
AVIATRIX	a female pilot/flyer
AVANT-GARDE *(ah-VAHNT-gard)*	French for advance guard; leaders of new or unusual movements (usually "arty")
AVKASTA *(AWV-kahs-tah)*	Swedish for yielding
AVSKAHFFA *(AWV-skahff-ah)*	Swedish for to abolish
AWENITA *(ah-way-NEE-tah)*	Indian girl's name for fawn
AXMINISTER	a town in England (or the lovely cut pile carpets they make there)
AYASHA *(IGH-ish-ah)*	a very common Muslim girl's name (Egypt, Persia, etc.)
AYLETTE *(igh-LET)*	a French girl's name meaning sea bird
AZIMUTH *(AHZ-uh-muth)*	a measurement of distance (in degrees) from North or South points

AZIZA
(ah-ZEE-zah)
an African girl's name, "precious"

AZRAEL
(AZ-ray-ell)
the angel who separates a spirit from it's earthly body at the moment of death

AZUL
(ah-SOOL)
the Spanish word for blue

B

BABASU
(BAH-buh-soo)
a Brazilian palm tree

BABE IN THE WOOD
an innocent or naive person; one with sweetness of manner

BABE OF GRACE
a sanctified-looking person; innocent or without sin

BABU
(bah-BOO)
A Hindu gentleman

BABUSHKA
(buh-BOOSH-kuh)
a slavic head-covering tied under the chin; term of endearment for a grandmother

BABY BLUE
a light, pale blue shade

BABY-BLUE-EYES
term of endearment; a California shrub with blue flowers

BABY BUNTING
term of endearment; first line of a favored nursery rhyme

BABYLONIA
(bah-buh-LONE-ee-uh)
the ancient Tigris/Euphrates kingdom

BABY'S CRIES
a colorful slang word for eyes, (rhyming)

BABY TALK
baby gibberish; the cooing nonsense spoken *to* babies

BACARDI
(buh-CAR-dee)
a famous brand of rum distilled by the Cuban Bacardi family

BACCARAT
(BAC-uh-rat)
french card game of chance, played for high stakes

BACCIO
(BAH-choh)
Italian for to kiss

BACK ALLEY
any alley located in a notorious part of town

BACKFIRE
a fire started by forest rangers to stop an onrushing fire

BACK O' THE GREEN
a theatrical term for behind the scenes

BACK ROADS	an unpaved country road; the rural part of an area
BACK TALK	to argue; impudent contradiction
BAD AXE	a city in East Michigan (south of Saginaw Bay)
BAD BLOOD	feelings of hostility
BADLANDS	barren, unhospitable, desolate areas of eroded hills and gullies in South Dakota (east of the Black Hills)
BAGATELL *(bah-gah-TELL)*	Swedish for a trifle
BAGHDAD	a province in South Central Iraq
BAHAMA BANK	two areas of shoal water in the Bahama Islands (the LITTLE BAHAMA and GREAT BAHAMA banks)
BAHIA *(bah-EE-ah)*	Spanish word for bay
BAISER D'ADIEUX *(bez-ZAY de AD-jew)*	French for a *farewell kiss*
BAIT 'N SWITCH	a con scheme where an advertisement lures customers; then a salesman sends their focus to more expensive items
BALANIKI *(bah-lah-NEE-kee)*	Hawaiian girl's name, "pretty one"
BALBRIGGAN *(bal-BRIG-uhn)*	a seaport town on the NE coast of Ireland
BALDACHIN *(BOL-duh-kin)*	a rich silk and gold brocade fabric
BALDERDASH! *(BOWL-dehr-dash)*	expletive for nonsense
BALLADEER	someone who sings ballads
BALL OF FIRE	an energetic person who strives for success; a dynamo
BAMBINO *(bahm-BEE-no)*	Italian for child or infant
BAMBOLA *(BAHM-boh-lah)*	Italian word for doll
BANCO *(BAHN-koh)*	the Italian word for bank
BANDICOOT	an Australian, ratlike marsupial
BANDIERA *(bahn-dee-EH-rah)*	an Italian word for banner or flag
BANDMASTER	the conductor of a brass band

14

BANDOLEER	a militaristic shoulder belt carrying additional ammo
BANGKOK	the capital city of Thailand
BANJOEWANGI *(BAN-you-WANG-ee)*	seaport on the Bali Strait, East Java, in Indonesia
BANJORINE *(ban-jer-REEN)*	musical instrument like a banjo but tuned higher
BANSHEE *(BAN-shee)*	Gaelic folklore hag who visits a home with wailings to foretell a coming death
BANTU *(BAN-too)*	tribe of African natives in the southern Sahara
BANZAI *(BON-zigh)*	Japanese shout of honor; literally "10,000 Years!"
BAPTISM OF FIRE	a severe ordeal experienced for the first time
BARBARIAN	a person of little culture, uncivilized and savage
BARBIZON *(BAR-buh-zon)*	village in N France famous for art schools
BARCELONA *(BAR-suh-LOH-nuh)*	a province in Spain
BARGHEST *(barr-GUEST)*	a doglike goblin that foretells misfortune
BARKEEP	a bartender
BARLEYCORN	a grain of barley
BARMAID	a waitress who serves alcoholic drinks
BARN DANCE	a country dance or gathering held in a barn
BARNSTORM	a traveling flying circus that visits county fairs
BARONAGE	the rank, or dignity, of a baron; and his realm
BARONET	the next ranking office below the baron himself
BARTHOLOMEW BAYOU	a river in SE Arkansas and NE Louisiana
BASHI-BAZOUK *(BASH-uh buh-ZUUK)*	an irregular Turkish soldier; lawless
BASKERVILLE	an English printer/typesetter; also, "The Hounds Of ..."
BARN-BURNER	anything remarkable or sensational
BARRIO *(BAH-ree-yoh)*	Spanish for neighborhood
BASHAM *(BAH-shuhm)*	a Gypsy boy's name meaning born of the earth

BASTON *(bahss-TOHN)*	the Spanish word for cane
BATTLE CRUISER	a large, easily-manuevered warship
BATTLE ROYAL	a very furious fight to the finish
BATTLESHIP	a class of heavily gunned and armored warships
BAUDRONS *(BAWD-runz)*	an Old Scot word for a cat
BAUL *(BALL)*	a gypsy word for snail
BAYOU	a marshy inlet of the South US
BAYOU BLUE	cheap and inferior bootleg whisky
BAZAAR	a street full of shops common in the Middle East
BAZOOKA	a modern, tubelike, weapon used to fire rockets
BEACHCOMBER	a "shore hobo" who scavenges the beach for a living, or one who combs the beach for shells
BEAMISH	something radiant, or beaming with light
BEARCAT	a fierce person or animal
BEAR GARDEN	the scene of a fight
BEAR-PLAY	rough and noisy behavior from children
BEARWALLOW	a famous mountain peak in Yancy County, western North Carolina; any depression in the earth where animals can roll in mud or soft earth to rid themselves of insects
BEASTIE	an Old Scottish word for a little beast (though used endearingly)
BEAT THE BAND	doing something with flash, excessively or intently
BEAT THE RAP	being acquitted of a legal charge; escaping punishment
BEAT THE STREETS	to walk up and down; to pace back and forth
BEAUX-ARTS *(bo-ZAR)*	French word for fine arts; music, sculpture, etc.
BEAUCOUP *(bo-KOO)*	French word meaning much
BEAU GESTE *(bo-ZHEST)*	French for fine gesture
BEAU IDEAL *(bo I-deal)*	French for ideal beauty

BEAU MONDE *(bo-MAHND)*	French for fashionable society
BED AND BOARD	accommodations consisting of a place to sleep and meals
BEDEW *(bi-DOO)*	when something becomes lightly damp (as with dewdrops)
BEDFELLOW	someone who shares a bed; someone's bedmate
BEDLAM	a place of noise and confusion; Bedlam was originally the other name for St. Mary's Hospital For The Criminally Insane in London
BED OF ROSES	the perfect comfort or luxury; a state of blissful contentment
BEDRAGERI *(beh-drag-eh-REE)*	Swedish word for a fraud
BEDROCK	solid rock that lies beneath the soil's surface
BEDTIME STORY	a story told to children at bedtime
BEEFEATER	a slang term for an Englishman; a famous brand of gin
BEES WING	the filmy crust that forms on the surface of great old wines
BEFALLA *(beh-FAHLL-ah)*	the Swedish word for to order
BEFORE THE WIND	a nautical term that serves to mean well-placed/prospering
BEFRIA *(beh-FREE-ah)*	the Swedish word for to free
BEGORRA(H)!	an Anglo/Irish expletive; it means something like "good heavens!"
BEHEMOTH *(buh-HEE-muth)*	any huge animal or thing
BEHOLDEN!	any feelings of gratitude, or owing thanks
BEJABBERS!	an exclamation of surprise
BEL-ESPRIT *(bell es-PREE)*	a person of culture
BELGRAVIA *(bell-GRAY-vee-uh)*	a fashionable residential district in London's West End
BELLEZZA *(bell-LETS-tsah)*	the Italian word for beauty
BELLY DANCER	a person who performs an exotic, hip-rolling dance of the Near East
BEL-SHANGLE	Old English word for clown or buffoon

BELTANE	the Old Scottish name given to May Day
BELL THE CAT	when someone undertakes a very hazardous mission or task
BELLS DOWN	the last peal of a chapel bell, used as a warning notice
BELVEDERE	any "handsome fellow" (after Apollo Belvedere, a London playboy)
BELZONI *(bell-ZOE-nub)*	a small city in western Mississippi
BENEFIT OF CLERGY	getting married by a preacher instead of a Justice of the Peace
BENGAL BLANKET	refers to the sun, or a very blue sky
BENGALI *(ben-GAHL-ee)*	a person who is a native of Bengal
BENZI *(BEN-zee)*	popular Israeli boy's name; the shortened telescoping for Ben Zion ("excellent son")
BERGAMOT *(BER-gub-mo)*	any of several plants in the mint family
BERSERK and BERSERKER	a violent warrior found in Norse Mythology; a furious fighter who could take the form of a wild beast
BESANCON *(buh-zabN-SOHN)*	a city in eastern France
BESS O'BEDLAM	an Old English term for a person who acts irrationally
BETE NOIRE *(bet NWAR)*	literally "black beast"; French term for anything to be disliked or avoided
BETROTHAL	the act of betrothing (becoming engaged to be married)
BETWEEN THE FLAGS	as in steeplechase riding, a sporting event has the course marked off with flags; one must negotiate "between the flags"
BET YOUR BOOTS!	an expletive meaning yes or surely
BEVAL *(BAY-vahl)*	gypsy boy's name, meaning like the wind
BEVILJA *(beh-VILL-yah)*	Swedish word for to grant or give
BEZIQUE *(buh-ZEEK)*	A French card game similar to pinochle
BIANCO *(B-YAHN-ko)*	an Italian word for white
BIBELOT *(BEE-blow)*	French word for a trinket
BIEN-AIMÉ *(b-yahn-nay-MAY)*	the French word for beloved or sweetheart

BIFROST (*BEE-froast*)	Norse mythological word for rainbow; this was the Norseman's rainbow
BIG BAD WOLF	from the fairy tale "Little Red Riding Hood"; any sinister person or problem
BIJOU (*bee-ZHOO*)	French word meaning jewel; a girl's name
BILLABONG (*BILL-uh-bong*)	Australian word for the backwaters of a stream
BILLET-DOUX (*bill-uh-DOOZ*)	French for love letter
BILLINGSGATE	a fish market in London (complete with rough, uncultured, abusive citizens, and their language)
BILL OF FARE	a menu
BILL OF GOODS	a shipment (list) of goods sent for resale
BILLY BLUEGUM	affectionate Australian nickname for the Koala bear
BIMISI (*bee-MEE-see*)	an American Indian boy's name; "slippery"
BIRD OF PARADISE	a brightly colored bird of New Guinea
BIRD OF PASSAGE	a person who is constantly traveling
BIRD'S EYE SPEEDWELL	a Eurasian plant having bright blue flowers
BIRDSHOT	small shot used in shotgun shells; particularly in ammo used to hunt birds
BIRTHRIGHT	a "right" bestowed on someone simply by being born into a certain family
BISTRO (*BEES-trow*)	a second-rate tavern/restaurant
BITKI (*bit-KI*)	a Turkish girl's name meaning plant
BIZZARRO (*beeds-DSAHR-rob*)	Italian word for quaint
BJORK (*B-YORK*)	the Swedish word for birch; often used as a boy's name
BJORN (*B-YORN*)	the Swedish word for bear; often used as a boy's name
BJORNBAR (*B-YORN-bair*)	Swedish word for blackberry
BLACK ART	black magic
BLACK FRIAR	a Friar of the Dominican Order
BLACKHEATH	a pleasure resort southeast of London
BLACK HILLS	a mountainous area of South Dakota and Wyoming

BLACKJACK	a card game; a variety of oak; a leather bludgeon
BLACKMAIL	payments made for a threat of some kind of disclosure
BLACKOUT	putting out all the lights (during an air raid)
BLACKPOOL	a county, and seaside resort, in Lancashire, NW England
BLACK PRINCE	generally associated with Edward (Prince of Wales)
BLACKSTRAP	a crude, thick, unrefined molasses
BLACKTHORN	the American hawthorn
BLACK TIE	a black bow tie worn with a dinner jacket; a formal affair
BLACK WATCH	famous Highland regiment of the British Army; known for the somber tartans they wore and their bagpipes
BLACK WIDOW	a poisonous spider
BLANKA *(BLENG-kah)*	the Swedish word for to glitter
BLARNEY STONE	a stone found at Blarney Castle in Ireland; kissing the Blarney Stone supposedly bestowed on someone the gift for gab/flattery
BLAZ *(blahz)*	a Slavic boy's name meaning unwavering protector
BLAZES!	a forcible exclamation equivalent to "the flames of hell"
BLAZING STAR	a plant with falling, starlike, flowers
BLAZON *(BLAY-zen)*	a coat of arms; a shield
BLENDED WHISKEY	a blend of 2 or more straight whiskeys
BLESS 'EM ALL!	a term used as a general-purpose thank you
BLESSING	an expression of good wishes; grace said before dinner
BLESS MY SOUL!	an exclamation of surprise
BLESS MY STARS!	an exclamation of surprise
BLINKA *(BLING-kah)*	the Swedish word for to wink
BLINKEN *(BLING-ken)*	the German word for to twinkle
BLINTZ	little Russian pancakes filled with fruit or cream cheese

BLISS	a state of serene happiness
BLITHE or BLYTHE	a girl's name; also meaning carefree or frivolous
BLITZ	a bombing run done by a country's air force with sudden ferocity; the German word for lightning
BLITZKRIEG	a German word meaning a sudden, swift military offensive
BLIXTRA (*BLICK-strah*)	Swedish word for to flash
BLOCKADE-RUNNER	a ship, person, or country that runs through blockades
BLOOD BROTHER	people bound by ceremony (blood-mixing) sealing loyalties
BLOOMER	a "blooming" plant; old-timey athletic trousers for ladies
BLOMSTER (*BLOHM-stehr*)	Swedish word for blossom
BLOW THE WHISTLE	to "tell" on someone; informing to expose scandal or deed
BLUE BLAZES	simply "Hell"
BLUE BLOOD	a person of noble birth, an aristocrat, one of noble descent
BLUEBLOSSOM	a West Coast shrub having blue flowers
BLUEBONNET	a common SW plant with tiny blue flowers
BLUE BOOK	a publication that gives the names of socially prominent people
BLUE CHIP	a stock that sells at high prices because the public has extreme confidence in it
BLUE CURLS	an herb belonging to the mint family
BLUE DEVIL	any particularly evil-doing demon
BLUE FIELDS	a seaport town in Central America
BLUE FLAG	the wild blue iris of North America
BLUE FIRE!	an exclamation for something that is sensational
BLUE FOX	the Artic Fox when it is in summer phase (a bluish-gray pelt)
BLUEJACK	a small oak tree found in the southern United States
BLUEJACKET	a man who enlists in the US Navy
BLUE JEANS	Levis; blue denim pants
BLUE LAW	the law that regulates Sunday hours of business

BLUE LIGHTS	a nickname used for naval gunners
BLUE MOON	a period of time that would happen during a blue moon, hence...*never*
BLUE-PLATE SPECIAL	an inexpensive restaurant meal
BLUESKY LAW	the law that protects us from bunco securities
BOADICIA *(bo-uh-dee-see-uh)*	British queen, defeated in 62 AD
BOARDING HOUSE	a private home that provides guests with rooms and meals
BOARDING SCHOOL	a school for students to live away from home, providing rooms and meals
BOARDWALK	a sidewalk made out of wooden planks
BOAZ *(BOH-ahz)*	a Hebrew boy's name meaning strong
BOBBIN LACE	(same as Pillow Lace); a very fine lace used for trimming
BOBBY SOCKS or BOBBY SOX	long, white, cotton socks worn with cuffs
BOCCA TIGRIS *(BOK-uh TEE-gris)*	"tiger's mouth"; a narrow channel running between Canton, China and Hong Kong
BODAWAY *(bob-DAH-way)*	American Indian boy's name meaning firemaker
BODI *(BOH-dee)*	Hungarian boy's name; "may God protect the king"
BODKIN	a very ornamental lady's hair pin
BOGALUSA *(BO-guh-LOO-suh)*	a city in eastern Louisiana
BOGAR *(boh-GAHR)*	a semi-legendary Hindu sittar and alchemist
BOGTROTTER	an Irishman (one who walks through the bogs)
BOGYMAN or BOOGIEMAN	the ultimate in spooks; the "awful" one
BOLD AS BRASS	being absolutely shameless or presumptuous
BOMBA *(BOHM-buh)*	the Italian word for bomb
BOMBAY DUCK	nickname for the 18th century British Bombay regiments
BOMBER BAY	nickname for a member of an RAF bomber crew
BONHEUR *(bo-NUHR)*	the French word for happiness

BONHOMIE *(bawn-o-MEE)*	the French word for good fellowship
BONITO *(bon-NEE-toh)*	the Spanish word for pretty
BOOBY PRIZE	a comical award for something insignificant; award for last place
BOOBY TRAP	anything (device or situation) that catches one off guard
BOOK LEARNIN'	something learned from reading (rather than experience)
BOOM TOWN	a town that grew up suddenly through prosperity
BOOT CAMP	the first training center to which military troops are sent
BOOTLEG	the making, selling, and transport of illegal liquor
BOOTS or MR. BOOTS	a valet or servant (one who shines the master's shoes)
BOOTSTRAP	leather loops sewn on boots as handholds to assist in putting them on
BOOTY	a pirate's treasure; plunder; any valuable prize or award
BORJAN *(BOR-yahnn)*	Swedish word for beginning
BOSSA *(BOSS-ah)*	the Swedish word for a gun
BOSS COCKIE	an Australian farmer who employs labor but also works himself; a "top dog" or boss man
BOSTON ROCKER	19th century rocking chair with a high, stencilled back
BOTANY BAY	a town in New South Wales (it began as a penal colony)
BO TREE	a type of Asiatic tree (where Buddha received his "enlightenment")
BOUDOIR *(BOOD-wahr)*	a woman's bedroom
BOUGAINVILLE *(BOO-gen-ville)*	a tropic flower; largest of the Solomon Islands
BOULEAU *(boo-LO)*	the French word for birch
BOULEVARDIER *(bool-uh-VAR-dee-yay)*	French for man about town
BOUNDER	one who bounds (taking great leaps)
BOUNTIFUL	generous, or an abundance of

BOUNTY	greatness; generosity; something given liberally
BOUNTY HUNTER	one who hunts man, or animal, for pay
BOUNTY JUMPER	one who deserts the army after receiving a cash incentive (bounty) to enlist (or re-enlist); Civil War usage
BOYSIE	an Australian term of address to a "boy" (used with affection)
BRANDYWINE	a battlefield in Pennsylvania where the British defeated George Washington's troops
BRAMBLES	the wild blackberries of Scotland
BRAMBLING	a European mountain finch
BRASS TACKS	the bare facts; only practical realities
BRASS WINDS	an orchestra's wind instruments made of metal (trumpet, etc.)
BRATCHET	a little brat (used affectionately)
BRAZORIA *(bruh-ZORR-ee-uh)*	a county in Texas
BRAZZAVILLE *(BRAH-zuh-ville)*	capital of the Congo
BEACH OF PROMISE	when someone fails to keep a promise
BREATHE EASY	to be relieved of worry; assurance of success
BREDE *(BREH-deh)*	a popular Scandinavian boy's name meaning glacier
BREEZE	poetically; "a whisper of wind"; light air currents
BRIERLEY HILL *(BRIAR-lee)*	a county district in Staffordshire, in west central England
BRIGHOUSE	a borough in West Riding, Yorkshire, north England
BRIGHT EYES	one who is active or alert
BRIGHTWATERS	a village in Suffolk County, in southeast New York
BRILLARE *(breel-LAH-reh)*	the Italian for to twinkle
BRING-'EM-BACK-ALIVE	a big game hunter who caters to zoos
BRIOCHE *(bree-OSH)*	a soft, sweet French yeast roll
BRINDIS *(BREEN-deess)*	the Spanish word for toast
BRINNA *(BRIN-ah)*	the Swedish word for to burn

24

BRISBANE *(BRIZ-bane)*	a seaport city, and capital, of Queensland, Australia
BRISHEN *(BREE-shen)*	gypsy boy's name meaning born during a storm
BRITTANIQUE *(bree-tah-NEEK)*	the French word for a *citizen of Britain*
BRITTANY BLUE	a moderate shade of blue
BROKEN ARROW	a city in Tulsa County, Oklahoma
BROMBEERE *(BRAWM-bay-ruh)*	the German word for blackberry
BROTHER BLADE	a nickname for a fellow soldier (1700-1800s usage)
BROTHERHOOD	state of being brotherly towards another; cultlike with some assemblages
BROWNSTONE	a red-brown sandstone facade on a building; or the actual building constructed out of this material
BRUSSELS LACE	an extremely fine handmade lace with appliqué design
BRUT *(BROOT)*	the legendary king of Britain; a very dry wine or champagne
BUBBLA *(BOOB-lah)*	the Swedish word for to bubble
BUCANEER'S BOOT	a pirate's booty, or treasure
BUCKAROO	a cowboy
BUCKBOARD	a 4-wheeled wagon with boards that actually sit on the axles
BUCKINGHAM PALACE	the official home of England's royalty
BUCK PRIVATE	an army private; a new recruit
BUCK 'N' WING	a fast, solo tap dance with lots of jumping
BUFFALO BAY	an inlet of Lake Of The Woods, SE Manitoba, Canada
BUFFO *(BOOF-foh)*	the Italian word for funny
BULL FINCH	a European singing bird
BULL MOOSE	a male moose; Teddy Roosevelt's Progressive Party
BULL OF THE WOODS	any important person; one who acts with authority
BULL PEN	the enclosed area near a baseball diamond where pitchers limber up; or referencing "those who wait to be called" for something

BULL RUN	area in Virginia; site of 2 famous Civil War battles
BUM AROUND	to loaf; to do nothing; to wander aimlessly
BUNKER HILL	Revolutionary War battleground (located near Boston)
BUNKHOUSE	a ranch house for the hired hands (cowboys)
BUON GIORNO *(bwohn JOHR-no)*	Italian for good morning
BUONA SERA *(BWOH-nah SEH-rah)*	Italian for good evening
BURDEN OF PROOF	the presentation of overwhelming evidence
BURLESQUE	striptease, comedians, or other vaudvillian-type acts
BURMA ROAD	a highway through Burma/China
BURN IT BLUE	said of a person who acts outrageously
BURNT CINDER	a colorful slang word for a "window" (rhyming)
BURRO *(BOO-rroh)*	the Spanish word for a donkey
BUSHFIRE BLONDE	the Australian slang term for a redhead
BUSHMAN	an Australian dweller (or farmer), living in the "bush"
BUSHRANGER	an Australian outlaw who lives in the "bush"
BUSHRIDER	an Australian professional ranger on a "bush farm"
BUSHWHACK	to ambush (guerilla-type fighting)
BUSMAN'S HOLIDAY	a vacation where one continues to do their job for recreation
BUSY SIGNAL	when a series of sharp buzzes reveals that the number dialed is already in use
BUSYWORK	activities designed to keep one busy, (not necessarily productive)
BUTTERFLY KISS	a caress given by winking one eye so that the lashes brush the receiver's cheek
BUZZARDS BAY	an inlet of the Atlantic Ocean in southeast Massachusetts
BWANA *(BWAH-nah)*	the African word for boss or master

C

CABALA *(kuh-BALL-uh)*	occultism; darkly kept secrets
CABALLERO *(kah-bay-L-YEE-roh)*	Spanish word for gentleman or knight
CABALLITO *(kah-bah-L-YEE-toh)*	the Spanish word for pony
CABAÑA *(kah-BAHN-yah)*	the Spanish word for little house
CABIN CLASS	traveling class aboard a ship (between 1st and tourist class)
CABOODLE	the entire lot; a bunch or group of things
CABOOSE	the last car in a freight train (usually painted red)
CACCIA *(KAHCH-chah)*	the Italian word for hunt
CACCIATORE *(CATCH-uh-torrey)*	an Italian chicken casserole
CACHER *(kah-SHAY)*	the French word for to hide
CACHUCHA *(cah-CHOO-chah)*	an Andalusian dance resembling a "bolero"
CADENCE/CADENCY	any rhythmic, balanced flow (as in riding or music)
CADIZ *(kuh-DIZ)*	a province of Spain
CAFE AU LAIT *(cah-FAY oh Lay)*	French coffee with milk
CAHIL *(kah-HILL)*	the Turkish word for young, used as a boy's name too
CAHOOTS	a collaboration of a questionable nature, as "in cahoots"
CAJUN	a native of the state of Louisiana (particularly from the Bayous)
CAKES AND ALE	phrase coined to mean: "all the good things in life"
CAKEWALK	began as an entertainment where a cake was the prize for the most unusual manner of walking
CALABASH *(CAL-uh-bash)*	a tropical, gourdlike fruit

CALIBER	the size of a bullet shell (measured by its diameter)
CALLIOPE HUMMINGBIRD	the smallest US hummingbird, this "hummer" is common to the western US
CALL IT A DAY	a term for "calling it quits"; going no further
CALL IT EIGHT BELLS	nautical term—an excuse for a drink before noon
CALMARE *(kahl-MAH-reh)*	Italian word for to soothe
CALUTE *(kah-LOOT)*	Turkish development for the word "Goliath"
CALYPSO	a kind of orchid; the mythic Greek sea nymph; West Indian music
CAMARADE *(kah-mah-RAHD)*	the French word for companion
CAMARADERIE *(kahm-RAHD-uh-ree)*	goodwill and a lighthearted rapport
CAMARILLA *(kohm-uh-REE-uh)*	the secret advisors of the Spanish kings
CAMBRIDGE FORTUNE	marrying a woman with no dowry; marrying for love, not money
CAMELOT	the legendary town of King Arthur's court
CAMISOLE *(camma-SOLE)*	sleeveless undershirt ladies wear as a blouse
CAMPAGNA *(kahm-PAH-nyah)*	region of southern Italy surrounding Rome; (flat plains—site of many battles)
CAMP-FOLLOWER	a person who follows military units around for their business
CANDLE-KEEPER	privileged person; one singled out for recognition
CANDLEWICK	a needlework made of knottings; fibers of which candle wicks are made
CANNELURE *(cannel-LOOR)*	the fluting around the rim of a bullet
CANOA *(kah-NO-ah)*	the Swedish for canoe
CANTARE *(kahn-TAH-reh)*	the Italian word for to sing
CANTEEN COWBOY	World War II RAF term for "ladies man"
CANTINA *(kahn-TEE-nah)*	the Italian word for cellar or small saloon
CAN'T KEEP STILL	a lively, or active personality

28

CANTRIP *(kan-TRIP)*	Old Scottish for a magic spell, witch trick or prank
CANUCK *(cub-NUCK)*	slang term for a French Canadian
CAP AND BELLS	slang term for a "jester" (since a cap with bells was an essential part of a court jester's outfit
CAPE FLYAWAY	a nautical term for the imaginary land on every horizon
CAPE SMOKE	a brandy from the South African, vine-growing, area that makes it
CAPITAINE *(kah-pee-TEN)*	the French word for captain
CAPITAL GAINS	the profit generated from the sale of capital assets
CAPITANO *(kah-pee-TAH-no)*	the Italian word for captain
CAPPI *(KAHP-pee)*	a gypsy boy's name meaning good fortune
CAPPUCCIO *(kahp-POOCH-choh)*	the Italian word for a hooded garment
CAPRICCIO *(kah-PREECH-choh)*	the Italian word for fancy
CAPRICE	changeableness; the inclination for changes
CAPTAIN CORK	used for the person who is slow in passing the bottle around
CAPTAIN KETTLE	the famous character in the Cutcliffe Hyne stories
CAPTAIN MACFLUFFER	theatrical name for an actor who "goofs" (fluffs) their lines
CARAMBA! *(cub-RAHM-bub)*	an American Spanish exclamation of surprise
CARAVEL *(CARE-uh-vell)*	small and fast 16th century sailing ship
CARDIGAN	a jacket of knitted wool
CARDSHARP	someone who cheats at cards
CARELESS TALK	gossip or a loose tongue concerning delicate issues
CARIBOU *(CARE-uh-boo)*	a Canadian/French word for a large North American, elklike deer
CARIBOU ROAD	a highway in British Columbia; also CARIBOO ROAD
CARILLON *(CARE-uh-lahn)*	a set of bells played as a musical instrument

CARINTHIA *(kuh-RIN-thia)*	a province of Austria
CARIOCA *(care-ee-OH-kuh)*	a South American ballroom dance
CARRY ON	to flirt; to endure hardship; to raise a ruckus
CARRY THE LOAD	to be depended upon, by others, to do most of the work
CARTE BLANCHE *(kart-BLAHNSH)*	unlimited authority, unconditional spending
CARTEL *(car-TELL)*	an international conglomerate of independent enterprises
CASABLANCA *(cah-suh-BLAHNG-kuh)*	seaport of the NW coast of Morocco
CASBAH *(CAZ-bah)*	old, crowded area of a North African city; usually full of vendors, sleazy bars and "intrigue"
CASHIER'S CHECK	a check drawn by a bank on it's own funds
CASHMERE *(kaj-MEER)*	the fine, soft, and costly fabric made from a Cashmere goat's hair
CASIMIR *(kah-SEE-mer)*	Polish boy's name meaning he brings peace
CASINO *(kuh-SEE-no)*	a room or building for public gambling or entertainment
CASTALIA *(cas-tuh-LEE-uh)*	the fountain near Delphi that gives inspiration to those who drink from it
CASTAWAY	any vessel, or person, cast away from a ship; shipwrecked person
CASTEL *(kah-STEHL)*	Spanish word for belonging to a castle
CASTILE *(cas-TEEL)*	the former kingdom of northern Spain
CASTLE SHANNON	a borough in Allegheny County, SW Pennsylvania
CATAVA *(chah-TAH-vah)*	an African girl's name
CATAWAMPUS	a hobgoblin or boogieman; something that is wild
CATAWBA *(cuh-TAW-buh)*	Choctaw Indian tribe; a reddish wine grape
CATBRIER	a thorny vine in the lily family
CAT BURGLAR	a burglar who enters through the roof or upstairs window

CATER-COUSIN *(CAT-ehr CUZZ-in)*	fourth cousins; any *remote* relative
CATFIT	a fit of anger; emotional outburst due to extreme anger
CATHAY *(cath-AYE)*	a lyrical old name for China
CAT-O'-MOUNTAIN	a mountain lion (cougar)
CATON *(kah-TOHN)*	a common Spanish boy's name; "wise"
CAVALLA *(kah-VAHL-lah)*	Italian word for mare; any pretty, feminine horse
CAVALLINO *(kah-vahl-LEE-no)*	Italian for pony or little horse
CEDARBIRD	another name for the common waxwing/cedar waxwing (bird)
CEDRO *(CHEH-droh)*	the Italian word for cedar
CELLO *(CHEL-low)*	4-stringed instrument pitched between a viola and a bass
CEMAL *(ke-MAHL)*	Arabic word for beauty; used as a girl's name
CERELLA *(se-REH-luh)*	a girl's name meaning spring
CEREZA *(seh-REH-sah)*	the Spanish word for cherry
CERISE *(suh-REEZ)*	the French word for cherry
CE SOIR *(suh SWAHR)*	the French word for tonight
CHABLIS *(shuh-BLEE)*	a very dry, white burgundy wine
CHABOUK *(SHAH-book)*	Eastern Indian word for a leather horsewhip
CHA-CHA or CHA-CHA-CHA	a Latin American ballroom dance
CHACONNE *(shuh-KAHN)*	a slow, stately 18th century dance
CHAIN GANG	prisoners chained together; a prison work crew
CHAIN REACTION	a series of events where each induces it's influence on it's successor
CHALLIS *(shall-EE)*	a light, printed fabric made of rayon
CHAMBERMAID	a female servant or cleaning lady in a hotel

CHAMBER MUSIC	a small group of instruments (usually strings) suitable to play music in a private room or concert hall
CHAMBRAY *(SHAM-bray)*	a strong, cotton cloth woven with colored warp
CHAMONIX *(SHAH-mo-nee)*	a valley on the Arve River in northern France
CHAMPAGNE WEATHER	ironically it means *bad* weather
CHANCE-MEDLEY	something occurring at random
CHANSON *(shahn-SOHNG)*	French word for song
CHAPERONE *(SHAP-uh-rone)*	an older person who protects (supervises) a young person or an unmarried couple
CHAPELLE *(shah-PELL)*	the French word for chapel
CHARADES	a parlor game where words and phrases are pantomimed
CHARGE ACCOUNT	credit arrangement when purchases are made prior to payment
CHARISMA	rare quality (power) that attracts attention, worship, or adoration to the person possessing it
CHARITY	a feminine name; something given to help the needy
CHARLA *(CHAHR-lah)*	Spanish word for to talk
CHARLEROI *(shahr-luh-RWAH)*	mining town in SW Belgium
CHARYBDIS *(kuh-RIB-dis)*	mythological character, a ravenous woman who turned into a huge whirlpool off Sicily
CHASE-ME-CHARLIE	a German, radio-controlled glider used in World War II
CHATELAINE *(SHAT-uh-lane)*	mistress of the chateau (or castle)
CHATTERBASKET	a prattling child (used by their nannys with fondness)
CHATON *(shah-TOHNG)*	the French word for kitten
CHATOYANT *(shuh-twah-YAHN)*	the French word for having a changeable luster (like a cat's eyes in the dark)
CHAVI *(CHAH-vee)*	gypsy girl's name, it means child
CHAYA *(ki-YAH)*	Hebrew word for life, used as a boy's or girl's name

CHAZY *(shay-ZEE)*	village in Clinton Co., NY (near Lake Champlain)
CHE *(cheh)*	Spanish name (the pet form of "Jose")
CHEECHAKO *(chee-CHOCK-oh)*	an Alaskan word with local usage for newcomer or tenderfoot
CHEERIBYE	English usage, meaning goodbye
CHEERIO	British usage, either as a greeting or a parting word
CHELSEA	a feminine name, recent in popularity with British origin
CHEMINEAU *(shuh-mee-NO)*	the French for hobo or tramp
CHEMISETTE *(shem-uh-ZETT)*	French for the ornamental lacework used to fill-in the open neck of a dress or fancy blouse
CHESMU *(CHEHS-moo)*	American Indian boy's name meaning sooty
CHENOA *(chay-NOH-ah)*	American Indian girl's name meaning dove
CHEQUERS *(CHEK-erz)*	a Tudor mansion/county seat of the Prime Minister of England (located NW of London)
CHERCHEZ LA FEMME *(shair-SHAY luh FAM)*	French for seek the woman, implying that the woman is the motive for the action
CHERI *(sher-EE)*	originated in France with Miss Rose Cheri (1900s); a feminine name meaning charming woman
CHERISH	to treat with affection or to hold dear
CHEROKEE ROSE	a large, white, climbing rose that began with Chinese stock
CHEROKEE STRIP	12,000 acres in Oklahoma given to the Indian and taken back
CHERRYBIRD	another name for the cedarbird
CHEVALET *(SHEV-uh-lay)*	the French for bridge (as on a stringed musical instrument)
CHEVALIER *(shev-uh-LEER)*	French word for knight or nobleman
CHEWINK	one of several eastern United States finches (buntings)
CHIARO *(K-YAH-roh)*	Italian word for clear, natural or unadorned
CHIARO DI LUNA *(K-YAH-roh dee LOO-nah)*	Italian word for moonlight

CHIANTI *(key-AHN-tee)*	a dry, red wine from Italy
CHIC *(SHEEK)*	sophisticated, stylish, or fashionable
CHICKAHOMINY	a river in eastern Virginia
CHICKAMAUGA *(chik-uh-MAH-guh)*	a city in NW Georgia where the Confederates defeated the Union soldiers
CHICKASAW	member of Oklahoma's Muskogean Indians
CHICKAREE	the American red squirrel
CHI-CHI *(SHE-she)*	French word meaning stylish or showy
CHIK *(cheek)*	a gypsy boy's name meaning the earth
CHIKA *(chee-KAH)*	a Japanese girl's name meaning close
CHILD'S PLAY	anything that is very easy to do
CHILL FACTOR	the effects of cold wind and low temperature on persons
CHIMENE *(shee-MEHN)*	French/Greek word for hospitable
CHIMERA *(kigh-MEE-ruh)*	mythical Greek fire-breathing monster, it had the head of a lion, a goat's body, and a serpent's tail
CHIMNEY SWEEP	someone who cleans soot out of chimneys for a living
CHINA ROSE	a fragrant red/pink shrub (the pre-hybrid rose)
CHINESE CHIPPENDALE	a very oriental influence in Chippendale furniture
CHINESE LANTERN	decorative (party) lanterns made from collapsible colored papers
CHINHAI *(chin-HI)*	a port city in east China
CHINCHOW *(JIN-JOE)*	a town in Manchuria at the Po Hai Gulf
CHINJU *(JIN-JOO)*	a town in South Korea
CHIN LING SHAN	a mountain range in north China
CHINOOK *(chi-NOOK)*	warm SW winds of the northern Pacific coasts; warm winter winds (also known as "snow eaters," since they are so unseasonal)
CHINWANGTAO *(CHIN-hwang-doo)*	a seaport town in NE China

34

CHIPPENDALE	the graceful rococo furniture of Thomas Chippendale
CHIPPEWA	a tribe of North American Indians near the Canadian border
CHIP SHOT	a golfing term; a short shot made to the green with a high curve
CHIRICAHUA *(CHEER-uh-CAH-wuh)*	Apache tribes of Arizona/New Mexico
CHIRRUP	to give a cheer
CHISHIMA *(chee-SHEE-mah)*	a chain of 47 volcanic islands owned by Japan
CHISOLM TRAIL	the cattle trail that ran from San Antonio to Abilene, Texas
CHITSA *(CHEEt-sah)*	the American Indian word for pretty, a girl's name
CHITTAMWOOD	a kind of North American tree; the "smoke tree"
CHOCTAWHATCHEE *(CHOCK-tah-HATCH-ee)*	a river in NW Florida
CHOOMIA *(CHOO-mee-uh)*	a gypsy word meaning kiss, a girl's name
CHOSHU *(CHOE-SHOE)*	a feudal Japanese clan that rebelled against the emperor
CHUBASCO *(choo-BAHS-ko)*	a violent thunderstorm off Central America's west coast
CHUCHA and CHUCHITA	a pet form of "Jesusa" (heh-SOO-sah) Spanish girl's name
CHUCKIESTONE	an old Scottish game played with pebbles that you "chuck"
CHUKKA	a man's fleece-lined, boot-shoe
CHUN *(CHWUN)*	a common Chinese girl's name meaning spring
CHUNGCHOW *(JOONG-joe)*	a city in central China's Szechwan Province (on the Yangtze River)
CHURCH-FOLK	members of established churches
CHUTZPAH *(HOOTS-puh)*	the Hebrew word for bold, brassy behavior
CIEL *(see-ELL)*	French word for sky, also a girl's name
CILKA *(CHEL-kuh)*	a Slavic girl's name, a pet form of Cecilia
CINDERELLA	the fairy tale heroine; any "rags to riches" girl

35

CINNAMON TEAL	a small, west US duck (head and breast are cinnamon-red)
CIPHER/CYPHER	any Arabic figures, numerals, or numbers
CIRCUIT BREAKER	an automatic switch that stops electric current in the event of an overload
CIRCUIT RIDER	the old-time preacher who rode from town to town
CISCO	a French Canadian word for a type of whitefish found in the waters off the NE United States and Canada
CITY SLICKER	a city dweller; rural people regard them as shrewd, worldly, stylishly-dressed swindlers
CIVIL DEFENSE	emergency measures taken during natural disasters
CLAIR DE LUNE *(claire-dub-LOON)*	French for moonlight; some usage as the blue-gray glaze used on ceramics
CLAMBAKE	a seaside picnic of clams, corn, etc., covered with seaweed and steamed in the sand upon heated rocks
CLAMJAMFERY *(CLAM-jam-furry)*	an Old Scottish word for fluffs (worthless finery or gaudiness)
CLARABELLA	an organ stop with open wood pipes (soft and sweet sounds)
CLARET *(CLAIRE-aye)*	a dry, red wine from Bordeaux, France
CLEAR SAILING	something that is easy to do (without worry or strain)
CLEMENCY	mild temper; the granting of an easier criminal sentence
CLIPPER	the old, sharp-bowed sailing ships (prior to the steamship)
CLISHMACLAVER *(KLISH-mub-KLAVER)*	Old Scot word for gossip or foolish talk
CLOAK-AND-DAGGER	a scenario of melodramatic intrigue
CLOISONNE *(clwab-zo-NAY)*	method of producing designs on wares by filling wire forms with bright enamels
CLOOT/CLOOTIE	what the Old Scottish called the devil
CLOWN ALLEY	the aisle of tents or wagons where circus clowns lived and prepared for their performances
COALSACK	(as in NORTHERN COALSACK) a dark nebula near the Southern Cross constellation

COAST ARTILLERY	artillery used to defend a country's coastal areas
COBBLER	a deep-dish fruit pie; a person who makes or repairs shoes
COCKLESHELL	a scallop shell
CODE NAPOLEON	a code of French Civil Law prepared by Napoleon Bonaparte
CODICIL *(cod-uh-sill)*	an addendum to one's Last Will And Testament
CODY	(as in Buffalo Bill Cody) The American scout/frontiersman
COME-HITHER	seductive or alluring
COHUNE *(cuh-HOON)*	feather-shaped palm of South America; Hawaiian for big boss or leader
COLLIESHANGIE *(collie-SHANGEE)*	Old Scottish word for brawl or fight
COLONUS *(kuh-LONE-us)*	an ancient village in Greece (now called Attica)
COLOR GUARD	US Army, or Navy Guard use (3 men assigned to protect the American flag during ceremonies and parades)
COMET-SEEKER or **COMET-FINDER**	a small telescope created just for comet watching
COMMANDEER *(common-DEER)*	to appropriate (confiscate) possessions or people to fight, or be used, during time of war
COMMANDO	a small force (or a person) trained for quick destructive raids
COMMAND **PERFORMANCE**	an entertainment performance given upon the request of some head of state
COMMONWEALTH	the entire people of a state
COMPANY MAN	an employee, usually white-collar, whose loyalty is more with management than with his fellow employees
CONCORDIA	the Roman goddess of "concord" (peace)
CONFEDERATE ROSE	a Chinese rose with pink flowers
CONGOU *(CONG-goo)*	a grade of black tea from China (a third picking)
CONQUISTA *(kohn-KEESS-tah)*	the Spanish word for conquest
CONSORT	a companion (a mate, husband, or a wife)
CONTRABAND	prohibited; forbidden goods or trade

COOK-OUT	a meal cooked out-of-doors; a camping trip or scouting adventure where an outdoor meal is prepared
COPENHAGEN *(KO-pen-HAG-ehn)*	a seaport and capital city of Denmark
COPPER CAPTAIN	a pretended captain (faking a military rank)
COPPERSMITH	someone who manufactures, or is a worker, in copper metal
COPPER-TOP	the Australian nickname for a redhead
COQUINA *(ko-KEEN-uh)*	a tiny, brightly-colored shell common to Florida
CORDERO *(kohr-DEH-roh)*	the Spanish word for lamb, a common boy's name
CORDON BLEU *(kohr-dahn BLUE)*	French word, literally "blue ribbon" (usually refers high honors to expert chefs)
CORDUROY	the thick, corded (ribbed) durable cotton fabric used in clothes
CORNBREAD	a bread used extensively through the South US, made from cornmeal
CORN PONE	(sometimes called PIG PONE), small oval loaves of cornbread
CORN WHISKEY	whiskey made from corn
CORSAIR *(core-SAIR)*	a pirate (also, the ship of a pirate)
COSMIC DUST	fine particles found in interstellar space
COSMOS *(koz-MOS)*	the universe seen as an orderly system
COSSACK	the fierce horsemen warriors of southern Russia (Mongols)
COTILLION	a formal ball given to present a young lady to society
COTTON CANDY	a fluffy, spun-sugar candy common at fairs and circus
COUNCIL BLUFFS	an old Indian meeting ground (now a city) in SW Iowa
COUNTER-ESPIONAGE	the detection and countering of enemy espionage
COUMAROU *(KOO-muh-roo)*	the caribe name for the bean of the tonka
COUNTRY CLUB	a social club outside of a town, exclusive to the use of the town's well-to-do, and snobs
COUNTRY COUSIN	rustic (yokels) and their ways—as seen by city dwellers

COUNTRY-DANCE	an English folk dance with 2 lines facing each other
COUNTRY FOLK	the people who live in a rural area
COUNTRY GENTLEMAN	the rich landowner of a country estate
COUNTRY MILE	a term to mean "a very long way"
COUNTRYWOMAN	a woman who lives in the country
COURTLY LOVE	a debonair code of chivalrous conduct/devotion to any married woman (in medieval times); knightly devotion to all women
COUSCOUS *(KOOS-koos)*	a North African meat and grain dish
COVEN *(KUV-ehn)*	a gathering of witches
COVENANT *(KUV-ehn-nent)*	promises made
COVENTRY *(KUV-ehn-tree)*	a manufacturing town in central England
COVENTRY BLUE	a superior blue embroidery thread made in Coventry, England
COVER-UP	an alibi, distraction, or attempt to conceal something
COWALKER *(KO-walker)*	a person's spiritual double; one's "other"; the unseen one that "walks" with us all; a doppelganger
COYDUCK	slang for *acting as a decoy* (combining the words de*coy* and *duck*)
CRADLESONG	a song to soothe a child to sleep (i.e., Rock-A-Bye-Baby)
CRAWDAD	a crawfish (freshwater crustaceans of the United States)
CRAZY QUILT	a wildly-colored patchwork quilt
CREAMCUPS	ornamental annual flower of the poppy family
CRINKUM-CRANKUM *(CRING-kum CRANG-kum)*	Old Scottish word for whimsies (useless adornments)
CRISTALLO *(kree-STAHL-lo)*	the Italian word for crystal
CRITTER	any living creature
CROSSFIRE	when 2 or more lines of fire are aimed at one objective from both sides
CROSS MY HEART	the mild, childlike oath taken to affirm truths

CROSS-PATCH	a nickname for a peevish child or young woman
CROWN PRINCE	the heir apparent to a throne
CROW WING	a river in central Minnesota; or the inference of being "as dark as a crow's wing"
CRUSADO (croo-ZAH-doe)	an old Portuguese gold coin
CRUZAR (kroo-SAHR)	the Spanish word for to cross
CUCHARITA (koo-chah-REE-tah)	the Spanish word for teaspoon
CURARE (coo-RAH-ree)	a South American plant extraction that is highly poisonous; Indians dipped arrows/darts in curare insuring fatal results
CURTAIN CALL	performers in a play, concert, etc., asked to return to the stage through the applause-level of their audiences
CYBELE (SIGHB-uh-lee)	mother of the gods; "goddess of mysteries"
CYGNE (SEEN-yuh)	French word for swan
CYGNET (SIG-net)	a young swan
CYTHERIA (sigh-THEH-ree-uh)	another name for Venus (goddess of love and beauty)
CZARDAS (CHAR-dash)	an intricate Hungarian dance

D

DABIR (dah-BEER)	this Egyptian word means teacher, also a boy's name
DAIQUIRI (DAK-er-ee)	a sweet Jamaican rum & lime drink
DAISY RECRUIT	an innocent—fresh off the farm
DAKOTA	a tribe of Indians; a former US territory that was divided into two states
DAME (DAH-muh)	the German word for lady
DAMEK (DUH-mek)	the Czech word for earth, used as a boy's name

DAMMERUNG *(DEM-uh-roonk)*	the German word for twilight
DAMOSEL/DAMOISELLE/ **DAMOZEL/DAMSEL** *(dam-zelle)*	French for young girl
DANDELION	a common plant (weed) with yellow flowers
DANDIPRAT *(DANDY-prat)*	a little fellow (used fondly *and* derogatorially)
DANSEUR *(DAN-soer)*	the French word for ballet dancer
DANSK *(DAHNSK)*	the Swedish word for something that is Danish
DANUBE *(dan-YOOB)*	a famous river in central Europe
DANYA *(DAHN-yah)*	a Russian boy's name meaning given by God
DAR *(dahr)*	a Hebrew boy's name that means pearl
DARIO *(DAH-ree-oh)*	the Spanish word for wealthy, a boy's name
DARKLING	being, or happening, in the dark of night
DARLING SHOWER	an Australian dust-storm occurring in the vicinity of the Darling River
DARK SHADOWS	a dark brown color; a 1960s TV soap opera with vampires
DASHA *(DAH-shah)*	the Russian pet form of the name Doroteya (Dorothy)
DASHY	stylish, showy, or dashing
DAX	a recently popular boy's name (origin unknown)
DAVY JONES LOCKER	the bottom of the sea
DAY'S DAWNING	the "morning"
DAYS OF GRACE	extra time permitted to make a payment on a bank loan
DEAR JOHN	a farewell letter to a lady's fiance; any letter that breaks off an engagement or dismisses a sweetheart
DEBT OF HONOR	a gambling debt
DEERLET	a small deer or fawn
DEERSTALKER	one who hunts deer by stalking, or the helmet-shaped cloth cap worn by deer hunters
DELICE *(day-LEESS)*	the French word for delight

DELIVER THE GOODS	when you accomplish something
DEMOS *(DEE-mus)*	the people of one of ancient Greece's states
DEMURE *(di-MYOOR)*	having sedate manners; reserved
DENARO *(deh-NAH-roh)*	the Italian word for cash (money)
DEN MOTHER	the woman who supervises a den of cub scouts
DEPUTY	a person authorized to act for another
DERORA *(deh-ROH-rah)*	a Hebrew girl's name meaning bird
DESIDERIO *(deh-zee-DEH-ree-oh)*	the Italian word for desire
DESPERADO	a bad hombre or desperate criminal (used often in the Old West)
DESTROYING ANGEL	nickname for a deadly mushroom
DEUCE	gambling device (cards or dice) bearing 2 (two) spots
DEUCES WILD	a variation of poker where the deuce can represent any card
DEUTZIA *(DOOT-see-uh)*	a white-flowered shrub of Appalachia
DEVAKI *(dah-vah-KEE)*	a Hindu girl's name meaning black
DEVIL BEATS	the rain falling when the sun is still shining
DEVIL-CATCHER	the preacher
DEVIL DODGER	a very religious person
DEVILKIN	an imp or small devil; the apprentice of a devil
DEVIL-MAY-CARE	something done carelessly or recklessly
DEVIL'S ADVOCATE	someone who takes a critical position for validity's sake
DEVIL'S COLOURS or DEVIL'S LIVERY	the colors black & yellow in combination
DEVIL'S DAUGHTER	a spiteful or shrewish woman
DEVIL'S DELIGHT	creating a din or disturbance (yelling and screaming)
DEVIL'S DINNER-HOUR	the midnight hour
DEVIL'S ISLAND	former penal colony (prison) off French Guiana
DEVIL'S LUCK	"no luck at all!"

DEVIL'S OWN	someone who is devilish, troublesome and impish
DEVIL'S OWN BOY	a devilish, troublesome and impish little boy
DEVIL'S OWN DANCE	any situation that is particularly troublesome
DEVILSHINE	demonic power and skill
DEVIL'S SMILES	one minute sunshine and the next minute rain showers
DEVIL'S TATTOO	when someone unconsciously drums their fingers on a table or taps their foot on the floor
DEVIL'S WOODYARD	an area on Trinidad Island (in the Caribbean) where mud volcanoes have taken over and ruined a forest
DEVIL TO PAY	actions leading to very unpleasant consequences
DEVILTRY	wickedness or reckless mischief
DEVILWOOD	a southern US tree with green flowers
DIABLO *(DYAH-bloh)*	the Spanish word for devil
DIEGO *(dee-EH-goh)*	a common Spanish name for boys (like our James)
DIGGER'S DELIGHT	a wide-brimmed felt hat
DIGGUMS	slang term or nickname given someone who likes to garden
DING-BOY	English slang for a bully or rogue (used in 1700-1800s)
DINNER BELL	a rurally common practice where people are called for a meal by ringing a bell (because it can be heard from a great distance)
DINNER JACKET	a tuxedo
DIRTY SHIRT	soldier in the British Fusiliers, so named because in the Battle at Delhi they fought bravely to the last man in their shirtsleeves after many days of bloody combat
DISASTRO *(dee-ZAH-stroh)*	the Italian word for disaster
DISCIPLE *(duh-SIGH-puhl)*	a pupil or follower of a person (or school of thought)
DISMAL SWAMP	the marshy swamps of Virginia/North Carolina coasts
DJARKARTA *(juh-KAR-tuh)*	the capital city of Java, Indonesia

DJARV *(YAIRV)*	the Swedish word for bold
DJAVUL *(YAY-vuhl)*	the Swedish word for devil
DOCTOR LIVINGSTONE	someone met (encountered) unexpectedly
DODGE CITY	former frontier town in Ford County, Kansas; home address of TV's Marshall Matt Dillon
DOLCEZZA *(dohl-CHETTS-tsah)*	the Italian word for sweetness
DOMANI *(doh-MAH-nee)*	the Italian word for tomorrow
DOMINGO *(doh-MEEN-goh)*	the Spanish word for Sunday; a boy who is born on Sunday
DOMINI *(DOH-mee-nee)*	a girl's name meaning born on Sunday
DONNER *(DAWNN-ehr)*	the German word for thunder
DOOR PRIZE	a lottery-type prize given away at an assembly
DOUBLOON *(duh-BLOON)*	former Spanish gold coin (in actual money it was worth about $16)
DOVEKIE	a small, North Atlantic coastal bird brought inland during storms
DOWN YONDER	rural Southern US usage meaning "down there"
DRACHE *(DRAH-khuh)*	German word for dragon
DRACHMA *(DRAK-muh)*	the modern gold monetary unit of Greece
DRAGO *(DRAY-go)*	the northern constellation of stars known as the dragon
DRAGOON *(druh-GOON)*	a soldier who served on horseback (European origin)
DREADNOUGHT *(DRED-not)*	a class of heavily-armored British warships
DRESS PARADE	a military parade that demands wearing a dress uniform
DRINK-HAIL!	a courteous reply to a drinking toast (early British use)
DRUM & FIFE	military musical instruments played on a "marching command"
DUCKLING	a young duck
DUKKER *(DOOK-kuhr)*	gypsy boy's name (it implies some evil doing)

DULZURA *(dool-SOO-rah)*	Spanish word for sweetness
DUMBARTON OAKS	a famous mansion in Georgetown (outside Washington DC)
DUNCANNON	a borough/summer resort in south central Pennsylvania
DUNDER *(DOON-dehr)*	the Swedish word for thunder
DUNKEL *(DOONG-kel)*	the German word for dark
DURUM	a hard wheat
DUTCH COMFORT	equivalent to the phrase "thank God it isn't any worse!"
DYBBUK *(DIB-uhk)*	the Hebrew zombie (folklore where spirits of the dead possess the bodies of the living)
DYRBAR *(DUR-bawr)*	the Swedish word for costly
DYRKA *(DUR-kah)*	the Swedish word for to adore

E

EAGLET	a young eagle
EAGLE PASS	a city in Maverick County, Texas (on the Rio Grande)
EAGLE RIVER	a village in northern Michigan (on Lake Superior)
EARLY HOUR	during the early morning; predawn
EARTHSHINE	when sunlight is reflected from the earth as it lights those parts of the moon that the sun's rays do not reach
EASTBOUND	going in an easterly direction
EAST INDIES	southeast Asia and Indonesia
EBB TIDE	the receding (outgoing) tide
ECHO	a repetition of sounds; an imitator
ECLAIR *(ay-KLEHR)*	French word for lightning; also, a hollow pastry filled with custard and iced with chocolate
ECLIPSE	when one celestial body is hidden by, or in, the shadows of another

EDEN	being in a state of bliss; Adam & Eve's garden home; a common girl's name
EFFENDI *(ah-FENN-dee)*	the Turkish title of respect, "master"
EGO IDEAL	all of a person's positive attitudes about himself
EIDER DOWN	refers to the down of the eider (a large sea duck of the far North), used for stuffing expensive silk pillows
EKORRE *(ECK-or-eh)*	the Swedish word for squirrel
ELECTRIC BLUE	a bright, metallic blue color
ELFCHILD	a child left by elves in place of a human infant which they have kidnapped
ELFIN	relating, or belonging, to elves
ELF-LAND	a fairyland that is the supposed home of elves
ELF-LOCK	a dangling lock of hair (such as found on babies or puppies); a lock of hair that gets tangled all the time (as if done by elves)
ELIXIR	a sweetened alcoholic medicinal preparation; a cordial
ELKAN *(el-KAHN)*	Hebrew for he belongs to God; a boy's name
ELSU *(EHL-soo)*	an Indian boy's name meaning falcon
ELVET	a little elf (young or baby elf)
EMBASSY	the residence and offices of an ambassador
EMBER GOOSE	another name for the American loon
EMBEZZLE	the misappropriation of something in violation of a trust
EMPEROR GOOSE	the beautiful Snow Goose of the Alaskan coasts
EMPORIA	a city in east Kansas (SW of Topeka)
ENCHANTER *(ahn-shahn-TAY)*	the French word for to delight
ENEMY SHIPS	the vessels of nations at war
ENFANT TERRIBLE *(AHN-fahn tuh-REE-bl')*	the French for an unmanageable or mischievous child
EQUATORIA *(eck-wuh-TOR-ee-uh)*	a sometimes used name for the equatorial regions of Africa
EQUINOX *(ECK-wuh-knox)*	when the sun crosses the equator making day and night equal in length

46

ERKANNA *(AIR-khen-ah)*	the Swedish for to acknowledge
ERLKING *(URL-king)*	the King of the Elves (as found in German folklore)
ERIC THE RED	the famous 10th century Scandinavian who founded Greenland
ERMINE STREET	an ancient Roman road in Britain that ran from London to York
EROVRA *(AIR-ov-rah)*	the Swedish word for to conquer
ESCAPADE	carefree or reckless adventure (escape from restrictions)
ESPIONAGE	the act of spying on others
ESPIRITU *(ess-PEE-ree-too)*	the Spanish for spirit
ESPRIT *(ess-PREE)*	the French word for mind or spirit
ETERNITY	time without beginning or end
ETHEREAL *(eth-AIR-ee-uhl)*	having the nature of air (heavenly or airy)
ETOILE *(ay-TWAHL)*	the French word for star
EUREKA *(yoor-EE-kuh)*	the Greek for "I have found it"
EUROPE MORNING	to rise from bed late in the day; not an early riser
EVENFALL	the beginning of evening, twilight
EVENSONG	an evening hymn; the time of day used for evening services
EVEN-STEVEN	when something is fair or equal
EVERLASTING	something that is eternal, or lasts forever
EVER SWORDED	someone who takes pride in being in a constant state of readiness (military usage is common)
EVERY MAN JACK and EVERY MOTHER'S SON	this means "absolutely everybody"
EXCALIBUR	the legendary King Arthur's famous sword
EX CATHEDRA *(eks 'kuh-THEE-druh)*	the Latin for with authority
EYEBRIGHT	an annual herb used in making eye lotions
EYEWINKER	a person's eyes or eyelashes
EYEWITNESS	someone who witnesses (with one's own eyes) an occurrence

EZRAELLA
(ehz-RAY-luh)
an Israeli girl's name meaning God is my strength

F

FABERGE
(fab-er-ZHAY)
Peter Carl (the Frenchman) who became Russia's court jeweler, particularly noted for the jewel and gold imperial eggs

FABRICIA
(FAHB-bree-kah)
the Italian word for plant; a girl's name

FAFANG
(FOH-feng)
the Swedish for vain

FAHNE
(FAH-nuh)
the German word for flag

FAIRBANKS
a city in east central Alaska

FAIR FA'
(FAIR-fah)
Old Scottish/English word meaning good luck

FAIR-SPOKEN
a person who has mastered grace of speech

FAIR ROEBUCK
a woman in the bloom of her beauty

FAIR WIND
good weather; good things

FAIRY LIGHT
something that is lightweight; the flicker of a lightning bug

FAIRY BABE
a very tiny child

FALBALA
(fahl-BELL-uh)
French word for flounce or ruffle

FALCHION
(foll-SHEN)
the short, broad sword of medieval times

FALCO
(FAHL-koh)
the Italian for hawk; a popular man's name

FALCON-GENTLE
another name for the European goshawk (a small falcon); also, a female falcon (particularly a peregrine falcon)

FALDERAL
(FALL-duh-ral)
any trifling fancy or ornamentation

FALKE
(FAHLL-kuh)
the German word for hawk

FALKENSTEIN
(FAHL-ken-shtine)
an industrial city in Saxony, East Germany; literally "stone hawk"

FALLA
(FAHLL-ah)
the Swedish for to fall

FALLEN TIMBERS	the historical site on the Maumee River (SW of Toledo, Ohio) where Mad Anthony Wayne beat the French and Indians
FALSE ALARM	an incorrect, or groundless alarm
FALSE ARREST	being arrested unjustly
FANCYFREE or FANCY-FREE	a person who is not involved in a love affair
FANCY GOODS	small wares or ornamental cloth, ribbons, silk and lace
FANCYWORK	embroidery, tatting, crocheting, lacework, and other fancy stitchery
FANGO *(FAHN-go)*	the Italian for mud
FANTASMA *(fahn-TAHS-mah)*	the Italian for ghost
FANYA *(FAIIN-yah)*	a pet form of the Russian girl's name Fayina "fair one"
FARBE *(FAR-buh)*	the German for color or paint
FARCEUR *(fahr-SIR)*	one who acts a farce; a jester
FARFA *(FAR-fah)*	the Swedish word for grandfather
FARFALLA *(fahr-FAHL-lah)*	the Italian word for butterfly
FARO *(FAIR-oh)*	a card game where the bet is on the first card turned
FATHOM	a nautical word for a measure equal to 6 feet
FAUNA *(FAWN-uh)*	the animals that live in any given area
FAVOLA *(FAH-voh-lah)*	the Italian word for fairy tale
FAWN/FAWNA/FAWNIE	recently popularized girl's name; a young deer
FEARBABE	something that is used to scare babies or young children, (a story, making a face, threat of the boogieman, etc.)
FEATHER & FLIP	an old slang term for a bed (since a feather bed was often "flipped" to plump up the feathers)
FEATHER ME!	a mild Australian expletive meaning something like "good grief!"
FEATHERS	slang term for money or wealth
FEDERACY	an alliance or confederacy

49

FEE *(FAY)*	German word for elves and fairies
FEE-FI-FO-FUM	the nonsense words used by the giant in "Jack And The Bean Stalk"
FELICITA *(feh-lee-chee-TAH)*	an Italian girl's name; "happiness"
FELICITY	great happiness
FELLOWSHIP	a union of friends; a companionship
FEMINIE *(FEM-uh-nee)*	another name for the country of the Amazons, (Land Of The Amazon Women)
FEMME FATALE *(FAM fuh-TAL)*	seductive woman who can lead an unsuspecting man into danger
FENGCHENG *(fung-chung)*	a railroad town in South Manchuria
FENGTU *(fung-doo)*	a city in the Szechwan Province of central China (on the banks of the Yangtze River)
FETERITA *(fet-uh-REE-tuh)*	a Sudanese variety of sorghum (cane sugar)
FIANZA *(F-YAN-sah)*	the Spanish word for bond or joining
FIAT *(FEE-ott)*	the Italian make of fast, classy, sports car
FIDDLER	one who plays the fiddle
FIDDLER'S FARE	meat, drink and money
FIDDLER'S GREEN	the traditional heaven of sailors who die ashore
FIDDLER'S PAY	a phrase meaning "a thanks and wine"
FIDDLESTICKS	an expression of mild annoyance or impatience
FIDGET	to play or fuss; to fiddle impatiently
FIELDER'S CHOICE	baseball term; option of play offered to a fielder
FIELD JACKET	a lightweight cotton, olive-drab, jacket worn by soldiers
FIELD MUSIC	those who play for marching troops (drummers, buglers, etc.)
FIELD NOTES	surveyor's, or naturalist's notes taken in "the field"
FIELD OFFICER	an officer who is intermediate between a company and a general officer (could be a Major, Colonel, or Lt. Colonel)
FIFE	a musical instrument like a flute, but pitched higher

FI-HEATH!	an Old English term for a thief or a mild expletive used alone
FIJI *(FEE-gee)*	British crown colony in the SW Pacific
FINCASTLE	a little town in west central Virginia
FILIBUSTER	any action designed to obstruct (usually a prolonged *speech*)
FINESSE	delicacy of behavior; refinement
FIRE-AND-BRIMSTONE	a very zealous personality
FIRE-AWAY!	"go ahead!" (expletive of encouragement)
FIREBUG	an arsonist
FIRE COMPANY	a fire station, or the organized band of firemen in a community
FIRE-EATER	a bold, or very brave person
FIRE-WATER	whisky (common pioneer or American Indian terminology)
FIREWORKS	excitement; a spectacular display of something
FIRING LINE	the area of most danger, or where all the action is
FIRST-NIGHTER	a person who likes attending opening performances
FIVE NATIONS	the Iroquois Indian Federation (Seneca, Mohawk, Oneida, Onondaga and Cayuga tribes)
FJADER *(F-YAD-ehr)*	Swedish word for feather
FLADDERMUS *(FLAHD-ehr-moos)*	the Swedish word for bat
FLAGSHIP	a ship carrying an officer entitled to display his flag (the flag of his country)
FLAG-WAVER	an aggressively patriotic person
FLAMBEAUX *(flam-BO)*	French word for small flame
FIXED BAYONETS	a brand of good Bermuda rum; to attach a bayonet to a rifle
FLAMINGO	the tall, pink, stilt-legged tropical wading bird
FLAMME *(FLUMM-uh)* *(FLAHM)*	the German word for flame the French word for flame
FLANDERS FORTUNE	a very small fortune

FLAPDRAGON	a drinking game where raisins are snatched out of burning whisky and *quickly* swallowed
FLASH JACK	a showy fellow, or boaster
FLEET STREET	a street in London (center of the newspaper and printing industry)
FLEUR (*FLUHR*)	the French word for blossom, or flower
FLICKEN (*FLICK-ehn*)	the German word for patch
FLITTERMOUSE	an old-time word for a bat
FLOOZY or FLOOZIE	a cheap-looking and disreputable woman
FLORIDA KEYS	the chain of islands that run off the southern tip. of Florida
FLUFFY RUFFLES	a girl in rustling petticoats and feather boa
FLUGEL (*FLEW-gull*)	the German word for wing
FLYGMASKIN (*FLUG-mah-sheen*)	the Swedish word for airplane
FLYING CIRCUS	an exhibition of stunt flying
FLYING COLORS or FLYING THE COLORS	a victory or success
FLYING COUNTRY	Old English usage; in rural English countrysides this was a "hunt" district where one could literally ride or drive their horses safely and quickly (no dangers or obstructions)
FLYING DUTCHMAN	a sailing clipper "the Dreadnought"; also a famous English railway
FLYTTA (*FLUT-ah*)	the Swedish word for to move
FOLK MUSIC	music of the common people
FOLK SONG	a song created and sung by the common people of the area
FOLKWAYS	traditional habits, customs, and behavior of any group
FOLLOW-ME-LADS	old-time use; a woman's curls or ribbons, that hang over one shoulder
FOOL'S ERRAND	any fruitless errand or undertaking
FOOL'S GOLD	iron pyrite (nuggets of a false, goldlike mineral)
FOOL'S PARADISE	being content in one's ignorance of something

FOOTLIGHT FAVOURITE	a theatrical *ham*; one who always eases his way forward (into the footlights)
FORBIDDEN CITY	Lhasa; the capital city of Tibet (outer China); named the Forbidden City because of the hostile attitude (by the lamas, or holy men) toward visitors/strangers
FORENA *(fir-AY-nah)*	Swedish word meaning to associate or to join
FOREVER GENTLEMAN	a man in whom good breeding is *ingrained*
FORFAKTA *(fir-FEK-tah)*	the Swedish word for to agree or advocate
FORGET-ME-NOT	the low-growing garden flower having tiny blue flowers
FORLOVNING *(fir-LOHV-ning)*	the Swedish word for *engagement*
FORTHWITH	immediately; an order to be carried out at once
FORTUNA *(fohr-TOO-nah)*	Italian word for fortune or luck
FORTY WINKS	a short sleep or nap
FOX-BRUSH	an orchid that has a "trailing" (hanging) habit; like a fox's tail
FOXTAIL	a wild grass with dense spike flower plumes like a fox's tail
FOX'S SLEEP	feined sleep, veiling an extreme alertness; pretending to be asleep or pretending not to care what is going on
FOXWOOD	the venerable wood of old, fallen trees (found at timberlines or on the forest floor)
FRAMBOISE *(fram-BWAZ)*	French raspberry brandy
FRAME-UP	to victimize an innocent person by conspiracy; especially when a person is arrested by means of falsified evidence
FRANCISCO *(frahn-SEES-koh)*	the Spanish boy's name meaning free man; also appears in the forms of: CHICO, CHICHO, PACO, PANCHO, PANCHITO, PAQUITO, and QUICO
FRANGIPANI *(fran-je-PEN-ee)*	perfume made from the tropical Plumeria
FRAULEIN *(FROY-line)*	German word for woman or Miss
FRAXINELLA *(frax-uh-nell-uh)*	a Eurasian herb in the Rue family

FREEBOOT or FREEBOOTER	a pirate, buccanneer, or plunderer
FREE ENTERPRISE	freedom of private businesses to operate for a profit
FRENCH CREAM and FRENCH LACE	other colorful names for brandy
FRENCH FARE	when someone indulges in elaborate (extraordinary) politeness
FRIENDLY HOSTILE	used during World War II, when an enemy plane flew over an area and did not drop bombs
FROLICH *(FRO-lish)*	the German word for merry
FRONT AND CENTER	commanding someone to present themselves *immediately*; a stern way of commanding "Come here!"
FROSTWORK	the delicate tracery that hoarfrost decorates leaves and windows with
FUJIYAMA *(FOO-jee-YAH-muh)*	a sacred mountain in south central Japan
FUCHS *(FOOCKS)*	the German word for fox
FUEGO *(FWEH-go)*	the Spanish word for fire
FUSS BUDGET	a very fussy person; someone who is very difficult to please; very demanding
FUTURE PERFECT	a grammatical term; verb tense expressing action in the future

G

GABBY	talking excessively
GABRIEL	the archangel
GAGE	a test or challenge; a variety of plum; a currently popular boy's name
GALAXY	an assembly of brilliant, beautiful, or distinguished persons or things; the heavens or stars
GALENO *(gah-LEH-noh)*	the Spanish word for little bright one
GALICIA *(guh-LISH-ee-uh)*	former Austrian crownland that the 1918 peace conference gave to Poland

GALIVANT	to roam about aimlessly and frivilously
GALLANT	to be brave or courageous
GALT	a Scandinavian boy's name meaning high ground
GANDY DANCER	a railroad track laborer; one who lays railroad tracks
GATEAU *(gah-TOH)*	the French word for cake
GATO *(GAH-toh)*	the Spanish word for kitten
GATTINO *(gaht-TEE-no)*	the Italian word for kitten
GAZEBO *(guh-ZEE-bo)*	pavilion or belvedere (ornamental garden structure)
GEE WHIZ	an exclamation of wonder, like "gee!"
GEGENSCHEIN *(GAY-gen-shine)*	German astronomy's word to describe the patch of hazy light seen at night on the point of ecliptic opposite of the sun
GEHENNA *(guh-HEN-nuh)*	the place of future torment, "Hell"
GELYA *(GAYL-yah)*	the pet form of the Russian name Angeline (Angel)
GEMMA *(JAM-mah)*	the Italian word for gem or jewel
GENDARME *(zhan-DARM)*	a French policeman
GENERALISSIMO *(jen-er-all-ISS-ee-mo)*	the supreme military commander
GENESIS *(JEN-uh-sis)*	"creation," the first book of the Bible
GENGHIS KHAN or JENGHIZ KHAN	the famous mongol conqueror of Asia
GENTLEFOLK	people coming from a good family; persons of good breeding
GENTLEMAN'S AGREEMENT	an agreement guaranteed only by the honor of the persons involved
GENTLEMAN'S GENTLEMAN	one's manservant or valet
GENTRY	people of gentle birth, good breeding, or high social position
GESCHWIND *(guh-SHVINNT)*	the German word for to glitter
GHOST STORY	a tale about spooks, spirits or hauntings

GIFTA SIG *(YIF-tah seeg)*	Swedish for to marry
GIGLIO *(JEE-lyoh)*	an Italian word for lily
GILDERSLEEVE	an American scholar (1831-1924); fictional radio personality
GIMCRACK *(JIM-krak)*	a knickknack, a cheap or showy object of little value
GIN AND JAGUAR	anything that is both good *and* expensive
GIOVANNA *(joh-VAHN-ah)*	an Italian girl's name meaning God is gracious
GITANA *(hee-TAH-nah)*	a Spanish girl's name, meaning gypsy
GIUDITTA *(joo-DEET-tah)*	the Italian for Judith
GIUSEPPE *(joo-SEPH-peh)*	the Italian for Joseph
GIZMO	a gadget or gimmick
GLAD RAGS	one's best clothes; fancy or party clothes
GLITZERN *(GLIT-sehrn)*	the German word for to glitter
GLOCKENSPIEL *(GLOCK-ehn-shpeel)*	a musical instrument where bell-like notes are made by striking metal bars with little, flocked hammers
GOLDEN RULE	the one that goes: "Do unto others as you would have them do unto you"
GOODFELLOW	a companion, or a good person
GRANILOQUENT *(gran-DILL-uh-kwent)*	fancy (snooty or snobbish) language that sounds more important than it is
GRASS ROOTS	the common people
GRIESHOCH *(GREE-shuk)*	the Irish/Scottish for ember, a fire without a blaze
GRODA *(GROO-dah)*	the Swedish word for frog
GRYNING *(GRU-ning)*	the Swedish word for dawn
GUNDA *(GOON-dah)*	a common Scandinavian girl's name meaning battle maiden
GUDINNA *(good-IN-ah)*	the Swedish word for goddess
GUIDO *(GWEE-doh)*	the Spanish word for life
GUN METAL	a vibrant blue/gray color; the color of a gun barrel

GUN MOLL	a female thief or criminal, especially when she acts as the accomplice to a male criminal
GUNNAR *(GOO-nahr)*	a common Scandinavian boy's name meaning battle army
GUNRUNNER	a smuggler of guns, weapons, etc., into a country
GUN SLINGER	a gunman or hired killer (much usage in the Old West)
GUSTAF *(goo-STAHF)*	the Swedish boy's name, it means slave of the Goths
GYLLENE *(YULL-eh-neh)*	the Swedish word for golden
GYPSY'S WARNING	a colorful slang phrase for morning, (rhyming)
GYRFALCON *(JUR-fal-ken)*	a beautiful white Arctic falcon

H

HABIB AND HABIBAH *(hah-BEEB) (hah-BEE-bah)*	a common Arabic boy's name, "beloved"
HACKENSACK	a city in NE New Jersey; a river on the New York/New Jersey border
HADAD *(hah-DAHD)*	the Syrian god of virility
HAGBORN	born of a witch or a hag
HAGEL *(HAH-gel)*	the German word for hail
HAGRIDDEN	tormented or harrassed (ridden); as if by a witch
HAIDAR *(HIGH-dahr)*	the East Indian word for a lion
HAIL-FELLOW	being on very cordial terms; a close companion
HAKEEM *(HA-keem)*	a common Arabic boy's name meaning wise
HALSA *(HELL-sah)*	the Swedish word for to greet or to salute
HALF-A-CROWN or HALF-CROWN	the British coin worth 2 shillings and sixpence

HALF MOON	the moon when only half its disk is illuminated
HALLELUJAH GALLOP	a hymn in a quick, lively measure
HALLELUJAH LASS	a girl in the service of the Salvation Army
HAND-IN-GLOVE	in close intimacy
HANDMAIDEN	a female servant or attendant
HAND-ME-DOWNS	an item used by one person and then given to another
HANDSOME HARRY	a Lothario (love-'em-and-leave-'em) kind of guy
HANGFORA (*HAN-fir-ah*)	the Swedish word for to charm
HANGCHOW (*hang-chou*)	capital city of E. China (in the province of Chekiang)
HANGFIRE	a delay in an explosion; a misfire
HANKY-PANK	something crooked or unethical; funny business
HAPPY LANDINGS!	an expletive meaning good luck
HARBORMASTER	an officer who oversees and enforces regulations of a harbor
HARDECANUTE (*hardy-cuh-NOOT*)	King of England and Denmark (1010-1042)
HARD HAT	construction worker
HARD TIME	difficult/troublesome job, time of adversity, a "hard" prison term
HAREM	a woman's (the wives, servants, and concubines) presence or position in a Moslem household
HAROUN (*hah-ROON*)	a common Arabic boy's name meaning exalted
HASTA (*AHSS-tah*)	the Swedish word for until
HARVEST HOME	completion of the harvest; in the time of the harvest
HARVEST MOON	the full moon that occurs during the autumnal equinox
HASTA LA VISTA (*AHS-tuh luh VEES-tuh*)	the Spanish for goodbye or until we meet again
HATTERAS (*hat-uh-rus*)	a cape and an island off the North Carolina coast (it is a long, narrow sandbar)
HAUTE COUTURE (*OAT KOO-tuhr*)	the French for "high sewing"; it refers to fashion designers and their creations
HAVERSACK	a hiker's canvas bag used to carry food

HAXA *(HECK-sah)*	the Swedish word for witch
HAYMAKER	a heavy blow with the fist; a knockout punch
HAYWIRE	crazy; in a confused or unusual manner
HEAD HUNTER	the owner of an executive employment agency; South American Indians who decapitate their victims and shrink their heads for display
HEADS UP!	a warning to get out of the way quickly, or to watch out
HEARTBEAT	a single, complete, pulsation of the heart
HEARTSEASE	peace of mind; also, a wild pansy
HEARTS AND FLOWERS	sentimentality; something said or done for sympathy
HEAT LIGHTNING	lightning without thunder; seen on the horizon on hot summer evenings
HEAVENS ABOVE	rhyming slang words for love
HEGEN *(HAY-gen)*	the German word for to cherish
HEIR APPARENT	one who must, by course of law, become heir if he survives an ancestor
HELGON *(HELL-gohn)*	the Swedish word for saint
HELL-BENDER	a wild spree
HELL CAT	an extremely spirited, reckless young woman
HELLDIVER	the American Dabchick (a small water bird in the Grebe family)
HELLER	a person who behaves recklessly, or wildly
HELLFIRE PASS	what the British soldiers called Halfaya Pass (in extreme NW Egypt) after many bloody battles were fought there
HELL GATE	the narrow part of the East River in New York (between Long Island and Manhattan Island)
HELLHOUND	a hound from Hell; a fierce or cruel pursuer
HELLKITE	a fierce bird of prey; a wantonly cruel person
HELL'S BELLS!	an exclamation of surprise or anger
HELLS CANYON	canyon of the Snake River on the Idaho/Oregon border (7,000 feet deep)
HELL'S DELIGHT!	an exclamation of surprise

HEN PARTY	a talking or gossiping party attended by women and girls
HEXE *(HEX-uh)*	the German word for witch
HIAWASSEE *(HI-uh-WAH-see)*	a small town in northern Georgia
HIGHFALUTIN'	pompous or high class
HIGH-FLIER	a person who is overly enthusiastic or ambitious
HIGH-HAT	a snob, one who acts superior, aloof, or conceited
HIGHLAND FRISKY	a slang word for whisky, (rhyming)
HIGHPOCKETS	nickname for any tall person
HIGHROAD	a main road or highway; the "sure" path
HIGH ROLLER	one who frequently gambles large sums of money
HIGH SEAS	open waters of an ocean, or sea, beyond the limits of any nation's jurisdiction
HIGH-STRIKES	many successes
HIGH TEA	the British people's late afternoon meal; it includes tea, a hot course, bread and butter
HIGH-TEST	meeting the most exacting requirements
HIGH TREASON	treason against a ruler or government
HIGH WINE	grain spirits distilled to a high percentage of alcohol
HILL 609	a height (hill) commanding near Mateur, N. Tunisia, where after severe fighting the Americans captured it on May 1, 1943
HIS LORDSHIP	address towards the lord of the manor
HJALPA *(YELL-pah)*	Swedish word for to help
HJALTE *(YELL-teh)*	the Swedish word for hero
HOBOKEN *(HO-boh-kin)*	a city in Hudson County, New Jersey
HOBOMOKO *(HOBO-mo-ko)*	evil spirit of the Algonquian Indians
HOEDOWN	a rural square dance; a rural party or dance
HOME-FOLK	one's relatives
HONEST FELLOW	a good person
HONEST INDIAN! or HONEST INJUN!	the absolute truth

HONEY-CREEPER	a small, brightly-colored bird of the warmer areas of the US, there is also a Bahama honey-creeper
HONEY-LOTUS	the white melilot (a sweet clover)
HONEYSUCKLE	a very fragrant shrub with white, pink and yellow flowers
HONEY SHUCKS	the beans of the Honey-Locust tree
HONIG *(HOH-nig)*	the German word for honey
HOOCHINOO *(HOOCH-uh-new)*	a strong liquor made by the Alaskan Indians (it is made out of ferns)
HOOLIGAN	a hoodlum, ruffian, or tough guy
HOP-THUMB or **HOP-O'-MY-THUMB**	a dwarf or small person or thing; the tiny hero in the Charles Perrault fairy tale
HORSEBREAKER	one who trains horses
HORSE MARINE	a mounted Marine; and since there is no such thing this means that one is as out of place as a Marine on horseback
HORSE-SUGAR	a sweetleaf shrub from the southern United States
HOSHI *(hoh-SHEE)*	a Japanese girl's name, it means star
HOT STUFF	a person of notice; superior, charming, dashing, and reckless
HOTTENTOT *(hot 'n tot)*	people of southwest Africa
HOUYHNHNM *(HOO-in-em HWIN-em)*	the humanlike race of horses found in the book *Gulliver's Travels*
HOWITZER	a short cannon
HSINGAN SHAN *(SHING-an SHAN)*	a mountain range in southwest Jehol, northeast China
HSUCHOW *(SOO-joe)*	a town in N. Honan Province, east central China
HUG-ME-TIGHT	a woman's close-fitting, knitted jacket
HUKONG *(HOO-kong)*	a remote valley in N. Burma (upper Chindwin)
HUNTAWAY	an Australian word commanding a sheep-dog to drive the sheep forward when mustering
HUNTER'S HILL	a group of islands off Cape Grim, northwest Tasmania in Australia
HUNTER'S MOON	a full moon following the harvest moon; a late autumn full moon
HUNTRESS	a woman who hunts

HUNT'S UP	a tune played on a horn to awaken huntsmen in the morning
HURRAH-BOY	a noisy, loud supporter of an idea or political party
HURRAH'S NEST	a situation of utmost confusion
HURRY BACK	an RAF (Royal Air Force) hurricane fighter plane
HUTE *(HOO-teh)*	American Indian boy's name, it means North Star
HWANG HO *(hwang ho)*	the Yellow River in north central and eastern China
HWANG PU *(hwang poo)*	a river that flows to the Yangtze in east China
HYACINTH-BLUE	a medium purplish-blue, the color of hyacinths in bloom
HYACINTHINE	pertaining to, or like, the hyacinth; a graceful girl's name

I

IAKTTOG *(EE-ahk-tog)*	the Swedish for watching
ICE BLINK	coastal ice cliff; the yellow glare in the sky over ice fields
ICHANG *(ee-CHANG)*	a walled city in S. Hupah Province in east central China
IDEE FIXE *(EE-day FEEKS)*	obsession; the literal French is "fixed idea"
IDYLL *(EYED-l)*	a scene or event of rural simplicity; picturesque short poem describing such a scene
IGAR *(ee-GOHR)*	the Swedish word for yesterday; a name sometimes used to describe some ugly little hunchback in a Frankenstein movie
IKVELL *(ee-KVELL)*	the Swedish for tonight
ILE-DE-FRANCE *(EEL-duh-frahnz)*	region/former province in north central France
ILE-DU-DIABLE *(EEL-doo-dee-ahbl)*	French for Devil's Island
ILKA *(ILL-kuh)*	an Old Scottish word for each, every and each one

ILLUSION	the erroneous perception of reality; a delusion
IMAGERY *(IM-uhj-ree)*	mental pictures or images
IMMORTELLE *(IM-ohr-tell)*	French for everlasting
I MORGON *(E MOHR-rohn)*	Swedish for tomorrow
IMPROMPTU	done on the spur of the moment; done on impulse
INAMORATA *(in-AMOUR-ah-tuh)*	a woman with whom one is enamored; a sweetheart
INCA DOVE	a tiny-bodied, long-tailed dove of the arid Southwest
INDIAN AGENT	official of the government who deals with Indians on a reservation
INDIAN CORN	brightly-colored ornamental corn
INDIAN GIVER	one who gives a present and then takes it back
INDIAN PIPE	a low, waxy-white flower common in the woods of America
INDIAN PUDDING	a cereal of cornmeal, milk and molasses (pioneer use)
INDIGO BUNTING	a gorgeous iridescent blue bird of the eastern US
INESITA *(EE-neh-SEE-tah)*	the Spanish spelling of Inez/Ines
INGENUE *(AHN-zhuh-new)*	French for innocent young woman
INGLENOOK	a British word for a corner by the fireplace
INJUN	the facetious respelling of Indian
INKBERRY	an eastern US shrub with black berries
INKLING	a hint, intimation, or vague idea
INKY	stained or smeared with ink
INNSBRUCK *(INNZ-brook)*	a city in the Tirol, West Austria
INNUENDO *(in-yoo-EHN-doh)*	suggestion or hint about some person
IRISH UP	(as in "Get your Irish up"), a term meaning to become angry
IRONDEQUOIT *(uh-ROHN-du-kwoit)*	a town in western New York state
IRON GATES	a 2-mile-long gorge, with rapids, on the Danube River on the Yugoslav border

IRON HAND	severe control
IRON HORSE	an old-time prairie Indian term for a train
IRONSIDES	nickname for the Englishman, Oliver Cromwell
ISHTAR	the Babylonian goddess of love
ISIS *(EYE-sis)*	the Egyptian goddess of love
ISTAS *(EE-stahs)*	an American Indian girl's name meaning snow
IVORY GULL	a rare, pure white Arctic gull
IVY LEAGUE	characteristic of the Ivy League schools (i.e., Princeton, Yale, Harvard), and the manners, and fashions of the students; usually connotes wealth, sophistication, refinement, and social prominence
IWALANI *(ee-wuh-LAH-nee)*	a Hawaiian girl's name meaning sea bird
IZHMA *(EASE-muh)*	a navigable river in central Komi Republic, Russia

J

JABIRU *(JAB-uh-roo)*	a tropical American wading bird (white)
JACKANAPES *(JACK-uh-napes)*	a monkey; a cocky young person
JACKBOOT	a tough military boot that reaches above the knee
JACKDAW	a European, crowlike bird
JACKFIELD	a village in Shropshire, West England
JACK-O'-LANTERN	a lantern made from a hollowed-out pumpkin
JACKPOT	top prize or an award, cumulative pool or kitty in a game
JACKSTRAW	a game played with a pile of straws or sticks
JACOB'S LADDER	a ladder on a ship; it is made of rope
JACQUARD *(juh-KARD)*	a special loom for weaving figured fabric; a fabric with an intricate woven pattern
JAEGER *(YAY-gehr)*	a type of sea bird (it bullies other birds into giving up their catches/prey)

JAFAR *(jah-FAHR)*	Muslim boy's name, it means little stream
JAGDHUND *(YAGHT-hoont)*	the German word for hound
JAGGERY	an unrefined sugar made from pine sap
JAGUARIBE *(zha-gwuh-REE-buh)*	a river in northeast Brazil, flowing eventually to the Atlantic (JAGUAR RIVER)
JAI ALAI *(HIGH-LIGH)*	a fast court game played with long, hand-shaped baskets
JAIPUR *(JIGH-poor)*	former Indian state in East Rajputana, NW India
JAKTHUND *(YAHKT-hoond)*	the Swedish word for hound
JAL *(jahl)*	a gypsy boy's name
JAMAICA BAY	an inlet (20 miles square) off the Atlantic Coast (west of Long Island, NY)
JAMBU *(JAHM-boo)*	a Hindu believer's mythical rose-apple tree that was so large that it shaded the earth, thus it makes the night
JAMILA *(jah-MEE-lah)*	Muslim girl's name, it means beautiful
JANIZARY *(JAN-uh-zer-ee)*	Turkish word for a very loyal supporter (one of the Sultan's guards)
JAQUETTE *(zhah-KETT)*	French word for jacket
JARN *(YAIRN)*	Swedish word for iron
JAROSLAV *(YAH-roh-slahf)*	a Czech boy's name, it means spring
JAYHAWKER	someone from Kansas (nickname of a Kansas resident)
JEFE *(HEH-feh)*	Spanish boy's name, it means boss or leader
JEHOSHAPHAT *(juh-HOSS-uh-fat)*	a 9th century BC king of Judah; also, the modern expletive of "Jumpin' Jehoshaphat!"
JELENA *(yah-LAY-nah)*	a common Russian girl's name
JENICA *(zhye-NEE-kah)*	a Rumanian girl's name, it means God is gracious
JERICHO	the ancient city of Jordan
JESAJA *(yehs-EYE-ah)*	the Swedish form of Isaiah
JEWEL OF ASIA	a rare gemstone

JIN	a Chinese boy's name, it means gold
JINGO	a person who loudly supports his country
JINNI *(JIN-ee)*	the mythical character of Moslem legend, who lives in magic lamps and grants wishes (but there are also evil jinni's)
JINRIKISHA *(jin-RICK-shaw)*	oriental, 2-wheeled, man-pulled carriage cab
JIPIJAPA *(HEE-pee-HAP-uh)*	a palmlike plant from South America (used in making panama hats)
JIRO *(ji-ROH)*	Japanese boy's name, it means the second male child
JOHN BARLEYCORN	a nickname for corn liquor
JOHN HENRY	the famous black American folk hero who supposedly died proving that he was faster with a sledgehammer than the steam drills were
JOHNNIE GALLAGHER	an Irish policeman's term for any hobo or tramp
JOHNNIE JUMP-UP	the heartsease plant
JOHNNY-ON-THE-SPOT	a person ready, and available, to act when necessary
JOHNNY REB	a confederate soldier
JOKER	a person who tells a joke; a prankster
JOLI *(zoh-LEE)*	the French word for pretty, also used as a girl's name
JOLON *(JOH-lohn)* *(YOH-lawn)*	American Indian boy's name meaning valley of the oaks Hungarian girl's name meaning violet blossom
JOLLY ROGER	the black flag with white skull and crossbones flown on a pirate's ship
JONQUIL *(JONG-kwill)*	the narcissus, a yellow, trumpet-shaped flower that blooms in the spring
JOSE *(hoh-SEH)*	a very common Spanish name for a boy; it can also be in the forms of PEPE, PEPITO, CHE, CHEPITA, JOSEITO
JOURNEY'S END	reaching a goal; ending up in jail; etc.
JOUET *(zhoo-AY)*	the French word for toy
JOV *(johv)*	a Russian pet name meaning God will establish
JOVEN *(HO-venn)*	the Spanish word for young
JOYA *(HO-yah)*	the Spanish for jewel

JOY OF MY LIFE — slang words for wife (rhyming)

JUDGE ADVOCATE — a commissioned officer in the US Army assigned to the legal branch

JUGADOR *(hoo-gah-DOHR)* — the Spanish word for gambler

JUGGERNAUT *(JUG-ehr-not)* — from the Sanskrit, meaning lord of the world; it is a wild, untamed force

JUMBUCK — an Australian word for a sheep

JUTE *(JOOT)* — a fiber used in making rope and burlap

K

KABIR *(kah-BEER)* — an ancient Hindu mystic

KABUKI *(kuh-BOO-kee)* — Japanese drama dance and song with much pantomime

KAFEE *(KUFF-ay)* — the German word for coffee

KAFEE KLATSCH *(KAF-fee KLATCH)* — when housewives gather informally for coffee and gossip

KAI *(KIGH)* — the Hawaiian word for sea, used as a boy's or girl's name

KAILI *(KIGH-lee)* — a Hawaiian goddess, the name is now used for girls

KAIMI *(KIGH-mee)* — a Hawaiian girl's name, it means searcher

KAISER *(KIZE-ehr)* — German word for emperor

KAKALINA *(kah-kuh-LEE-nuh)* — a Hawaiian girl's name, it means virtuous

KALLA *(CHELL-ah)* — the Swedish word for spring

KAMASUTRA *(KOM-muh-SOO-truh)* — a *very* explicit Hindu love manual

KAMIKAZE *(KOM-muh-KAWZ-ee)* — World War II Japanese suicide pilots

KANGA *(KANG-guh)* — the Australian nickname for a kangaroo

KANINCHEN *(kah-NEEN-shen)* — the German word for rabbit

KANJI *(KAN-jee)*	a Japanese system of writing (based on Chinese)
KANOA *(kuh-NOH-uh)*	a Hawaiian boy's name meaning free
KANON *(kah-NOON)*	the Swedish word for cannon
KANTU *(KAHN-too)*	the Hindu god of love
KARAMELL *(kah-rah-MELL)*	the Swedish word for candy
KARISIMBI *(kar-uh-SIM-buh)*	a mountain peak in the east Congo
KARIF *(kah-REEF)*	a popular Arabic boy's name, it means born in autumn
KARLIK *(CHAIR-lake)*	the Swedish word for love
KARNAK *(KAR-nak)*	site of ancient Thebes (along the Nile in S. Egypt)
KASHAN *(kuh-SHAN)*	a city in central Iran famous for its beautiful velvet and brocade fabrics
KASIM *(kah-SEEM)*	popular Muslim boy's name, it means divided
KASSIA *(kahs-SEE-uh)*	Greek/Polish girl's name, it means pure
KATCHEN *(KETZ-shen)*	the German word for kitten
KATT *(KAHTT)*	the Swedish word for cat
KATMANDU *(KAT-man-DOO)*	the capital city of Nepal (in the Himalayas)
KATOOMBA *(kuh-TOOM-buh)*	a town in E. New South Wales, Australia
KATYDID	a green, grasshopper-looking insect that lives in trees and makes very shrill (unmistakeable) sounds
KATZENJAMMER	a German word for any loud, or discordant noise
KAYAK	an island off the coast of SE Alaska; a small, one-man canoe
KAZATSKI *(kuh-ZATT-skee)*	the Russian folk dance where a man kicks his legs out from the squatting position
KEALOHA *(keh-uh-LOH-huh)*	the Hawaiian word for loved one, a girl's name

KEELHAUL	a sailor's punishment, he is tied with a rope and then hauled back and forth through the water, under the keel of the boat
KEFIRA *(kah-FEE-ruh)*	the Hebrew word for lioness, used as a girl's name
KEJSARDOME *(CHAY-sahr-do-meh)*	the Swedish word for empire
KEJSARE *(CHAY-sah-reh)*	the Swedish word for emperor
KELPIE	found in Old Scottish folklore, a water spirit that can change into a horse and then entices people to cross the river on its back, where halfway across he drowns them
KENNEBEC *(KEN-uh-BECK)*	a river in west central and southern Maine; a variety of potato that was developed there
KENSPECKLE	Old English word that is used on something that is striking because of well-defined or peculiar markings; something that is conspicuous or showy
KESAR *(keh-SAHR)*	a Russian boy's name, it means longhaired
KETCHIKAN *(KETCH-uh-kan)*	seaport town in SE Alaska, famous for its fine furs and salmon
KETCHUM	a village in central Idaho
KETTLEDRUM	a drum in an orchestra (very large with a brass shell and a parchment head) that is sounded with soft drumsticks; it can also be used to describe an informal afternoon get-together
KEY LARGO	one of the larger of the Florida Keys
KHOJAK PASS *(KOE-jack)*	a pass on the west ridge of the Sulaiman mountains of Pakistan
KHYBER PASS	a mountain pass between Pakistan and Afghanistan
KIBBE *(KEE-beh)*	an American Indian girl's name, it means night bird
KIBITZER	a Yiddish word for a meddlesome person; one who is both nosey and very free with giving out unrequested opinions/advice
KICHI *(KEE-chee)*	a Japanese girl's name, it means lucky
KICKSHAW	a fancy food; fancy delicacies or fancy trinkets

KID BROTHER	slang for someone's younger brother
KID SISTER	slang for someone's younger sister
KIEFER *(KEE-fer)*	the German word for pine
KIKILIA *(ke-ke-LEE-uh)*	the Hawaiian form of the name Cecilia
KIKU *(kee-KOO)*	a favorite Japanese girl's name, it means chrysanthemum
KILIMANJARO	the famous mountain near the Kenya border in NE Tanzania, Africa (Mt. Kilimanjaro is the often-photographed, snow-capped peak)
KILKENNY CATS	the legendary Irish cats that fought until only their tails were left
KILLARNEY *(kill-ARE-nee)*	an old urban district in County Kerry, SW Eire in Ireland (now a tourist attraction)
KIMIKO *(kuh-MEE-ko)*	a popular Japanese girl's name, it means princess
KINDU *(KIN-doo)*	a town in the West Kivu province of the East Congo
KINEKS *(KEE-nehks)*	an American Indian girl's name, it means rosebud
KINGCHOW	pronounced JING-joe and sometimes KING-chow; it is the former name of the walled city on the north bank of the Yangtze River in central China
KINGCRAFT	the art, style, or method that a king decides to use to rule
KING'S BIRTHDAY	Old English slang term for pay day
KING'S COUNSEL	in the British empire it is the *barristers*; they can council the crown but cannot go back later on and speak against the crown without permission
KING'S SILVER	a soft, very pure silver (used in only the most costly of pieces)
KING'S UP	in a poker game this means a pair of kings
KINSMAN	someone's blood relations, whether close or distant
KIRITAN *(keer-ee-TAHN)*	the Hindu word for wearing a crown
KIRSCHE *(KEERR-shuh)*	the German word for cherry
KIRSI *(KEER-see)*	a popular girl's name in India, it is a plant name

70

KISA *(KEE-sah)*	a popular Russian pet name; it means kitty or pussycat
KISKA *(KEES-kah)*	a Russian girl's name, it means pure
KISMET *(KIZ-met)*	a contemporary American word for fate or destiny
KISSING COUSIN	constant companions (of the same or opposite sex) regardless of any true blood relationship, they are granted the same closeness accorded a blood relation
KISSING-KIN	something that is "like," a very close match
KISS-ME-QUICK	the old-time bonnets that ladies wore on the back of their heads
KISS THE MAID	(late 17th century use) losing one's head on the guillotine
KITTLA *(CHITT-lah)*	Swedish word meaning to tickle
KITTIWAKE	a gull of the North Seas
KIWI	a flightless bird of New Zealand; also used to refer to an Air Force person not qualified to fly
KIYANG *(KEE-yang)*	a town in S. Hunan Province, southeast central China
KIYOSHI *(kee-YOH-shee)*	a Japanese boy's name, it means silence
KLIPSPRINGER	a small, agile African antelope
KLONDIKE	a gold-mining region of the Yukon; a chocolate-covered ice cream bar
KNICKERS and KNICKERBOCKERS	loose trousers gathered just below the knees
KNIGHT ERRANT	a medieval knight who went out to redress wrongs or to seek out his own adventures
KNIGHT OF THE BLADE	a bully
KNIGHT OF THE FIELD	a tramp
KNIGHT OF THE MOON	a drunk
KNIGHT OF THE RAINBOW	a footman, or valet
KNIGHT OF THE ROAD	a highwayman, or robber
KNIGHT OF THE SUN	an adventurer
KODIAK	an island off the SW coast of Alaska; the grizzly bears common to the area
KOGNAK *(KAWNN-yahk)*	the German word for brandy

KOHINOOR or **KOH-I-NOOR**	the name of a huge diamond that came from India but is now with the crown jewels of England
KOHL *(coal)*	a black eye makeup substance used in Mid-Eastern countries; much used during the time of the pharoahs of ancient Egypt
KONGMOON	a town in Central Kwangtung Province in SE China
KONGO	the Bantu language spoken in the lower regions of the Congo
KONGOLO *(kong-GO-low)*	a town on the Lualaba River in N. Katanga Province in thc SE Congo
KONGJU *(GONG-joe)*	a town in South Chusei Province, western Korea
KONIG *(KO-nig)*	German word for king
KONIGIN *(KO-nee-gin)*	German word for queen
KONJAK *(KOHN-yahk)*	the Swedish word for brandy
KOOKUBURRA *(KOOK-uh-burr-uh)*	an Australian bird (Kingfisher) that has a cry sounding like loud laughter
KOPECK or KOPEK	a Russian coin (worth 1/100th of a ruble)
KOVAR *(KOH-vahr)*	the Czech word for blacksmith, used as a boy's name
KRAKA *(KROH-kah)*	the Swedish word for crow
KRIG *(KREEG)*	The Swedish word for war
KRIKOR *(kree-KOHR)*	the Armenian spelling of Gregory
KRISTALL *(kris-TOHL)*	the Swedish for crystal
KRISTO *(KREE-stoh)*	the Greek form of Christopher
KRISTOFORO *(KREE-stoh-FOR-oh)*	the Italian form of Christopher
KRONA *(KRO-nah)*	the Swedish for to crown
KRONEN *(KRO-nen)*	the German word for to crown
KRUT *(KROOT)*	the Swedish word for gunpowder
KUBLAI KHAN *(KOO-bligh khan)*	the grandson of Genghis Khan (the Kublai was, himself, a Mongol ruler of China)

KUCHEN (*KOO-khen*)	the German word for cake
KUDOS (*KOO-doughs*)	glory or fame; to give lavish praise for an accomplishment
KUGEL (*KOO-gel*)	the German word for bullet
KUMAR (*koo-MAHR*)	an Anglo-Indian word meaning prince
KUMI (*KOO-mee*)	a common Japanese girl's name, it means braid
KUSHKA (*KOOSH-kuh*)	Russian military post and railhead in southeast Turkmen S.S.R.
KUSSEN (*KUSS-ehn*)	the German word for to kiss
KYCKLING (*CHUK-ling*)	the Swedish form of chicken
KYOKO (*KYOH-koh*)	a common Japanese girl's name, it means mirror

L

LACET (*lay-SAY*)	the French for lace
LACEWOOD	the handsomely figured furniture wood of the American Sycamore
LA-DI-DA (*LAW-dee-dah*)	slang for something that is pretty; or used as an expletive for "how cute!"
LADYBELL	a perennial herb with bell-shaped, violet flowers
LADY-IN-WAITING	a lady of the British royal household in attendance at court
LADYKIN	a small woman
LADY OF THE MANOR	equivalent to Lord of the Manor (lady of the house)
LADYSHIP	the rank or position of a lady; a titled lady (Her Ladyship!)
LADYSMITH	a town in W. Natal, East Union in South Africa (it was the scene of the famous siege of the Boer Wars)
LADY-TRESSES	an orchid with slender stems and small flowers that bloom on trailing arms

LAFAYETTE	French general and a marquis; he served with the Americans during the Revolutionary War
LAGNIAPPE *(lan-YAP)*	a French Creole word meaning tip; a small gift given with a purchase
LAGOON	a South Sea pool of water surrounded by coral; a calm pond of water offshore protected from the battering waves by coral reefs
LAHELA *(luh-HE-luh)*	a Hawaiian girl's name, it means lamb
LAKENHEATH *(LAKE-'n'-heath)*	a village in NW Suffolk (east England)
LAMBKIN	a little lamb; figuratively meaning "cherished child"
LAMPBLACK	a fine soot (as found in the glass chimney of candle lamps), and used as a black pigment
LANCASHIRE LASS	colorful slang for a "glass" (rhyming)
LANCE JACK	a slang term for a Lance Corporal
LANCHOW *(lan-JOE)*	capital city of Kansu Province in north central China
LANCIA *(LAHN-chah)*	the Italian word for spear
LANGCHUNG *(lang-JOONG)*	city in N. Szechwan Province in south central China
LANI *(LAH-nee)*	a very common Hawaiian girl's name meaning heaven
LANTANA *(lan-TAN-uh)*	a town in Palm Beach County, SE Florida
LANZA *(LAHN-sah)*	the Spanish word for spear
LAPIS LAZULI *(LAP-is LAZ-yoo)*	an azure-blue, semiprecious stone
LARAMIE	a city in Albany County, SE Wyoming (near Cheyenne)
LARCENY	theft (it includes both GRAND LARCENY and PETTY LARCENY)
LAREDO *(luh-RAY-do)*	city in Webb County, south Texas (settled by the Spanish in 1755)
LARGESSE *(lar-JESS)*	a generous giving (gift)
LARGO	music in a slow, stately tempo
LASHI *(LAH-shee)*	a gypsy boy's name meaning the same as Louis

LATIGO *(LAH-tee-go)*	the Spanish word for whip
LAVALAVA	a draped, kiltlike garment of cotton prints worn by the Polynesian and Samoan natives
LAVALIERE *(lav-uh-LERR)*	a French word for the ornament on a necklace (a charm, locket, heart)
LAZY SUSAN	a revolving tray that holds food or spices
LEATHERNECK	nickname for a Marine
LEAVENWORTH	a city in NE Kansas, site of a Federal Prison
LEGERDEMAIN *(lej-ehr-duh-main)*	French for sleight-of-hand; magic or trickery
LEILANI *(lay-LAH-nee)*	a Hawaiian girl's name meaning heavenly child
LEITMOTIF *(light-moe-teef)*	a recurring musical phrase (German)
LEJON *(LEH-yohn)*	the Swedish word for lion
LE MANS *(luh MAHN)*	a city in W. France, site of the famous Gran Prix car race of the same name
LEMON SQUASH	a carbonated lemon drink (lemonade with fizz)
LESE MAJESTY *(LEEZ maj-us-tee)*	French for injured majesty; crimes or treason against the king
LETTERPERFECT	correct to the last detail
LIANG *(lee-AHNG)*	a Chinese boy's name meaning good
LICKETY-SPLIT	slang for "going at full speed"
LIEBLING *(LEEP-link)*	the German for darling
LIEN HUA *(lay-ehn hwah)*	a Chinese girl's name meaning lotus flower
LIGHT AIR	official designation for a wind speed of 1-3 mph
LIGHT FANTASTIC	slang term for foot; commonly: "Tripping The Light Fantastic"
LIGHTHOUSE	a tall tower with a bright light used for guiding ships at night
LIGHTNING BUG	a firefly
LIGHTNING-ROD	metal conductor that protects buildings by carrying lightning strikes into the ground
LIGHT-O'-LOVE	an old-time dance tune; a coquettish woman

LIGHT'S OUT!	slang term for turn out the lights or out go the lights
LI HUA *(lay HWAH)*	a Chinese girl's name, it means pear blossom
LILJA *(LILL-yah)*	Swedish word for lily
LILLIBULLERO *(lily-buy-LAY-roh)*	an English revolutionary song used to kindle people to revolt (1688)
LILIPUT	the country of the tiny people (from *Gulliver's Travels*)
LINDO *(LEEN-doh)*	Spanish word for lovely
LINE-RIDER	cowboy who rides fences looking for breaks or stray stock
LINE STORM	a severe storm occurring at, or near, the equinox
LINGO	language, vocabulary or dialect of a people or country
LINSEY-WOOLSEY	a coarse fabric made of cotton and woven with wool
LIONET	a small lion cub; a young lion
LION'S LAIR	a very dangerous place to be
LIRIT *(li-REET)*	an Israeli girl's name, it means lyrical
LIS *(LEESS)*	the French for lily
LISBON *(LIZ-buhn)*	capital and seaport city in Portugal
LITTLE BLACK	a river in northern Maine
LITTLE BLUE	a river in Nebraska and Kansas
LITTLE BRITCHES	a little, or young, boy
LITTLE ENDIAN	one who argues over small and umimportant things
LITTLE-GO	the preliminary exam for a B.A. degree at Cambridge
LITTLE SLAM	a Bridge term when someone wins every trick but one in a deal
LITTLE STEPS	slang term used endearingly for children
LITTLE SILVER	a river flowing from Minnesota to Iowa
LITLIT *(LEET-leet)*	a North American Indian girl's name meaning butterfly
LIVERPOOL BLUES	the 79th division of foot soldiers in the British Royal Army

LOBO *(LOH-boh)*	the Spanish word for wolf
LOCKE *(LAWK-uh)*	the German word for curl
LOCH RAVEN *(Lock Raven)*	Scottish for Lake Raven (or Raven's Lake); an urban community in Baltimore County, Maryland
LOCOMOTION	the power to move from one place to another
LODESTAR	a star used to direct a course (the North Star)
LOGJAM	a barrier of logs on a river's course
LOKELANI *(loh-ke-LAH-nee)*	A Hawaiian girl's name meaning heavenly rose
LOKNI *(LOHK-nee)*	an Indian boy's name, meaning born during a storm
LONDONDERRY	a county in NW Ireland
LONDON FOG	a type of manufactured raincoat (a trademark/brand)
LONDON IVY	slang for a thick, London fog
LONDON PARTICULAR	a thick, heavy London fog
LONDON SMOKE	a gray color (similar to London's foggy atmosphere)
LONDONY	anything that is characteristic of London (weather, accents, etc.)
LONGSHIPS	rocky islets west of Lands End in Cornwall, SW England; also, the great sailing ships of the Vikings
LORDLING	a little lord or petty chieftain
LORIKEET	any of several varieties of Polynesian parrots
LOSHAN *(LOE-shan)*	a city in SW Szechwan Province, south central China
LOVEDRURY	a keepsake or love token
LOVE-IN-A-MIST	a European plant with blue flowers
LOVING-KINDNESS	the type of kindness that comes from personal attachment
LOX *(locks)*	expensive smoked salmon, (as in lox and bagels)
LUCHOW *(LOO-joe)*	a city in Anhwei, east China
LUCIFER HUMMINGBIRD	a hummingbird of the southwest US, violet-throated and green-crowned

LUIGI *(loo-EE-jee)*	the Italian form of Louis
LULANI *(loo-LAH-nee)*	a Hawaiian girl's name meaning highest heaven
LUJO *(LOO-ho)*	the Spanish word for luxury
LUPERCALIA *(loo-pehr-KAY-lee)*	the ancient Roman fertility festival, it is held in February and the Romans would pray for good and productive harvests
LUVVADUCK! *(LOVE A DUCK!)*	a mild expletive
LUXUS *(LOOX-ooss)*	the German word for luxury
LUZ DE LA LUNA *(looss deh lah LOO-nah)*	the Spanish for daylight
LUZ DEL SOL *(looss dell SOHL)*	the Spanish for sunshine
LYCIA *(LISH-ee-uh)*	an ancient Roman province in SW Asia Minor
LYCKA *(LUK-ah)*	the Swedish word for happiness
LYX *(LUX)*	the Swedish word for luxury

M

MACADAM *(muh-KAHD-uhm)*	a road made of a mixture of broken stone, tar, and asphalt
MACHISMO *(muh-CHEEZ-muh)*	Spanish word for having "macho" (being aggressively manish)
MACHO CABRIO *(MAH-choh ka-BREE-oh)*	Spanish word for buck (male deer)
MACHREE *(muh-KREE)*	Ango-Irish word for my dear; a term of endearment; also "Mother Machree"
MACKINAW	a short, double-breasted coat (plaid, heavy-wool)
MACKINTOSH	any raincoat; a variety of apple
MADISON AVENUE	philosophies and social ideas that exist with mass-media advertising business: wealth, youth, style, success, good looks, life in the fast lane

MAELSTROM *(MALE-struhm)*	dangerous, violent whirlpool off the northwest coast of Norway
MAESTRO *(mah-EH-stroh)*	the Italian word for master
MAFEKING *(MAFF-uh-king)*	a town in North Cape Province, South Union in South Africa; site of the 217-day siege during the Boer Wars
MAGGIO *(MADGE-ee-oh)*	an Italian boy's name, "born during the month of May"
MAGNETIC NORTH	spot on the earth that a magnetic needle on a compass points
MAGNETIC STORM	sudden disturbance in magnetic fields surrounding the earth, occurring all over the earth at the same time and connected with sunspots
MAGNIFICIO *(mahg-NEE-fee-koh)*	the Spanish word for magnificant
MAGNOLIA WARBLER	a common hemlock/spruce warbler; they are bright yellow with spots and wing bars
MAGNUM	a bottle holding over two-fifths of a gallon of wine or champagne, a very powerful caliber handgun
MAHALA *(mah-HAH-lah)*	American Indian girl's name meaning woman
MAHARAJAH	a king or prince of India
MAHARANEE	a queen or princess of India, the wife of a maharajah
MAHINA *(muh-HEE-nuh)*	a Hawaiian girl's name meaning moon
MAHAJAMBA *(muh-huh-JAM-buh)*	bay on the inlet of Mozambique Channel on the NW coast of Madagascar
MAHOUT *(muh-HOOT)*	an elephant driver or keeper in India
MAID'S ADORNING	colorful slang term for morning (rhyming)
MAIL ORDER	to order goods by the mail; sent and filled through the mail
MAINGKWAN *(MING-kwan)*	a town in N. Burma on the Chindwin River
MAJESTAD *(mah-hess-TAHD)*	Spanish word for majesty
MAJORDOMO *(major-DO-mo)*	head steward or butler; butler of a nobleman's house
MAJS *(MICE)*	Swedish word for Indian corn

MAKUMMA *(muh-KOOM-uh)*	river (the Morona) that flows south across the Equador/Peru border where it changes it's name to The Makumma
MALKIN *(MAHL-kin)*	a kitchen maid; a scarecrow in the image of a woman; a cat
MAMBO *(MOM-bo)*	a voodoo priestess
MANAKIN *(MAN-uh-kin)*	a small, colorful South American bird
MAÑANA *(mahn-YAH-nuh)*	the Spanish word for tomorrow
MANCHU *(mahn-joo)*	a Chinese boy's name, it means pure
MANDINGA *(man-DEENG-guh)*	a port city in north central Panama
MANDO *(MAHN-do)*	Spanish shortened version of the boy's name Armando
MANDRAKE	a poisonous May Apple (roots sometimes used as a narcotic)
MANIFESTO	public declaration of the government's plans/policies
MANIKIN	little man, dwarf, model (also spelled MANNEQUIN)
MANTILLA *(man-TEE-uh)*	Spanish woman's lace scarf worn over the head and shoulders
MANITOU *(MAN-uh-too)*	spirit or force of nature (good or evil) found in Algonquian Indian religion
MAO-TAI *(MOU-tee)*	a strong, clear Chinese grain liquor
MAPLE CREEK	a town in SW Saskatchewan, Canada
MAPLE SHADE	an urban township in Burlington County, south central New Jersey
MARABOU *(MARE-uh-boo)*	a large stork and the soft feathers that come from the Marabou Stork
MARACAIBO *(mare-uh-KIGH-bo)*	seaport city in NW Venezuela
MARCHEN *(MAIR-shen)*	the German word for fairy-tale
MARCHESA *(mar-KAY-zuh)*	an Italian wife of a marchese
MARCHESE *(mar-KAY-zay)*	an Italian nobleman, ranking above a count and below the prince
MARAUD or MARAUDER	to rove/raid in search of plunder
MARCH HARE	rabbit in breeding season (regarded as an excuse for madness)

MARCHING ORDERS	orders for a battalion to march
MARDI GRAS *(MAR-dee graw)*	famous New Orleans carnival of parades where participants are lavishly costumed
MARE'S-NEST	a hoax; a jumble or a mess
MARINER	one who navigates a ship; a sailor or seaman
MARIONETTE	a jointed puppet operated by strings and wires attached to the limbs
MARSH HAWK	a slim, common hawk found in grasslands and marshes
MARRAKESH *(MARE-uh-kesh)*	city and one of the traditional capitals of a Sultanate of Morocco
MARZIPAN	a confection paste containing ground almonds and molded into many decorative forms
MARIPOSA *(mah-ree-POH-sah)*	the Spanish word for butterfly
MARSCHERA *(mar-SHAY-rah)*	the Swedish word for to march
MASHA *(MAH-shah)*	the Russian pet form of Mara; a girl's name
MASAI *(MASS-i)*	a member of a pastoral African tribe in Kenya
MASTER-AT-ARMS	naval petty officer on a warship who acts as a chief of police
MATSU *(MAHT-soo)*	a Japanese girl's name meaning pine
MATSUMOTO *(mat-soo-MOE-toe)*	city in Nagano prefecture, central Honshu in Japan
MATTAMUSKEET *(mat-uh-MUS-keet)*	lake in SE Hyde County, North Carolina
MATTOON *(muh-TOON)*	a city in Coles County east central Illinois
MAVOURNEEN *(MAY-voor-neen)*	Irish word meaning my darling
MAYOUMBA *(muh-YOOM-buh)*	a seaport in S. Gabon, equatorial Africa
MAZELTOV *(MAH-zuhl-tov)*	Hebrew for good luck
MEDICINE DANCE	ritual dance of the Plains Indians to ask for spiritual assistance
MEDICINE MAN	an Indian healer, shaman, sorcerer
MEDICINE SHOW	a traveling show that peddled medicine between acts

MEGABUCK *(MEG-uh-buck)*	one million dollars
MEI HUA *(may hwah)*	a Chinese girl's name, it means plum blossom
MELODEON *(mel-LOW-dee-uhn)*	a small reed organ
MELODIA *(MELLOW-dee-uh)*	an organ stop having wood pipes and being toned nearly like the clarabella
MELOSA *(meh-LOH-sah)*	the Spanish for honeylike, or sweet and gentle
MEMDI *(MEHM-dee)*	Indian plant (the henna), used in ceremonies
MEM-SAHIB *(mehm-suh-heeb)*	Anglo-American-Indian for the lady or the mistress of the household; it is the name bestowed on her by her native servants
MENDELEY *(men-de-LAY)*	Russian boy's name, it means intelligent
MERRY-ANDREW	a prankster, jester, or clown
MERRYBELLS	May/June wildflowers (yellow), found in rock gardens
MERELY FOOLING ABOUT	standard child's answer (in England) when a child is asked what he has been up to
MESTIPEN *(MEHS-tee-pen)*	A gypsy boy's name, it means lucky
MICHI *(mee-chee)*	Japanese girl's name it means of good character
MICHMASH *(MICK-mash)*	a town in NE Judaea, Palestine
MIDDEN-JAVA	a province in Indonesia
MIDNIGHT SPECIAL	an island drink of dark rum, coconut rum, tia maria, grenadine, pineapple juice and milk
MIDNIGHT SUN	the sun visible at midnight due to the latitude of the place from which it is viewed being greater than the polar distance of the sun
MIDWINTER	middle of winter; time of the winter solstice
MIEL *(M-YELL)*	French for honey
MIKADO *(muh-KAH-do)*	title for the emperor (Japan)
MILADY *(muh-LAY-dee)*	"my lady"; title of respect used in Europe when addressing a noblewoman

MILLRACE	the channel that the water takes through a mill where it is used to turn the mill wheels (that grind grain or saw logs)
MILORD *(muh-LORD)*	"my lord"; title of respect used in Europe when addressing a nobleman
MINETTE *(mee-NET)*	French girl's name, it means unwavering protector
MINGAN *(MEEN-gahn)*	a North American boy's name, it means gray wolf
MINGO JUNCTION	a city in Jefferson County, E. Ohio
MINNETONKA *(minnuh-TONG-kuh)*	a village in Hennepin County; SE Minnesota
MINSK	the city capital of White Russia in central USSR
MINSTREL SHOW	a comic traveling variety show
MINUET *(mee-nu-EE)* *(min-yoo-WET)*	the French word for midnight the 17th-18th century French dance done with very tiny steps
MINX	a pert girl
MIR *(MEER)*	a Czech name for a girl, it means peace
MIRADA *(mee-RAH-dah)*	the Spanish for glance or look
MISSIONARY'S DOWNFALL	a "zombie" and other rum drinks
MISSIONARY RIDGE	a ridge running northeast to southwest in Hamilton County, Tennessee and Dade County in Georgia; it was the site of the Union Army victory
MISSISSIPPI KITE	a beautiful hawklike bird; graceful and swallowlike in flight
MISSOULA *(muh-ZOO-luh)*	a city in western Montana
MISSUS	the mistress of a household; one's wife
MISTLETOE	an evergreen plant with white berries, common as a plant decoration at Christmas
MITTERNACHT *(mit-tehr-NAH-kht)*	the German word for midnight
MIYOKO *(MEE-yoh-koh)*	a Japanese girl's name, it means beautiful
MIZELLA *(mee-ZEH-luh)*	a gypsy girl's name
MJUK *(M-YOOK)*	the Swedish word for gentle, or soft

MOJOG *(MOH-yahg)*	an American Indian boy's name, it means noisy baby
MONEY TALKS	where "money can buy anthing" is the ideology; wealth is power
MOHEGAN and MOHICAN	"a wolf"; member of the Algonquian Indian's "Mahican" tribe
MOGENDAMMERUNG *(MAWR-gen-dem-muh-roonk)*	the German for dawn
MONKEY BRAND	making an ugly face
MONKEY PUZZLE	a prickle-tipped evergreen native to Chile, South America
MONKEY-SHINES	monkeylike antics or tricks
MONKEY'S ALLOWANCE	a job where the employee receives more rough treatment than money for his work
MONTANA	the Spanish word for mountain; the northwest state by that name
MONTECRISTO *(mon-tuh-KRIS-toe)*	an Italian island in the Tyrrhenian Sea (south of Elba); also, from the book *The Count Of Montecristo*
MONTEGO BAY	a seaport resort in northwest Jamaica Island in the West Indies
MOONBEAM	a ray of moonlight
MOON DOG	a bright spot on a lunar halo
MOON-RAKER	a smuggler (he does his work by the light of the moon)
MORGONROCK *(MOR-ron-rok)*	the Swedish word for a robe
MOSI *(MOH-see)*	a Swahili boy's name, it means first born son
MOSS-TROOPER	a raider or maurauder who operated on the bogs of 17th century England and Scotland's border
MOUCHE *(MOOSH)*	a French word that means to fly
MOUNTAIN DEVIL	another name for The Tasmanian Devil
MOYSHE *(MOY-shuh)*	the Yiddish form of Moses; a common boy's name in Israel
MOZAMBIQUE *(moe-zam-BEEK)*	Portuguese East Africa
MOZELLA *(moh-ZEH-le)*	a Hebrew girl's name, meaning taken from the water (it is the feminine form of Moses)
MUCHACHA *(moo-CHAH-chah)*	the Spanish word for girl

MUCHACHO *(moo-CHAH-choh)*	the Spanish word for boy
MUKLUK *(MUCK-luck)*	Eskimo boots made of sealskin or reindeer skins
MUSIK *(moo-SEEK)*	the Swedish word for music
MUGWUMP	an Algonquian Indian chief (somewhat of an "independent")
MUSIQUE *(mu-ZEEK)*	the French word for music
MUSQUASH	the American Indian word for muskrat
MYCET *(MUK-eh)*	the Swedish word for very or much
MYCKET LITEN *(muk-eh LEE-ten)*	the Swedish word for wee

N

NAGID *(nah-GEET)*	a Hebrew boy's name, it means prince
NAIROBI *(nigh-ROH-bee)*	the capital of Kenya, Africa
NAMIR *(nah-MEER)*	an Israeli boy's name, it means leopard
NANKING	a city in eastern China
NANTUCKET	an island in the Atlantic Ocean, south of Cape Cod, Massachusetts
NANTY-GLO	a borough in Cambria County, southwest central Pennsylvania
NAPLES	seaport capital of Campania Region in Italy
NAPOLEON	Bonaparte, emperor of France; a flaky pastry
NAPOLI *(NAH-poh-lee)*	the Italian spelling and pronounciation of Naples
NARTHEX *(NAHR-theks)*	a church entrance hall
NARRAGANSETT	a town and summer resort in Washington County, Rhode Island
NASHIRA *(na-SHIGH-rah)*	one of the brightest stars in Capricorn

NASHOTA *(nah-SHOH-tah)*	an Indian girl's name, it means twin
NASHVILLE	captial of Tennessee; country music center
NASHVILLE WARBLER	common hybrid of North American warbler, it has a bluish-gray head and a lemon-colored body
NASSAU	capital city of the Bahama Islands
NATCHITOCHES *(NAK-uh-TOSH-ez), or* *(NAK-uh-TOSH)*	oldest city in Louisiana
NATIONAL BANK	bank associated with national finances and usually owned by that country
NATIONAL DEBT	debt owed by any state/country, particularly the "funded debt"
NATIONAL GUARD	state-controlled military reserve units (like the Air National Guard and Army National Guard)
NATURAL NUMBER	one of the set of positive whole numbers (term often associated with gambling)
NATURAL RESOURCE	material source of wealth in its natural state (like the forests, minerals, etc.)
NATURAL VIRTUES	(also called Cardinal Virtues) they are the virtues of justice, prudence, fortitude, and temperance
NAUTICAL MILE	a unit of length used by sea and air travelers (1,852 meters)
NAUTILUS *(NAW-til-us)*	an Indian/Pacific Ocean mollusk that has a spiral shell having a series of air-filled chambers
NAVAL BRASS	a brass metal containing some tin for hardness and to resist the corrosion of the salty sea water; used, nearly exclusively, to make marine fittings for boats and ships
NAVARINO *(nav-uh-REE-noh)*	a Chilean Island south of Tierra del Fuego
NAVEGAR *(nah-veh-GAHR)*	the Spanish for to sail or to navigate
NAVIGATOR	a person who calculates direction and plots routes
NAVY CROSS	a US Navy decoration for extreme heroism
NED KELLY	a famous Australian bushranger and buccaneer (outlaw)

NEEDFIRE	in German folklore it means a purificatory fire (a fire made by rubbing two sticks together—"new fire"), as opposed to fire carried from an existing one. Needfire (new fire) was necessary for kindling sacred bonfires.
NEFERTITI *(NEF-ehr-TEE-tee)*	14th century Egyptian queen and the wife of Pharoah Akhenaton
NESTLING	a bird too young to leave the nest; any young person or thing
NEW RICH	people who recently have acquired riches, as opposed to the "old rich"
NIABI *(nee-AH-bee)*	an American Indian girl's name, it means fawn
NIBELUNG *(NEE-buh-loonj)*	legendary Germanic dwarfs who guarded a magic ring and a hoard of gold
NICABAR *(nee-kah-BAHR)*	a gypsy boy's name, it means thief
NICKEL SILVER	silvery-hard alloy (copper, zinc and nickel combined); also called German Silver
NICODEMUS *(nick-oh-DEE-mus)*	one of the Pharisees who defended Christ
NIELLO *(KNEE-ell-loh)*	a black metallic alloy (sulfer with copper, silver, or lead)
NIGHTBIRD	a bird that flies, or sings, at night
NIGHT HERON	a fresh water swamp or tidal marsh heron that fishes at night
NIGHT JASMINE	a West Indian shrub with fragrant white flowers
NIGHT LETTER	a telegram sent at night at a reduced rate
NIGHT PEOPLE	people who work (a night job) or live (by desire) at night, and then sleep all day
NIGHT-RAVEN	the night heron; a bird with nocturnal habits
NIGHT RIDER	masked men, outlaws, highwaymen or bandits who travel at night and seek to intimidate their victims by attacking in the darkness of night
NIGHT SCHOOL	school that hold classes in the evening; usually because the building or the teachers are in use during the day
NIGHT TERRORS	a disorder of children (something like nightmares) but more pronounced with fits of semiconscious screaming
NIGHTWALKER	a sleepwaker, or someone who frequents the streets at nights

NIGHT WATCH	a guard for night duty; a watch period thru the night hours
NINEZ *(nee-N-YESS)*	the Spanish word for childhood
NIOBE *(NIGH-oh-bee)*	a Greek mythological woman who was the daughter of Tantalus who was turned to stone while wailing over the loss of her children
NOB HILL	a district of San Francisco that symbolizes fashion and wealth
NOBLESSE *(no-BLESS)*	the French word for nobility or noble birth
NOCTURNE	romantic composition intended to make a person "feel" sentiments that are appropriate to evening or night
NODAWAY	a river rising in Cass County, Iowa and flowing into the Missouri River in northwestern Missouri
NOEL	a Christmas carol; the French word for Christmas
NO MANS LAND	a small island in the Atlantic (southwest of Martha's Vineyard in southeast Massachusetts); also used when one is talking about a portion of land that is unowned, or when talking about a battlefield
NORDVAST *(NOORD-vest)*	the Swedish word for northwest
NOR'EASTER	a gale or storm, with wind and rain, when it comes from the northeast
NORMANDY	a region in northwest France on the English Channel, made famous by the ally's Normandy Invasion during WW II
NO-SEE-UM	North American Indian word for the mosquito; used in the southern US frequently to describe the tiny mosquito-like insect that bites and is gone before the victim knows what hit him
NOTTINGHAM	a city in central England, made famous in the Robin Hood tales where there is frequent reference to The Sheriff Of Nottingham
NOVIA *(NO-vee-yah)*	the Spanish word for bride
NYCK *(NUK)*	the Swedish word for fancy
NURSERY RHYME	a short, rhymed tale written especially for children

O

OBEAH *(oh-BEE-uh)*	the West Indies name for the religious beliefs in sorcery and witchcraft
OBERON *(OH-ber-ohn)*	the husband of Titania; he was King Of The Elves in the old French fairy-tale
OBJET D'ART *(OB-zhay DAWR)*	literally "objects of art"; valuable for the artistry required to create them; in France it is used particularly to describe *small* objects of artistic value
ODALISQUE *(ODE-uh-lisk)*	an oriental harem chambermaid or concubine
ODIN *(OH-din)*	the chief god of Norse mythology, considered the source of wisdom and culture
OFFICE HOURS	hours that any office is open for business
OFFICER OF THE DAY	a military officer who is responsible for the safety of his command for a given 24-hour time period
OJIBWA *(oh-JIB-way)*	the Algonquian Indian tribe of Michigan and North Dakota
OKALANI *(oh-kuh-LAH-nee)*	a Hawaiian girl's name, it means from heaven
OKEFENOKEE *(OKIE-fuh-NOKIE)*	the great swamp in southeastern Georgia and northeastern Florida
OISEAU *(wah-ZOO)*	the French word for bird
ONIDA *(oh-NEE-dah)*	North American Indian girl's name meaning desired one
ON THE TOWN	to enjoy the entertainment, etc., of a city in the way of a tourist; stopping at all the best restaurants and night-clubs
OPEN HOUSE	hospitality extended to all comers; a welcome
OPERA HOUSE	a theater specially constructed for the performance of operas
ORIFLAMME *(ORE-uh-FLAMM)*	founded in the French; it means the ancient royal flag (a red silk banner with flame-shaped streamers)
ORIGINAL SIN	tendency to evil, found in all human beings, as the result of Adam's first act of disobedience
OSHKOSH	an American Indian chief; a city in eastern Wisconsin

OUTLANDER	someone living beyond the limits of civilization
OUTPOST	troops that are stationed at some distance from the main body; they usually act as a guard against surprise attacks
OUTRIDER	a cowboy who rides along the edge of a herd to prevent stampedes; a mounted servant who rides alongside a carriage
OVERRASKA *(o-vehr-rahss-kah)*	the Swedish word for to surprise
OYEZ *(OH-yayhz)*	Hear! Hear ye! as by a court crier; usually said three times it is used to get the attention of all those assembled

P

PABLO *(PAH-bloh)*	the Spanish form of Paul
PACE	a step made in walking
PACHISI *(puh-CHEE-zee)*	an ancient game from India (it is similar to backgammon)
PACIFICO *(pah-CHEE-fee-koh)*	the Italian word for peaceful
PACIFIQUE *(pah-see-feek)*	the French spelling for the Pacific Ocean
PACO *(PAH-choh)*	an Indian boy's name, it means eagle
PADDINGTON	a city in east New South Wales, SE Australia
PADDY	a contemporary pet form of Patrick
PADDYWHACK	a fit of temper; a baby's game; a thrashing
PADMA *(PAHD-mah)*	a Hindu girl's name, it means lotus
PADRONE *(pah-DROH-neh)*	the Italian word for boss
PAGEANT *(PAJ-unt)*	an elaborate public drama, usually to show some historic event
PAGODA	an oriental temple with tapering towers and curved roofs
PAINTED GOOSE	a wild goose of America (the Emperor Goose)

PAINTED-LADY	another name for the thistle butterfly
PAISANO *(pie-ZON-nah)*	Italian word for a country man or compatriot
PAIUTE	a tribe of Indians within the Shoshone group
PAKI *(PAH-kee)*	a southern African boy's name, it means witness
PALADIN	any of Charlemagne's 12 peers; hence, "a paragon of knighthood"
PALAZZO *(pah-LAHTS-tsoh)*	the Italian word for palace
PALISADE *(PAL-us-sahd)*	a fence of poles that form a dense barrier
PALLA *(PAHL-lah)*	the Italian word for bullet
PALLATON *(PAHL-lah-tohn)*	American Indian boy's name, meaning fighter
PALM SPRINGS	a resort in southern California
PALOMA *(pah-loh-mah)*	the Spanish word for dove; a name often given to a happy baby—one that coos a lot
PALOMINO	the Spanish word for dove-colored; name given to cream- to gold-colored horses
PANACHE *(puh-NAHSH)*	a plume or bunch of feathers, especially when they are worn as decoration on a helmet
PANCHO *(PAHN-choh)*	a common Spanish boy's name, it means free one
PANDEMONIUM *(pan-duh-MOE-nee-uhm)*	the capital city of Hell; wild disorder or chaos
PANTALONES *(pahn-tah-LO-ness)*	the Spanish word for trousers
PANZER	a German word for an armored tank
PARADISE	the garden of Eden
PAR EXCELLENCE *(par EK-suh-lahns)*	French for the best; regarded as the highest degree of excellence
PARIS *(PAIR-us) or (pah-REE)*	it is France's capital city
PARK AVENUE	residential street in New York City, a place of wealth, fashion and glamour
PARLAY	to bet an original wager and it's winnings on the next event
PARTISAN *(PAR-te-zen)*	a militant supporter of a party, cause or idea

PARTY LINE or PARTY WIRE	a telephone line that serves more than one subscriber
PARVENU *(PAR-vuh-noo)*	a person who rises suddenly above his social or economic class
PASQUA *(PAH-skwah)*	the Italian for Easter
PASSIONAL	of, or pertaining to a passion
PASS THE BUCK	to pass along problems or responsibility to another
PASTEL *(pahss-TELL)*	the Spanish word for cake or pastry
PASTINA *(pas-TEE-nuh)*	tiny pieces of macaroni (usually found in baby food)
PATAMON *(PAH-tah-mahn)*	an American Indian boy's name, it means raging
PATENT LEATHER	a leather finished to a glossy, mirrorlike, black coat
PATHFINDER	one who is skilled in finding a way; a scout who mainly is involved in opening new trails into the wilderness
PAULOWINA *(puh-LOE-nee-uh)*	an oriental tree with heart-shaped leaves and clusters of white flowers
PAVEL *(PAH-vyel)*	the Russian form of Paul
PAVONINE *(PAV-uh-nine)*	of, or like, the peacock; flashy and brilliant like a peacock's tail (in color, design, or iridescence)
PAYROLL	the list of those who will receive a paycheck and what is due them
PAZ *(pahs)*	the Spanish word for peace
PEACEMAKER	a person who works to reconcile unfriendly parties; a rifle used in the Old West
PEACE OFFERING	an offering of some kind, made for the sake of peace
PEACE PIPE	(the CALUMET) the American Indian ceremonial pipe
PEACE RIVER	a river in eastern British Columbia and flows to Alberta
PEACETIME	whenever there is an absence of war
PEACHBLOOM	a pinkish-red glaze used on Chinese porcelain
PEARLY GATES	the gates of Heaven

PEEKABOO	a game for amusing children, by hiding your face and then taking your hands away to reveal it again saying "peekaboo!"
PELISSA *(puh-LEES)*	the French for a long cloak made from furs
PENANCE	feeling sorry for a sin or wrongdoing and promising not to do it again, mild punishment for such a deed
PENDRAGON	a supreme head; in early England it was a title awarded someone during a terrible confrontation (something like a field commission)
PENUCHE *(puh-NOOCH-ee)*	a brown sugar-based, fudgelike candy
PENZANCE	a municipal borough in Cornwall, England (as found in the famous operetta "The Pirate of Penzance")
PEPPER ALLEY	slang term for rough treatment
PEPPER'S DRAGOONS	nickname given England's Eighth Hussars (a military regiment)
PEP TALK	speech used to encourage (pep-up) a team or staff
PERCHANCE	perhaps or possibly
PERDITION *(per-DISH-uhn)*	the loss of the soul; being eternally damned
PERFECT PITCH	ability to identify pitch of any tone without having prior reference
PERSNICKETY	an Old Scottish word meaning very fussy or requiring unreasonable or special handling
PERSIKA *(PER-shee-kah)*	the Swedish word for a peach
PETTICOAT	a lady's underskirt
PETTICOAT LANE	Middlesex Street in London
PETTICOAT TAILS	a little, plain Scottish cookie
PETTIFOGGER	an inferior lawyer, who really doesn't much care whether his client is guilty or innocent *and* he is willing to use any trick to get his client "off"
PEWTER	an alloy (tin and lead), used much during Colonial America for making tableware
PFEFFER *(FEFF-ehr)*	the German for pepper
PHALANX *(FAY-lanks)*	an ancient military formation where the outer ranks protect the rest with their shields (something like a human tank)

PHANTASIE *(fun-tah-ZEE)*	the German word for imagination
PICAROON	one who lives by cheating and robbery; a pirate or rogue
PICADILLY FRINGE	1860s French way of fixing a lady's hair where the front lock was cut and curled over the forehead in fringes
PICCADILLY PATRIOT	an English politician
PICCOLO *(PEE-koh-lo)* *PICK-uh-loh)*	an Italian word for little or small a small flute having higher octaves than the standard
PICKAPEPPA	Pickapeppa Sauce is a brand-named sweet mango-based, all purpose Caribbean seasoning made in Shooter's Hill (Jamaica, West Indies), having a sightly sweet and moderately hot taste
PICOTEE *(PEE-co-tee)*	a type of carnation having pale petals bordered by a darker color
PICTURE SHOW	the motion pictures
PIECES-OF-EIGHT	silver Spanish coins (circa 1490s) worth 8 "reales" (8 bits)
PILGRIM	a wanderer, someone who journeys on foot
PILSNER *(PILS-nehr)*	the Swedish word for beer
PIMIENTA *(pee-M-YENN-tah)*	the Spanish word for pepper
PIÑA COLLADA	an island drink made from dark rum, coconut rum, pineapple juice and milk
PINAFORE	a child's sleeveless apron
PIN BALL	mechanical game enclosed in a slanted, glass-covered box
PIPIT	a songbird
PIQUET *(puh-KAY)*	a French card game for 2 people, everything below 7s are removed from the deck
PIROZHKI *(puh-ROZH-key)*	small Russian pastries with various fillings
PISTACHIO *(puh-STASH-ee-oo)*	a light green, delicate-flavored nut from western Asia
PISTOLEER	SW usage for someone who fires a pistol; a gunslinger
PIZZAZZ	power, force, or pep

PITAPAT	to move with a series of quick, tapping steps
PLAYFELLOW	a companion in play; a playmate
PLEAD THE FIFTH	literally, to plead the fifth ammendment (meaning, that you refuse to say something or answer a question for whatever reason—based on your fifth ammendment rights)
PLEDGE	to offer one's word of honor as security
PLUMA (PLOO-mah)	the Spanish word for feather
POCKET EDITION	edition, or copy, of something small enough to be carried in your pocket
POCKET MONEY	money for minor or incidental expenses
POCOMOKE (POH-kuh-MOKE)	a river in southeastern Maryland
PODESTA (po-DES-tuh)	a chief magistrate in an Italian medieval republic
POETIC JUSTICE	the idea that "good is rewarded—evil is punished"
POINSETTIA	the brightly-colored red Christmas flower from Mexico
POINT OF HONOR	something (usually an ideal) that could affect a person's own honor
POKII (POH-kee)	the Hawaiian girl's name that means baby sister
POLARIS	the North Star (also Polar Star and Polestar)
POLSKA (POLE-skuh)	the Polish name for Poland
POLTERGEIST	a ghost or spirit that makes itself known by noisy clatter
POMPEII	ancient city of Campania (near Naples) destroyed by Mt. Vesuvius
PONCHO	the blanketlike raincoat made with a hole in the center for the head
PONDEROSA	a variety of tomato; the TV home of Ben Cartwright and sons from the old "Bonanza" series
PONI (POH-nee)	a girl's name from Sudan, it means second-born daughter
POPINJAY (POP-ehn-jay)	a conceited person
PORT OF CALL	a port where ships dock to load and unload cargo during their voyages
POSITRON	a positively-charged particle of an atom

POTPOURRI *(POH-poo-ree)*	dried flower petals and spice fragrance mixes
POWDER HORN	the hollow horn of an ox/cow, used to carry gunpowder for the old muzzle-loaders
POWDER KEG	a keg of gunpowder, an explosive situation
POWER OF ATTORNEY	written legal authority to act for another person
PRAIRIE SMOKE	North American plant having plumed seed clusters
PREACHER	a Protestant clergyman or minister
PRECIEUSE *(press-UYHZZ)*	the French word for precious
PRESS CONFERENCE	a group interview granted to newsmen (by a celebrity or politician, etc.)
PRIMROSE PATH	a path of pleasure (or self-indulgence)
PRINCEKIN	a little prince (a young prince), or a lesser prince (in rank or by birth)
PRINCESS ROYAL	the eldest daughter of a sovereign
PRINSESSA *(prin-SESS-sah)*	the Swedish word for princess
PRIVATE ENTERPRISE	business activities not governed by state ownership or controls
PRIVATE EYE	a private detective
PRIVATE SNOOPS	a slang term for a private detective
PRIX FIXE *(PREE feeks)*	French for fixed price; the prices at which table d'hote meals are offered
PRIZE FIGHT	a match fought between professional boxers for money
PROMENADE	a leisurely walk
PROMISED LAND	"Canaan," the promised land which God gave to Abraham and his descendants; any place of anticipated happiness
PROPAGANDA	effort directed (planned out carefully) to gain public support
PROPHECY	a prediction
PROPHET	person who speaks by divine inspiration; a soothsayer
PROPHETESS	a female prophet
PSYCHE *(SIGH-kee)*	the soul or spirit; the mythological maiden who was loved by Eros
PUNCH LINE	the last line, sentence, or part of a joke that gives meaning to humor

PUPPETEER	one who operates and entertains with puppets/marionettes
PUSCAFE (*pooss-kah-FEH*)	the Spanish word for liquor
PUSHKIN	a town in northwest Leningrad Region, Soviet Russia (named Pushkin in honor of the great Russian poet)
PUTTIN' ON AIRS	to assume manners, refinement, or prestige that someone does not actually have
PUTTIN' ON THE HITS	playing record albums (what a disc jockey does)
PYTHON	a large, non-venomous snake that kills it's prey by coiling and crushing

Q

QUAESTOR (*KWES-tehr*)	an ancient Roman judge
QUAKER OATS	brand name oat grain cereal; something that is pure, wholesome and natural
QUAKER'S BARGAIN	a "take it or leave it" directness
QUAKERTOWN	a borough in Bucks County, southeastern Pennsylvania
QUANTICO (*KWON-tuh-koh*)	a town in Prince William County in northeastern Virginia
QUANTOCK (*KWON-tuck*)	a range of hills in northwestern Somersetshire in southwest England
QUANTRILL (*KWON-trill*)	William Quantrill, an American leader of Confederate raiders in Kansas and Missouri (1837-1865), known as the infamous Quantrill's Raiders
QUASAR (*KWAY-zahr*)	distant, starlike, celestial objects that emit much light
QUASSIA (*KWOSH-uh*)	a tropical American tree with red flowers
QUATRAIN (*KWAH-train*)	a poem of 4 lines; a stanza of 4 lines
QUEEN REGENT	a queen who rules in behalf of another; a queen who rules in her own right and not because she married the king
QUEEN'S PARADE	a term from the British Navy to refer to the quarter-deck

QUEEN'S PORTRAIT	a slang term in Great Britain for money
QUETZAL *(KET-sal)*	a colorful Central American bird with green and red tail feathers (long and flowing)
QUILLAN *(KWIL-luhn)*	an astrological child's name meaning cub, and given to a child born under the sign of Leo
QUINTAIN *(KWINT'N)*	a target mounted on a post to "tilt" at while the medieval knight was on horseback
QUINTESSENCE	an extract of anything containing the very essence of the product; hence "the purest and most essential part"
QUIRIN *(KWER-in)*	a magical stone supposedly found in the Lapwing bird's nest; also known as The Traitor's Stone (putting it under a person's pillow was supposed to make him reveal all his secrets)
QUIZAS *(kee-SAHSS)*	the Spanish word for maybe

R

RACIMO *(rah-SEE-moh)*	Spanish word for a cluster
RACINE *(ray-SEEN)*	an industrial city on Lake Michigan, in SE Wisconsin
RACKET	a clamor or uproar
RACKETEER	someone involved in illegal business (like bootlegging)
RADIANT ENERGY	energy associated with waves that come from some source
RADIO BEACON	a stationary radio transmitter which sends out characteristic signals for aircraft or ship guidance
RADJUR *(ROH yoor)*	the Swedish word for deer
RAFFERTY'S RULES	no rules at all
RAFFLES	a gentleman burglar; a society-linked thief
RAFI *(re-FEE)*	an Arabic boy's name, refers to someone held in high regard

RAGAZZA *(rah-GAHTS-tsah)*	the Italian word for girl
RAGBAG	a bag of rags; a collection of odds and ends
RAG DOLL	a cloth doll stuffed with rags
RAGNAR *(RAHG-nahr)*	the Swedish word for mighty army
RAGNO *(RAH-nyoh)*	the Italian word for spider
RAGWEED	a weed whose pollen is a common cause of hay fever
RASGAR *(rahss-GAHR)*	the Spanish word for to rip or to tear
RAIDING PARTY	a body of troops (oftentimes Indians) making sudden raids in enemy territory
RAINBOW-CHASER	one who seeks the pot of gold at the end of the rainbow; a dreamer
RAIN CROW	a black-billed cuckoo, so called from the belief that its cry is a sure sign of rain on the way
RAIN-MAKER	one who is supposedly able to cause rain, often associated with the American Indians
RAINI *(RAIN-ee)*	an American Indian god
RAIN SHADOW	an area of little average rainfall, it lies on the leeward side of high mountains that serve to break up the rain-laden winds
RAIZEL *(RAY-zel)*	a Hebrew girl's name, it means rose
RAKEHELL	acting with reckless abandon (caring little about what will result from their actions)
RAKEL *(RAH-kehl)*	a Scandinavian girl's name equivalent to Rachel
RAKNA *(RAKE-nah)*	the Swedish word for to count or to number
RAMADAN *(rah-mah-DAHN)*	the 9th month of the Muslim year
RAMPART	anything that serves to protect or defend
RAMROD	a rod used to clean the barrel of a rifle; a ''boss'' or the central figure
RAMUS *(RAY-mus)*	the branchlike part of any building, used for support
RANEE *(RAW-nee)*	the wife of a rajah; a Hindu queen or princess

RAMASAMMY (*RAMM-uh-sam-mee*)	what the people of southern India call a Hindu
RANGE-FINDER	something used to determine the distance of a target
RANGOON	the capital city of Burma
RAPIDAN (*RAP-uh-DAN*)	a river in northern Virginia that rises from the Blue Ridge Mountains
RAPPAHANNOCK (*RAP-uh-HAN-eck*)	the Algonquian name for a river in northeastern Virginia
RAPPAREE (*RAP-uh-ree*)	in the 17th century they called an Irish free-booter, a bandit, or a robber this
RAPPORT (*rah-POHR*)	a French word meaning relation, report, or respect
RAPPORTERA (*rah-port-AY-rah*)	the Swedish word for to report
RAPSCALLION (*rap-SKALL-yuhn*)	a rascal or rogue
RAPTOR (*RAP-tehr*)	a bird of prey
RASERI (*raw-seh-REE*)	the Swedish word for fury
RATAFIA (*rat-uh-FEE-uh*)	a sweet cordial flavored with fruit kernels
RATCATCHER'S DAUGHTER	a girl from a poor family, hence it means someone from such a low social background that they are unsuitable companions of the socially prominent
RATHSKELLER (*RAT-skel-ehr*)	the German-type restaurant that is found below street level; also pronounced (*RATH-skel-ehr*) in this country
RATSEL (*RATE-sell*)	the German word for puzzle
RAUWOLFIA (*ro-WOOL-fee-uh*)	tropical trees with roots that yield a medicinal sedative
RAV (*RAVE*)	the Swedish word for fox
RAVENSPUR	a former seaport town in East Riding, Yorkshire, NE England
RAWNIE (*RAW-nee*)	a gypsy girl's name, it means lady
RAZI (*RAH-zee*)	a popular Israeli boy's name, it means secret
RAZILEE (*rah-zi-LEE*)	a popular Israeli girl's name, it means my secret
RAZZLE-DAZZLE	flashy or deceptive displays

RAZZMATAZZ	flashiness, showiness, or vigor
REAL MCCOY	a thing, person or idea that is genuine
REAR ADMIRAL	a naval officer next in rank above the captain
REBELLE *(ruh-BELL)*	the French word for rebel .
REDCAP	a porter at a railroad station
RED CARPET	a carpet laid down for visiting VIP's; great hospitality given to someone of prominence
RED CENT	a copper penny
RED JACKET	an American Indian leader and speaker, chief of the Senecas
REGALO *(reh-GAH-lo)*	the Spanish word for gift or present
REGATTA *(ruh-GAHT-uh)*	a boat race
REGEN *(RAY-gen)*	the German word for rain
REGENBOGEN *(RAY-gen-bo-gen)*	the German word for rainbow
REGULUS *(REG-yoo-lus)*	the brightest star in the Leo constellation
REI and REIKO *(RAY) and (RAY-koh)*	a Japanese girl's name, meaning many thanks
REINO *(RAY-noh)*	the Spanish word for kingdom
REMBRANDT	a Dutch painter and etcher
REMINGTON	a type of rifle; a US painter and sculptor of the Old West (1861-1909)
RENA *(RAY-nah)*	the Greek word for peace, it is a girl's name
RENAISSANCE *(ren-uh-ZAHNZ)*	a rebirth, revival (the great revival of art and learning in Europe during the 14th to 16th centuries)
RENDEZ-VOUS *(rahn-day-VOO)*	the French word for an appointment
RENDOR *(REN-dohr)*	a Hungarian boy's name, it means policeman
REPERTOIRE *(REP-uh-twah)*	a list of songs, plays, etc., that a person (or acting company) is prepared to perform
REVEILE *(REV-uh-lee)*	morning bugle call to awaken the troops

REVERIE *(REV-uh-ree)*	a daydream
REVIVAL	a reawakening of faith; a series of impassioned preachings
REY *(RAY)*	the Spanish word for king
REYEZUELO *(reh-yeh-SWEH-lo)*	the Spanish for petty king; a sparrow
REYHAN *(REH-hahn)*	an Arabic boy's name, it means favored by God
REZ *(rhaz)*	a popular Hungarian boy's name, it means copper
RHAETIA *(ray-SHEE-uh)*	an ancient Roman province found in the Swiss and Austrian Alps
RHAPSODY	an exalted expression of feeling
RHINESTONE	a highly refractive, colorless glass; imitation gems
RHYTHM AND BLUES	popular Black American music, the origin of rock and roll
RIBELLE *(ree-BELL-leh)*	and Italian word for rebel
RICCHEZZE *(reek-KETTS-tseh)*	the Italian for riches
RICHESSE *(ree-SHESS)*	the French word for wealth
RICK-RACK	flat braid in zigzag form, used to trim garments
RIC-MA-TICK	slang word for arithmetic
RICKSHAW	a 2-wheeled oriental transport pulled by a man on foot, or a bike
RICOCHET *(RICK-oh-shay)*	rebounding off a surface
RIGADOON	a lively, jumping quickstep (dance) performed by one couple
RIGHT SMART	a large quantity; or "pretty well" (as in "I feel right smart")
RIKEDOM *(REE-keh-doom)*	the Swedish word for riches
RINGKLOCKA *(RING klohk ah)*	the Swedish word for bell
RINGLEADER	a leader or organizer of any undertaking
RINGMASTER	one who has charge of a circus ring
RING THE BELL	to succeed; to make a hit with someone
RIO DE JANEIRO	a seaport in southeastern Brazil

RIOT ACT	an energetic or forceful warning or reprimand
RIPCORD	a cord pulled to release the pack of a parachute
RIP CURRENT or RIP TIDE or TIDE RIP	tidal water current of water disturbed by an opposing current
RIPRAP	a wall made out of broken rock thrown together in a pile
RIQUEZA *(ree-KEH-sah)*	the Spanish word for riches or wealth
RISE AND SHINE	to get up in the morning
RITZY	elegant or fancy (originated as it relates to the Ritz-Carlton Hotel in New York City)
RIVER-RAT	a thief that waited in hiding along rivers and attacked passing boats
ROAD AGENT	a bandit who robs stagecoaches, a highway robber (highwayman)
ROAD HOUSE	an inn, restaurant, or night-club outside the city; a tavern catering to transient pleasure-seekers
ROADSHOW	a touring theatrical company
ROADRUNNER	a large, crested bird of the Southwest (it runs rapidly)
ROADSTER	a horse for riding on a road; any auto with a single seat
ROANOKE	a city in southwest Virginia
ROARING FORTIES	the most tempestuous part of the Atlantic Ocean, 40 degrees - 50 degrees N latitude nautical
ROBAR *(rob-BAR)*	the Spanish word for to kidnap or to rob
ROBBER BARON	a feudal lord who robbed travelers passing through his domain
ROBIN GOODFELLOW	an Old English folklore character; "Puck" the mischievious sprite
ROBIN HOOD'S CHOICE	"this ... or nothing!"; literally, no choice at all
ROB ROY	a Scottish freebooter and leader of the MacGregors
ROCKEFELLER	(as in John D. Rockefeller the very rich American industrialist) synonomous with wealth
ROGUE IN SPIRIT	a distiller or brandy merchant
ROGUE'S GALLERY	photographs of criminals that are kept in police files

ROGUE'S SALUTE	a single gun sounded on the morning of a court-martial
ROGUE'S WALK	English term for the area between Piccadilly Circus and Bond Street
ROHANNA (roh-HAH-nah)	the Hindu word for sandalwood, it is a girl's name
ROJO (ROH-ho)	the Spanish word for red
ROKA (RO-kah)	the Swedish word for smoky
ROLLING STOCK	a railroad's wheeled vehicles
ROMAN CANDLE	a firework consisting of a tube shooting balls of fire·
ROMANCE	a love affair, to think or behave in a romantic manner
ROMANTIQUE (ro-mahn-TEEK)	the French word for romantic
ROMANTISK (roo-MAHNN-tisk)	the Swedish word for romantic
ROMANY (ROE-muh-nee)	a gypsy, or the gypsy language
ROMANY RYE	a gentleman that talks and associates with gypsies
RONDEAU (RON-do)	a French lyric poem having 13 lines
ROOM AND BOARD	lodging and meals
ROSEBAY	another name for the Mountain Laurel; can be white or pink flowered
ROSELLE (ro-ZELLE)	a tropical, old world plant with yellow flowers
ROSELANI (roh-se-LAH-nee)	a Hawaiian girl's name meaning heavenly rose
ROSE MALLOW	a tall North American marsh plant with white/pink flowers
ROSES AND RAPTURES	the literary world's nickname for "beauty books"
ROSE WATER	fragrance made from steeping rose petals in water; a combination of water and attar or roses
ROSEWOOD	a semi-tropical hardwood tree
ROSIN-THE-BOW	a fiddler
ROSY FINCH	a lovely rosy-pink finch found in the western US and Canada
ROTC or R.O.T.C.	Reserve Officers' Training Corps

ROTH	a common German boy's name, it means red-haired
ROUGH DIAMOND	someone with a good heart but no manners
ROUGHRIDER	a person who breaks horses for a living
ROULETTE (ROO-let)	a gambling game played with a rotating colored bowl that is marked with numbers
ROUNDELAY (ROUN-duh-lay)	a poem or a song with a recurring refrain
ROUND-THE-CLOCK	throughout the entire day
ROVARE (ROH-vah-reh)	Swedish for robber
ROWDY	rough or disorderly person
RUBASSE (ROO-bass)	a ruby-red kind of quartz mineral
RUBICON (ROO-buh-kahn)	a small river in northern Italy
RUBY QUEEN	a young nurse of fresh complexion (used in Old England)
RUBY WINE	methylated spirits serving as liquor
RUCKUS	a noisy commotion
RUDDY DUCK	a stiff-tailed duck common in summer, having white cheeks and a ruddy-red body
RUFFIN'S HALL	an old section of London
RULE OF THUMB	a practical method (though seemingly crude or unscientific)
RUMBLEDETHUMPS	a Scottish potato dish made with cabbage and onion
RUMMAGE SALE	a sale of donated miscellaneous articles
RUMPUS	noisy clamor
RUMRUNNER	someone who illegally transports liquor
RUNABOUT	a small motorboat or any open auto
RUNAGATE	another variation of renegade (some Old English usage)
RUN-AROUND	to give evasive answers to direct questions
RUNNING EXPENSES	your daily expenses
RUNNING-LIGHTS	the sidelights of a vessel (boat) to make it visible at night
RUPEE	the monetary unit of India, it is equal to 100 "paise"
RURAL FREE DELIVERY or **R.F.D.**	government service of house-to-house free mail delivery in rural districts
RUSH HOUR	the time when traffic is at its worst

RUSSIAN ROULETTE	considered as the ultimate gamble; a revolver is loaded with only one bullet and then the barrel is spun before putting it to your head and pulling the trigger
RUSTY BLACKBIRD	another name for the common swamp blackbird
RYKTE *(RUK-teh)*	the Swedish for fame

S

SABBIA *(SAHB-bee-ah)*	the Italian word for sand
SABER RATTLING	open display of military power or threat of hostility
SABETHA *(suh-BETH-uh)*	a small city in northeast Kansas
SABOTAGE	deliberate subversion; covert actions intended to do harm
SABOTEUR *(sab-uh-TUR)*	someone who commits sabotage
SABRA *(SAH-bruh)*	a native born Israeli; a thorny cactus
SACHA *(SAH-shah)*	a Russian girl's nickname; also spelled Sasha
SACHET *(sah-SHAY)*	a small bag of perfumed powder to scent clothes
SACHI *(SAH-chee)*	Japanese girl's name, it means happiness
SADDLER	a maker of saddles; a saddle horse
SADDLE SHOES	style of white leather "Oxford" shoe with a wide, saddlelike brown leather insert over the instep
SADDLE SOAP	softening and preserving soap for leather (usually castile)
SAFARI	an expedition or journey on foot; especially an African Safari
SAFFRON HILL	a district in London (north of Holborn), where all the ballad singers frequented
SAGITTA *(sa-JEE-tuh)*	astrological girl's name for a girl born in December
SAGINAW	a city in northern Michigan

SAILING ORDERS	instructions given to a ship captain covering the details of his upcoming voyage
SAILOR'S BLESSING	a curse
SAILOR'S CHAMPAGNE	beer
SAILOR'S CHOICE	a variety of North American (Atlantic Coast) fish
SAILOR'S FAREWELL	a parting curse
SAILOR'S FRIEND	the moon
SAILOR'S PLEASURE	"yarning, smoking, dancing and growling"
SAILOR'S WEATHER	a fair wind and just enough of it
SAINT & SINNER	finding both good and bad in a person; vanilla ice cream and chocolate sauce
SAKI (SAH-kee)	a Japanese boy's name, it means cape
SAKURA (sub-KOOR-uh)	a Japanese girl's name, it means cherry blossom
SALAMA (sah-LAH-mah)	the Arabic word for peace
SALES TALK	talk aimed at making a sale; talk to persuade
SALES TAX	a tax placed on the sale of an item
SALOON	a bar, room, or hall where alcoholic drinks are sold
SALUTE	to honor or greet someone with a characteristic hand-to-brow motion
SALVATION	deliverance from an evil
SALVATION ARMY	an international evangelical/charitable organization that works to help the most derelict and pitiful of society
SALVO	a simultaneous release of a rack of bombs from an aircraft
SAMARINDA (sam-uh-RIN-duh)	a coastal town in east Borneo, Indonesia
SAMARKAND (sam-ahr-KAHN)	a former province of Russian Turkistan (an ancient seat of Arabic culture)
SANDOVAL (san-DOE-v'l)	a county in New Mexico
SAM HILL	the euphemism for "Hell"
SAMIEL (sam-YELL)	another name for the devil
SAMMET (SAHMM-met)	the Swedish for velvet

SAMOSET *(SAM-uh-set)*	an American Indian chief who aided the pilgrims
SAMT *(ZUMT)*	the German word for velvet
SAMTICKA *(SAHMM-tuk-ah)*	the Swedish for to agree or to consent
SAMURAI *(SAM-uh-rye)*	the military aristocracy of feudal Japan
SANDALWOOD	an aromatic oil of an Asian hardwood tree
SANDARAC *(SAN-duh-rack)*	North American tree that yields a resin used in very expensive varnishes
SANDBAR or SANDBANK	a ridge of sand formed in a river or along the shore
SANS A'-COUPS *(sans uh-KOO)*	French word for to go smoothly or without a hitch
SANS ADIEU *(sans ad-JEW)*	French for "goodbye for the present"
SANTIAGO *(san-tee-AH-go)*	capital city of Chile; a man's name
SAPAJOU *(SAP-uh-joo)*	the capuchin monkey
SARATOGA	a resort center in eastern New York
SARGENTLEMANLY!	an English transition of "so gentlemanly!"
SARI *(SHAW-ri)*	a Hungarian girl's name, it means princess
SAROJIN *(sah-roh-jeen)*	a Hindu boy's name, it means lotus
SARTAN *(SAHR-tuhn)*	a Hebrew boy's name
SASHAY	to strut or flounce
SASKATOON	a city in Saskatchewan, Canada
SASSAFRAS	a North American tree, known for the oil which is used as a flavoring
SATCHET	a small valese or bag
SATINKA *(sah-TEEN-kah)*	an American Indian girl's name, it means magic dancer
SAVANNAH	a newly popular girl's name; seaport city (oldest city) in Georgia
SAVANNAH SPARROW	a common ground sparrow found in the fields of the US
SAVOIR FAIRE *(sah-VWAH-fair)*	the ability to say and do the right thing
SCANDIAN	relating to Scandia (the Scandinavians)

SCANDAL	the act of doing something that offends the morality of others
SCAPEGRACE	a mischievious person; (combining the words escape and grace)
SCARABEE (*skah-rah-BEE*)	the French for the bracelets of ancient Egypt where beetles were carved out of gems)
SCARAMOUCH (*SCARE-uh-mowch*)	a boastful or swaggering buffoon
SCHARLATTO (*skahr-LAHT-toh*)	the Italian for scarlet
SCHARLAKAN (*SHAWR-lah-kahnn*)	the Swedish for scarlet
SCATTERGOOD	one who wastes money
SCATTERGUN	a shotgun
SCHEHEREZADE	the fictionary teller of tales in *The Arabian Nights*
SCENARIO (*suh-NAIR-ee-oh*)	the outline of a plot in a play
SCHNAPPS (*shnawps*)	a strong gin made in The Netherlands
SCHNITZEL (*shnits'l*)	a cutlet (small piece) of veal
SCHNOOK (*shnook*)	a Yiddish word for a meek person who is easily fooled
SCHUSSBOOMER	a skier; one who "schusses" expertly
SCHWARZWALD (*SHVORTS-valt*)	the German word for Black Forest
SCIMITAR (*SEM-uh-tahr*)	the short, curved, sword that the Arabs carry
SCOTCH WHISKEY	whisky made with a smoky flavor; originated in Scotland
SCOT-FREE	going unpunished, not having to pay for one's crimes; freed from "scot"
SCOTLAND YARD	the headquarters of the London Police
SCOTTISH MIST	a rain
SCOUNDREL	a villian
SCOUTMASTER	the adult leader of a troop of Boy Scouts
SCUPPERNONG	a wild, gold-green grape grown exclusively in the South US; the light, heady wine made from them
SCUTTLEBUTT	originated as a drinking fountain aboard a ship (hence, where a *rumor* began)
SEABEE	the US Navy's Construction Battalion

SEA BOOTS	an Old English turret battleship
SEABORNE	carried on, or over, the sea
SEAFARER	a sea traveler; a sailor
SEA FIRE	the phosphorescence of sea water as seen when the sun hits it
SEA-FOX	the "Thresher" (a long-tailed shark)
SEA KING	a viking pirate chief; a Norse pirate king of the Middle Ages
SEA LEGS	the ability to walk on board a ship with steadiness (especially when the seas are rough)
SEAMAID or SEAMAIDEN	a mermaid or sea nymph
SEANCE (say-AHNSS)	a meeting of persons to receive spiritual messages
SEARCHLIGHT	an apparatus containing a reflector and mounted so that the beam of intense light can be thrown in many directions for searching or signaling purposes
SEARCH WARRANT	a warrant directing an officer to search a house
SEA RISK	any danger of the sea (sharks, drowning, etc.)
SEASON TICKET	a ticket (or set of tickets) to be used for a series of games or concerts
SEAWORTHY	any vessel that is fit to sail
SECONDSTORY MAN	a burglar that enters through upstairs windows (see CAT BURGLAR)
SECOND WIND	a fresh ability to continue
SECRET SERVICE	US agency for guarding the President
SEDITION (sub-DISH-uhn)	conduct inciting to rebellion against the authority of the state
SEDUCTION	the act of enticing (seducing) someone into doing something
SEECATCH or SEECATCHIE	an adult male Alaskan fur seal
SEERSUCKER	a linen and silk fabric with stripes and a crinkled surface
SEIF (SIGH-eef)	an Arabic boy's name, it means sword
SENECA	a boy's name; a tribe of Indians; a river in west central New York
SEQUATCHIE (sub-KWACH-ub)	a river in southeastern Tennessee
SEQUIN	a small, shiny spangle (they are sewn onto clothes as decoration)

SEÑOR *(seh-NYOR)*	Spanish for mister
SEÑORA *(sen-YOH-rah)*	Spanish for Mrs.
SEÑORITA *(seh-NYOH-ree-tah)*	the Spanish for Miss
SENTIMENTAL JOURNEY	title of an old song; remembering something good (sentimental things and things long past)
SERAPE *(suh-RAH-pee)*	Mexican-Spanish colored wool blanket worn by a man as an outer garment
SERENADE	an evening song (usually sung by a lover under his lady's window)
SERGEANT-AT-ARMS	an executive officer in a legislative body who enforces order
SERGEANT MAJOR	a US Army enlisted person who is the assistant to someone of higher rank
SEVEN DEADLY SINS	pride, lechery, envy, anger, convetousness, gluttony, and sloth
SEVIN DEVILS	a mountain range in western Idaho
SEVENTH HEAVEN	the highest heaven (or condition) of happiness
SHADDOCK	a common citrus fruit found in the West Indies
SHAHAR *(shah-HAHR)*	the contemporary Muslim word for the moon
SHAINA *(SHAY-nah)*	a Yiddish girl's name, it means beautiful
SHAITAN or SHEITAN *(SHY-tan)*	the Arabic word for devil, satan, or evil spirit
SHAKEDOWN	a search of a person or place; to blackmail or extort money
SHALOM *(sha-LOHM)*	the Hebrew word for peace
SHAMASH *(SHAH-mahsh)*	the chief sun-god of Assyria and Babylon
SHAMIR *(shuh-MEER)*	a Hebrew boy's name, it means strong
SHAMROCK	a 4-leafed clover (symbol of Ireland)
SHANGHAI	to abduct a man, usually a sailor, and force him to work as an indentured sailor aboard another ship
SHANGAI GENTLEMAN	someone who is definitely *not* a gentleman
SHANGRI LA	a mythical land of eternal youth and beauty

SHANSI *(SHAN-see)*	a province of northeastern China
SHAPPA *(SHAH-pah)*	an American Indian boy's name, it means red thunder
SHARAI *(shah-RIGH)*	a Hebrew girl's name, it means royalty
SHARIF *(shah-REEF)*	an Arabic boy's name, it means honest
SHE-DRAGON	a forbidding woman
SHEET MUSIC	music printed on unbound sheets of paper
SHEIYE *(SHY-ah)*	the Yiddish form of Isaiah
SHE-LION	a forbidding woman
SHENANIGANS	tricks, pranks, nonsense, and petty deception
SHERBROOKE	a city in southern Quebec
SHERRY COBBLER	a mixed drink made of sherry, lemon, sugar, water and ice
SHERWOOD FOREST	a forest in central England (near Nottingham) made famous as the setting for the Robin Hood stories
SHETUCKET *(shu-TUCK-et)*	a small river in eastern Connecticut
SHEYENNE *(SHY-anne)*	a river in central North Dakota that flows to the Red River
SHICKSHINNY	a borough in Luzerne County in eastern Pennsylvania
SHIKA *(shee-KAH)*	a Japanese girl's name, it means deer
SHILLELAGH *(shill-AYE-lee)*	a club or cudgel
SHILOH	an area in Hardin County, southwestern Tennessee, site of a famous Civil War battle
SHINA *(SHEE-nah)*	a Japanese girl's name, it means virtue
SHINDY	a riotous quarrel; a noisy argument
SHING *(sheeng)*	a Chinese boy's name, it means victory
SHIPMATE	a fellow sailor
SHIPSHAPE	well-arranged; orderly and neat
SHIPWRECK	a wrecked ship; when something is a real mess
SHIRE TOWN	a county seat or county town

SHIRO *(shee-roh)*	a Japanese boy's name, it means fourth-born son
SHIVER ME TIMBERS!	a nautical expletive meaning: "Well I'll be!"
SHOCK TROOPS	seasoned and hand-picked men selected to lead an attack
SHOGAN	a Japanese warlord; a military governor
SHOOTING AFFAIR	an argument that results in the use of firearms
SHOOT THE AMBER	when a car driver speeds up to "run the amber" at a traffic light
SHOOT THE MOON	to risk it all
SHOOT THE WORKS	to go to the limit; to bet it all
SHOPTALK	to talk about work after duty hours
SHORE PATROL	Navy, Marine, or Coast Guard police on shore
SHORT CIRCUIT	a side circuit that deflects current
SHORT SUBJECT	a short film (sometimes an animated cartoon)
SHOTGUN WEDDING	a wedding demanded by a girl's father because she is pregnant, or has been intimate, with the groom
SHOWBOAT	to show off; a river boat with a traveling theater/company
SHUCKS!	a mild expletive to show annoyance
SIDE DISH	food served along with the main course
SIESTA *(see ESS-tah)*	the Spanish word for nap
SIGNAL FIRE	a fire used as a signal; a beacon fire
SIGNAL SMOKE	smoke from a fire used to signal with a series of puffs, plumes, or spirals that have meaning (Indian use)
SIGN OF THE ZODIAC	any of the 12 parts of the zodiac
SILHOUETTE *(see-loo-ETT)*	the French word for figure
SILKE *(SILL-keh)*	the Swedish for silk
SILLIKIN	a simpleton
SILVER CERTIFICATE	paper currency issued by the US Treasury Department and backed-up with silver currency or bullion
SILVER GLANCE	silver sulfide
SILVERHEELS	a mountain peak in Park County, central Colorado

SILVER PHEASANT	a society woman
SILVERSIDES	small fishes (related to the mullets) having a silver band along each side of the body
SILVERSMITH	worker in silver; maker of silverware
SILVER STANDARD	a monetary standard based on silver
SIMOON *(sub-MOOM)*	a ferocious hot wind blowing across African and Asian deserts
SIRIUS *(serious)*	the brightest star in the sky; the Dog Star
SIROCCO *(sub-ROCK-oh)*	hot or warm southerly wind
SISIKA *(si-SEE-kah)*	American Indian girl's name, it means little bird
SISYPHUS *(SIS-uh-fes)*	in Greek mythology it was the greedy king who went to Hell and was given the punishment of trying to roll a stone uphill as it keeps rolling back
SITTING DUCK	a person or thing easily attacked; naive
SITUATION COMEDY	a comic television series made up of episodes
SIX BITS	seventy-five cents
SIX-PACK	a package of six units (usually six cans of beer)
SJUNGA *(SHOONG-ah)*	the Swedish word for to sing
SKAGERRAK *(SKAG-uh-rack)*	the bit of North Sea that lies between Norway and Denmark
SKAGWAY	a city in southeastern Alaska (founded as a boomtown during the Yukon gold rush)
SKAR *(SHAIR)*	the Swedish word for pink
SKIPPSLAST *(SHIPS-lahst)*	the Swedish word for cargo
SKIRMISH	a light engagement (confrontation) between small parties
SKOAL!	a Danish/Norweigan toast: "To your health!"
SKUGGA *(SKOOG-ah)*	the Swedish for shadow
SKY-BLUE	another slang term for gin
SKY FALLS	a slang term for rain
SKY-HIGH	blasted to pieces; very high
SKYLARK	a Eurasian songbird, it sings as it rises up in the sky

SKY-LIGHT	a slang term for the moon
SKYMAN	an aviator (pilot)
SKY MARSHAL	a federal officer who is assigned to guard against skyjacking
SKYWAYS	routes of air travel mapped in the skies
SLAPJACK	a pancake or flapjack
SLEIGHT OF HAND	magic tricks; using your hands in a sly way to deceive
SLIVOVITZ *(SLIV-uh-vits)*	a dry, colorless plum brandy
SLUMGULLION *(slum-GULL-yehn)*	a stew made of miscellaneous ingredients
SLUMLORD	an absentee landlord of slum buildings
SLUSH FUND	money collected or spent for corrupt purposes (like bribery)
SLYBOOTS	a sly person or animal
SMITHEREENS	fragments and pieces (results of being smashed or blown up)
SMOCK-FROCK	a loose, shirt type garment worn by employees or artists
SMOKE SCREEN	a dense cloud of smoke, or an unrelated act committed to conceal (screen) an attack or action
SMORGASBORD	a large variety of Swedish appetizers
SMUTSA *(SMOOT-sah)*	a Swedish word that means to make sooty or dirty
SMYTHERIE *(SMYT-ri)*	a Scottish word for a collection of small things
SNAKE-CHARMER	someone who charms venemous snakes with music (flute)
SNAKE DANCE	an informal dance with many persons forming a long line
SNICKERSNEE	a Dutch word referring to "fighting with knives"
SNOWBIRD	a bird (like the Junco), seen only in winter months
SNOWBLINK	a white sky glow reflected from some far off snowfield
SOBEIT *(SO BE IT)*	an amen; meaning if so, or if only
SOIREE *(swar-AY)*	a French word meaning an evening party
SOLANA *(soh-LAH-nah)*	the Spanish word for sunshine

SOLAR FLARE	temporary outburst from the sun's surface
SOLDIER OF FORTUNE	a mercenary
SOLEIL *(so-LAY-yuh)*	the French word for the sun
SOLEDAD *(so-leh-DAHD)*	the Spanish word for solitude
SOIGNEUSE *(swann-YUHZZ)*	the French word for careful
SOLILOQUY *(suh-LIL-uh-kwee)*	when you talk to yourself in a drama; a poetic writing to oneself
SOLITAIRE	a gemstone or diamond set *alone* in a ring
SOLSKEN *(SOOL-shayn)*	the Swedish word for sunshine
SOMEWHERE IN FRANCE	used during WWI; to maintain secrecy the mail a soldier sent his loved ones came from "Somewhere in France"
SONAR *(so-N-YAHR)*	the Spanish word for to dream
SONAR *(SO-nar)*	the sound waves transmitted through water that assist in locating submarines
SONGAN *(SOHN-gahn)*	North American Indian boy's name, it means strong
SONG AND DANCE	an exaggerated (unbelievable) story
SONG SPARROW	a common Eastern fox sparrow (they are streaked on their breast)
SONIC BOOM	the explosive sound that jets make when they break the sound barrier
SONNENLICHT *(ZAWNN-en-lisht)*	the German word for sunlight
SONNER *(so-NAY)*	the French for to sound or to ring
SONRISA *(sohn-REE-sah)*	the Spanish word for smile
SOPWITH PUP	a Sopwith Aeroplane (Air Force/1914-1918 use)
SORA *(SOH-rah)*	the American Indian girl's name that means song bird
SORELLA *(so-RELL-lah)*	the Italian word for sister
SOROREAL *(suh-ROR-ehl)*	a sorority of women who gather for social functions
SORTILEGE *(SOR-tuh-lij)*	fortelling the future by drawing lots

SOUBRETTE *(soo-BRET)*	a saucy, flirtatious young woman
SOUCI *(soo-SEE)*	the French word for care
SOUDAIN *(soo-DANG)*	the French word for sudden
SOUND BARRIER or **SONIC BARRIER**	the increase in air resistance that occurs when aircraft near the speed of sound
SOUND EFFECTS	imitative sounds that are created for motion pictures/radio
SOUCHONG *(SOO-chonj)*	a black tea from China
SOUP KITCHEN	a charitable place that feeds needy people
SOUVERAIN *(soov-RANG)*	the French word for sovereign
SPANDEX	the synthetic elastic used to make girdles and tight pants
SPARTACUS *(SPAR-tuh-cuss)*	a 71 BC Roman slave who became a much respected gladiator and ended up leading a slave revolt
SPEEDWAY	a race track for cars
SPELLBINDER	one who holds others' attention with stories, etc.
SPELLBOUND	being entranced or fascinated
SPINDRIFT	wind-blown sea spray
SPIRIT OWL	another name for the Screech Owl
SPIRIT RAPPING	when communication with the dead comes via ''raps'' on the table where the seance is being held
SPLENDEUR *(splahn-DUHR)*	the French word for splendor
SPOKA *(SPO-kah)*	the Swedish word for to haunt
SPRATT *(SPRAHT)*	the Swedish word for trick
SPREE	a gay or wild outing
SPRINGBOK or **SPRINGBUCK**	a small brown and white gazelle from Africa
SPRINGEN *(SHPRING-ehn)*	the German word for to jump
SPINNAKER *(SPIN-uh-kehr)*	a large, triangular sail used on racing yachts
SPRITE	a pixie (small elf)

SPUMONE or SPUMONI *(spoo-MOE-nee)*	Italian ice cream with candy, fruit & nuts
SQUAW MAN	a frontiersman (white man) with an Indian wife
SQUIRE	young attendant to a knight; an English country gentleman
STAGESTRUCK	someone who is eager to become an actor
STALKING HORSE	(fronteir use) a horse trained to conceal his owner while stalking game
STAMP AND GO	Jamaican fried codfish cake
STAMPING GROUND	a regular gathering place
STAR-DRIFT	the common motion of stars
STARFLOWER	an American plant with white, starlike flowers
STAR-GAZER	a dreamer or idealist; an astronomer
STARLIGHT	the light that stars give off
STAR SHOWER	a meteor shower
STAR TRACKER	an instrument that uses stars to assist in rocket guidance
STEAM HEAT	heating system using a boiler and radiators to carry the heat
STELLARA *(steh-LAH-ruh)*	an astrological girl's name, it means "star child"
STESHA	a Russian boy's name, it means royalty
STIRRUP-CUP	a farewell drink, accepted by a mounted rider, before he leaves his host's grounds before the hunt
STJARNA *(SHAIRN-ah)*	the Swedish word for star
STORMALONG	a famous American folklore sailorman and whaler
STORMBOUND	when someone is delayed or cut off by a storm
STORM CENTER	the center of a circular storm, where calm and low pressure occur
STORM SIGNAL	when flags or lights are used as signals to warn sailors of an approaching storm
STRADIVARIUS *(STRAD-uh-VAIR-ee-us)*	a valuable violin made by the Italian A. Stradivari (or his sons)
STRATHBOGIE MIST	a Scottish gingered pear dessert
STREGA *(STREH-gah)*	the Italian word for witch

STROMBOLI *(strom-BOH-lee)*	an island volcano (active), north of Sicily
STYRKA *(STUR-kah)*	the Swedish word for strength
STYX	one of the rivers of Hell
SUEDE *(SWADE)*	a very soft, tanned leather used in making gloves, garments, etc.
SUENO *(SWEH-nyoh)*	the Spanish word for dream
SUJET *(su-ZHAY)*	the French word for topic
SUKE *(SOO-kay)*	the Hawaiian name for Susan
SULTAN *(sool-TAHN)*	a Moslem/African word applied to a ruler
SUMMERHOUSE	a small, open structure in a park or garden
SUNBOW	a rainbowlike display of colors created by sunlight
SUPPER CLUB	an expensive nightclub
SUZU *(SOO-zoo)*	a common Japanese girl's name, it means little bell
SWEET FLAG	a hardy, waterside wild flower with sword-shaped leaves and yellow flowers
SWEET-TALK	to gain advantage over another by flattery and sweet words
SVELTE *(SVELT)*	the French word for slender
SYCEE *(SIGH-see)*	lumps of pure silver that bear the stamp of a banker
SYNBAR *(SUN-bawr)*	the Swedish word for obvious

T

TABARET *(TAB-uh-ray)*	strong upholstery fabric, with satin and moire stripes
TABASCO	a brand name for a sauce made of very hot red peppers
TABLEHOPPING	going from table-to-table to greet people after entering a restaurant

119

TABLE TALK	casual mealtime conversation
TABLE WINE	a wine served with a meal; wine meant to accompany other foods
TABOO or TABU	something that is prohibited by moral or religious beliefs
TACMAHAC *(TACK-muh-hack)*	aromatic resin from the balsam poplar
TAFIA *(TAFF-ee-uh)*	a cheap rum made out of molasses and refuse sugar
TANGIER	seaport city in Morocco, at the extreme north of the Straits
TAHITI	principal island of the French Society group in the Pacific
TAILOR-MADE	something made "exacting" to fit by one's tailor
TAILOR'S TARZEN	a man who wears padded shoulders to enhance a "beefcake" image
TAILS UP	in good spirits
TAIL WIND	a wind that blows in the same general direction as an aircraft is flying, therefore, increasing it's speed
TAI SHAN *(tie shan)*	a sacred mountain in the Shantung Province of China
TALEBEARER or TALETELLER	one who tells stories (true or untrue)
TALKY-TALK	shallow or frivilous chatter
TALISMAN *(TALL-iz-muhn)*	an amulet or charm, an American Indian medicine bag, or any other magic thing
TALLYMAN	one who keeps tallies (records and counts)
TAMALE	a Mexican dish of cornmeal and meat, seasoned, wrapped in corn husks and steamed
TAMBOUR *(tahm-BOUR)*	the French for drum
TANGIERS *(tan-JEERZ)*	seaport and summer capital of Morocco
TANGLEFOOT	whisky; a bumbling person
TARADIDDLE	a little fib, or lie
TARGETEER	a soldier armed with a shield (drawing the enemy's fire)
TASARLA *(tah-SAHR-lah)*	a gypsy girl's name, it means morning
TASK FORCE	a military unit assigned to a specific task

TASKMASTER	one who assigns especially difficult tasks to others
TASMANIAN DEVIL	a ferocious burrowing carnivore
TASYA (*TAHS-yah*)	a Russian girl's name
TARNINGAR (*TAYRN-ing-ahr*)	Swedish for dice
TAUBE (*TOW-buh*)	the German word for dove
TAURA (*TAW-ruh*)	an astrological girl's name, it is for a girl born under the sign of Taurus
TAUREAU (*toh-RO*)	the French word for bull
TAVLA (*TAWV-luh*)	the Swedish for picture
TAVARISH (*tuh-VAR-eesh*)	a Russian word for friend
TAVERN-FOX	one who frequents taverns
TAWNO (*TAW-noh*)	a gypsy boy's name, it means small
TAXI DANCER	a girl who dances with a patron (in a dance hall) for money
TAZZA (*TAHTS-tsah*)	the Italian word for cup
TEA PARTY	a social gathering where tea and cakes are the main refreshments
TEN BONES	a person's fingers and thumbs
TEAZEL or TEASEL (*TEE-zle*)	a plant with thistlelike flowers
TEETOTUM (*TEE-tote-uhm*)	a top that is spun with the fingers
TEMPEST (*TEM-pest*)	violent storms with high winds
TEST PILOT	a pilot that flies experimental aircraft
TEUFEL (*TOY-fell*)	the German word for devil
THEME SONG	a song that is played especially for, written for, and associated with a certain person, television show, etc.
THESSALY (*THES-uh-lee*)	ancient division of eastern Greece
THIMBLEBERRY	an American raspberry having thimble-shaped fruits
THIMBLERIG	the gambling sleight-of-hand, using a single pea and 3 inverted thimbles (sometimes walnut shells)

THIRTEEN FIRES	an American Indian term for the 13 original states of the United States
THRASHER	any of several long-tailed songbirds; a threshing machine; another name for the Thresher Shark
THUNDERBIRD!	an expression of excitement, or enthusiasm
THUNDERER	a peak (10,600 feet high) in Yellowstone National Park
TICONDEROGA	an old fort in NE New York the American's took from the British during the Revolution
TIDERIP	water that is roughened by tides and currents
TIDINGS	news; as in "good tidings"
TIMBER WOLF	the large gray or brindle wolf found in Canada
TIMBUKTU	a town in central Mali, near the Niger River
TIME ZONE	any of the 24 divisions plotted for the sake of time-keeping
TINDERBOX	a very explosive situation (as used with a volatile problem, or in regards to a very dry forest floor)
TINDRA *(TIN-drah)*	the Swedish for to twinkle
TINHORN GAMBLER	a small-time gambler
TINKER	traveling mender of tin pots and pans; one who tinkers around
TINKER'S DAMN	something of no value (the tinker doesn't feel it is worth the money/labor to mend it)
TINKERTOY	a brand name for wooden toy pieces used as developmental tools for children
TIN PAN ALLEY	where popular songs were written and made popular
TIPPECANOE	an Algonquian Indian word given to an Indiana river
TIPPERARY	a county in S. Eire, Ireland
TIRANNO *(tee-RAHN-no)*	the Italian word for tyrant
TIRZA *(TEER-zah)*	a Hebrew girl's name meaning desireable
TO-AND-FRO	moving back and forth
TOASTMASTER	one who announces toasts, etc., at public dinners

TOBAL *(toh-BAHL)*	the pet form of the Spanish boy's name Cristobal
TOBBAR *(TOHB-bahr)*	the Gypsy boy's name, it means road
TOBIT *(toh-BEET)*	the Hebrew word for good, it is a boy's name
TOE DANCE	a ballet (dance done on the toes)
TOFFEL *(TOHF-el)*	the Swedish word for slipper
TOK *(TOO-K)*	the Swedish word for fool
TOLL CALL	a long-distance call (and charged for accordingly)
TOLLGATE	a gate across a bridge, roadway, etc., where money is charged for access to it
TOLLHOUSE	a booth (in olden days it was usually a lodge) for the toll-taker
TONGA	an island group in the South Pacific
TOPBOOT	a boot with a high top (sometimes decorated); army use for another nickname for a top sergeant
TOPFLIGHT	when something is excellent, or very good
TOPGALLANT	refers to the mast, sail, etc., that is above the topsail
TOP HAT	the tall silk hats worn by men during very formal occasions
TOPHET *(TOE-fete)*	Hell or a hellish place
TOP KICK	another name used to refer to the top sergeant
TOPO *(TOH-poh)*	the Italian word for mouse
TORA *(TOH-rah)*	the Japanese for tiger
TORCHBEARER	one who carries a torch; loud praise for someone/something
TORCHLIGHT	the light given off by one, or many, torches
TORCH SONG	a popular, very sentimental song
TORNADO GREY	a color (dark grey); a menacing grey (the color of a tornado)
TORPEDO	a submarine mine (it is self-propelled and cigar-shaped)

123

TORPEDO BOAT	a small, fast boat that flies along the surface of the ocean and is equipped to discharge torpedoes
TORTUGA *(tohr-TOO-gah)*	the Spanish word for turtle; it is also an island in the West Indies inhabited by pirates
TOTSI *(TOHT-shee)*	an Indian girl's name, it means moccasins
TOUJOURS *(too-ZHOOR)*	the French word for always
TOURIST	one who makes a pleasure trip somewhere
TOURIST CAMP	roadside cabins or strings of motels that cater to tourists
TOUR OF DUTY	when a member of the armed servies in on official duty
TOUT PETIT *(too puh-TEE)*	the French word for tiny
TOUT DE SUITE *(TOOT sweet)*	the French word for immediately
TOWN CRIER	a person who was hired to deliver statements through the streets of town
TOWNFOLK or TOWNSPEOPLE	the residents of a particular town
TOWN HALL	building where a town's public offices are located
TOWN MARSHALL	an officer of a town police force
TOWN MEETING	when townfolk gather to discuss, vote, etc., on town issues
TOWNSEND'S SOLITAIRE	an uncommon, robinlike bird of the West Coast of the US
TOY SHOP	a shop that sells only toys
TRACER BULLET	the line of actual "fire" that a bullet leaves as it travels from the gun to the target
TRACK MEET	where athletes gather for track contests
TRADE WIND	a wind that follows the same course (or *trade*) at the equator
TRADING POST	(early American use) the building where the trapper and the trading company set up station to trade furs for goods
TRANSVAAL *(TRAHNZ-vahl)*	a province in South Africa
TRANSYLVANIA	a plateau region in central Rumania (Dracula's hometown)
TRAVA *(TRAH-vah)*	a Slavic girl's name, it's meaning is found in nature

TRAVELING MAN	a traveling salesman
TREACLE *(TREE-kl)*	a syrup made during the refining of sugar (molasses)
TREASURE-TROVE	a hidden treasure that is found
TREFLE *(TREFL)*	the French word for clover
TRELLA *(TREH-yuh)*	the Spanish word for little star
TRIBESMAN	a member of a tribe
TRIBU *(tree-BU)*	the French word for tribe
TRIGGER-HAPPY	someone who is quick to resort to force
TRINIDAD	an island in the West Indies (off the Venezuelan coast)
TRINKET	a small ornament (often jewelry)
TRINKUMS	the Old English/Scottish word for trinkets (small ornaments)
TRIPP	the Swedish word for trip
TRISTAN	a love story from medieval times tells of the prince (Tristan) who goes to Ireland to ask for the hand of Iseult (''the beautiful'') for his uncle, then Tristan falls for her, himself
TRITON	the Greek god of the sea (son of Poseidon and Aphrodite)
TROGEN *(TROO-gen)*	the Swedish word for faithful
TROGLODYTE	a prehistoric cave dweller
TROIKA *(TROY-kuh)*	a Russian sleigh pulled by 3 horses abreast
TROMPER *(trohm-PAY)*	the French word for to err or to cheat
TROLLERI *(TROH-leh-ree)*	the Swedish word for magic
TROOPER	a mounted policeman; a cavalryman
TROOPSHIP	a ship used to transport army soldiers across the seas
TROOPTRAIN	a scheduled train, used mostly by military personnel (WW II)
TROPICBIRD	an oceanic bird (something like a tern) found mostly in the tropics; recognized by having 2 elongated middle feathers
TROUBADOUR	a strolling minstrel and 12th-13th century Italian court poets

TROUBLE-SHOOTER	an expert in his field who can locate and repair potential problems before they become serious
TRUEBLUE	someone who is an extremely loyal friend and supporter
TRUFFLE	a costly underground fungi (mushroomlike) black gourmet food item
TRUMPETER	someone who sounds a trumpet (or a position) loud and long
TRYCK *(TRUK)*	the Swedish word for using pressure; or written print
TRYGG *(TRUG)*	the Swedish word for secure
TRYST *(trist)*	when lovers arrange to meet at a certain time and place
TUCKAHOE	various plant roots used for food by the Algonquian Indians; a river in southeastern New Jersey
TUFFET	a tuft of grass; a low stool
TUFTHUNTER	a person who seeks to become acquainted with snobs and persons of society; originated when a student at Oxford/Cambridge would cozy-up to the students of titled parents (easily singled out because of the gold tufts they wore on their hats)
TULIPWOOD	the beautifully grained wood of the tuliptree
TULSA	a city in northeastern Oklahoma
TURKISH DELIGHT	a candy that originated in Turkey (made of colored, gelatin-flavored bases and coated with powdered sugar)
TUSCARORA *(tus-cuh-ROAR-uh)*	a tribe of Iroquoian Indians from Virginia and North Carolina
TUSKER	an elephant or wild boar, with large, dangerous tusks (usually used in reference to an extremely dangerous rogue animal)
TUTTI E DUE *(TOOT-tee eh DOO-eh)*	an Italian term meaning both
TUVALU *(TOO-vuh-LOO)*	a country made up of 9 small islands in the central Pacific Ocean
TVINGA *(TVING-ah)*	the Swedish for to force
TWALPENNIES	the Old Scottish for twelvepence (equal to one penny sterling)
TWAYBLADE *(TWAY-blade)*	a small terrestrial orchid

TWEED	a soft woolen fabric with a homespun appearance (made of 2 or more colors in a check or plaid pattern), used in suits and jackets
TWEED KETTLE	an Old Scottish salmon dish coming from the River Tweed area
TWELVE GODFATHERS	a slang term for a jury
TWILIT *(t'WHY-lit)*	when something is illuminated by the soft light of twilight
TWINIGHT	a baseball double-header played during late afternoon
TYCKA OM *(tuk-ah OHM)*	the Swedish for to like
TYEE *(TIGH-ee)*	an American Indian word for a chief; used for an Indian boy's name

u

U-BOAT	a German submarine (the term evolved by telescoping *U*ndersea and *boat*)
UMIAK *(OOH-me-ack)*	an eskimo canoe made of sealskin stretched over a whalebone, or wooden, frame
UNION JACK	the Union Flag
UPALA *(ooh-PAH-lah)*	a girl's name, it is a name from India that means colors of the rainbow
UP A SHADE, ADA!	an old-time appeal for more room, as "Move up a bit there!"
UP-COUNTRY	country property that is somewhat removed from the seashore or lowlands (property well above sea level)
UPS-A-DAISY	an encouragement of "get up" used on children after a fall
UP-TOWN	now universally accepted as being a person of money or social prominence (it once was used to refer to the upper part of town where the affluent residences were located).

V

VACKER *(VAHK-ehr)*	the Swedish word for handsome
VAGABONDO *(vah-gah-BAHN-doh)*	the Italian word for a tramp
VAHINE *(vuh-HEE-nay)*	a Polynesian woman
VAINGLORY	when a person is pompous; having a severe case of self-love
VALDSAM *(VOHL-sahmm)*	the Swedish word for violent
VALHALLA *(val-HAL-uh)*	the viking (Norseman) heaven; souls of battle heroes were taken here
VALIENTE *(vah-L-YENN-teh)*	the Spanish word for brave
VALKOMMEN *(VAIL-kohm-ehn)*	the Swedish word for welcome
VALKYRIE *(val-KEER-ee)*	in Norse mythology, the Valkyrie were the maidens of Odin whe escorted fallen heroes from the battlefield to Valhalla
VALSIGNA *(vel-SING-nah)*	the Swedish for to bless
VANDRA *(VAHNN-drah)*	the Swedish for to wander
VANADIUM *(vuh-NAY-dee-uhm)*	a metal element that is used in making steel alloys (originating from a shorter Vanadis—goddess of love)
VANGUARD	when an army is advancing, the vanguard is the front line
VANITA *(vah-nee-TAH)*	the Italian word for vanity, also, an often-used girl's name
VANQUISH	to thoroughly defeat one's enemy
VAPOR TRAIL and CONTRAIL	the white trail of vapor seen in the skies when a jet flies overhead
VAQUERO *(vuh-CARE-oh)*	the Spanish word for cowboy
VARDAR	a river in SE Yugoslavia and northern Greece
VARIETY SHOP	a store that deals in a wide range of merchandise
VARIETY SHOW	a show that has a lot of short acts (singers, dancers, etc.)

VARTAN *(VAHR-tahn)*	an Armenian boy's name, it's origin is in nature
VATUSIA *(vah-TOO-see-ah)*	an African girl's name meaning abandoned
VAUDEVILLE *(VAHD-uh-ville)*	a vaudeville show is an almost nonexistent form of entertainment now, but was a stage show made up of short comedy skits, dances, songs, etc.
VELD and VELDT *(velt)*	a South African term for an open, grassy plain with very few trees or shrubs
VELOCITA *(veh-lo-chee-TAH)*	the Italian word for *speed*
VELOURS *(vuh-LOOR)*	the French for velvet
VENDETTA	a blood feud carried on between warring families
VENEZIA *(vay-NAY-tsee-uh)*	the Italian spelling/pronounciation of Venice
VERMOGEN *(fehr-MO-gen)*	the German for fortune
VERY FAMILLIONAIRE	combining the word *familiar* x *millionaire* equals what is said of a person who cozies up to another person with considerably more money; patronizing a wealthy person for some psychological motive
VESTPOCKET	very small, particularly small for its kind of species
VESUVIUS *(vuh-SOO-vee-us)*	the active volcano of southern Italy
VICTRESS	a victorious person who is a woman
VIDUNDER *(VEED-oon-dehr)*	the Swedish word for a monster
VIEW-HALOO	when a fox breaks cover during a hunt the huntsman shouts "View haloo!"
VIGILANTE	a person who is always on the alert for lawbreakers and then takes the law into his own hands
VILDMARK *(VILLD-mark)*	the Swedish word for wilderness
VINEGARROON	a nonvenemous, scorpion-like little spider that gives off a vinegary odor when alarmed; also, a person who is basically harmless—but who can be nasty and noisy
VINKA *(VING-kah)*	the Swedish word for to wave

VINO *(VEE-noh)*	the Italian word for wine
VIOLETTA *(vee-oh-LET-tah)*	the Italian word for violet
VIRGA *(VUR-gah)*	the wisps of precipitation coming from a cloud only to evaporate before it can reach the earth
VIRGINIA RAIL	a common, but secretive, medium-sized bird found in brackish marshes
VIRTU *(VUR-too)*	knowledge of the fine arts
VITTORIA *(veet-TOH-ree-ah)*	the Italian word for victory
VIXEN	a female fox; a forbidding woman
VOGUER *(vo-GAY)*	the French word for to sail
VOLAR *(voh-LAHR)*	the Spanish for to fly
VOLCAN	the Roman mythological god of fire
VOLPE *(VOHL-peh)*	the Italian word for fox
VUNDERBAR *(VOON-der-bar)*	the Yiddish word for wonderful
VOULOIR *(voo-LWAHR)*	the French word for to wish
VULPINE *(VUL-pin)*	anything that resembles a fox in looks or character traits

WACO *(WAY-koh)*	a city in McLennan County in central Texas
WAHOO *(WAH-hoo)*	a shout of joy; a large game fish of the tropics
WAKASHAN	a North American Indian language
WALKAWAY	a contest that is easily won
WALK-ON	a minor role in a drama (usually just walking on stage, no lines)
WALLABY	an Australian animal like a small kangaroo

WALLABY, ON THE	Australian slang term for "on tramp" (walking through the bush)
WALLOON *(wuh-LOON)*	the people of Celtic descent who live in Belgium
WALPURGIS NIGHT *(VAHL-poor-gus)*	German for a witches gathering that takes place on the night of April 30th
WAMPUM	beads that the American Indians sometimes wove into belts, they were made from the lining of shells and used as money
WAMPUS	a cardigan; a heavy jacket made of coarse cloth
WANDERING TATTLER	an uncommon sandpiper that nests along mountain streams
WANDERLUST	German for impulse to travel; people who are constantly on the move
WANDEROO	a south Asian monkey
WANIGAN *(WAN-uh-gun)*	a shanty built on a raft (used by early American logging camps for cooking and sleeping)
WAPENSHAW *(WOP-ehn-shaw)*	an Old Scottish word for a show of weapons
WAPI *(WAH-pee)*	an American Indian boy's name, it means lucky
WAR BABY	a child born during a time of war while it's father is still in the service
WAR BELT	used by some American Indian tribes, it is a belt of wampum that is woven with certain symbols and summons others to war with them
WAR BONNET	a headdress made of long feathers and worn by American Indians during a battle
WAR COLLEGE	two "colleges" in the US where military officers are given advanced instruction in strategy, etc.
WAR CRY	a cry sounded during/before a battle to rally the participants to war
WARDROOM	a room aboard a warship for the use of officers only
WAR GAMES	staged conflicts to teach/test readiness of military divisions
WAR HAWK	a person who advocates war
WAR HORSE	a veteran, someone who is aggressive in politics
WARLOCK	a male witch or sorcerer

WARLORD	a military commander who exercises civil powers
WARMONGER	someone who encourages a warring condition
WARPAINT	colors that the American Indians applied to their faces and bodies in preparation for war
WARP AND WOOF	the underlying structure (foundation) on which you build
WARPATH	when the act of going to war begins (On the warpath!); it began as the actual path the Indians would take when they went off to war
WAR PLANE	an aircraft that carries weapons for combat
WAR POWERS	powers that are given to a government during time of war (granted under the Constitution)
WASSAIL (*WAH-suhl*)	a spiced ale that is used for drinking a ''health'' to someone (mostly Christmas use)
WATCHCRY	a password used while moving ''between the lines'' (during war, etc.) to identify friend or foe
WATCHER	one who watches; someone who is assigned to watch for the enemy
WATCH FIRE	a fire that is lit at night (see SIGNAL FIRE)
WATER-COLORS	concentrated pigments of color that are prepared for use by the addition of water
WATERLOO	the British and Prussians defeated Napoleon on this battlefield in central Belgium
WATER RAT	the American muskrat
WEE FOLK	fairies and elves
WEIDE (*VIDE-uh*)	the German word for willow
WELKIN	the sky; the area of the heavens
WELLAWAY	an Old English expletive for ''Alas!'' and ''Woe is me!''
WHIFFET	a little pesky person; a ''whiff'' or snappish person
WHIFFLER	a person who concerns himself with triflings; one who ''whiffs''
WHILOM	''Once upon a time''; at one time
WHINCHAT	an Old World, thrushlike song bird

132

WHISKY JACK	another name for the common Canadian Jay (blue jay bird)
WHISTLE STOP	a little town where a train stops only if it is "whistled" to
WHITECHAPEL WARRIOR	a nickname for the militia of the Aldgate District of East London
WHITEFRIARS	a section of London where outlaws and bandits hid out, or sought refuge in the slums and dingy alleyways
WHITE MAGIC	good magic; as opposed to black magic
WHITTLINGS	the fine shavings that remain when a whittler works on a piece of wood
WHODUNIT	"Who done it?"; a type of mystery fiction where the reader is encouraged to uncover the criminal before he is actually revealed
WICHITA	a city in southeast Kansas that began as a frontier cattletown
WICKET	a small door or gate that is found within the main entrance
WIDOW'S WEEDS	the black clothes that a widow wears during mourning
WIDOW'S TEARS	the name of a waterfall in Yosemite National Park
WILDCAT STRIKE	a strike that is not authorized by the union leaders
WILDFIRE	a fire that is uncontrollable, or raging out of control
WILD-GOOSE CHASE	when a search is practically without hope
WILD HUNT	found in European folklore, these were ghostly spirits/hunters who went dashing through the forest or flew through the skies on stormy nights; they were led by *The Wild Huntsman*
WILDING	something that grows in the wild; an animal that cannot be tamed
WILD MARE	another name for a nightmare
WILD RYE	a tall grass that is found in the southern US
WILDWOOD	a woodland escape; a natural woodland or forest
WILLET	a common upland sandpiper, it is mottled brown in color
WILLKOMMEN *(VILL-kawmm-ehn)*	the German word for welcome
WILL I, NILL I or WILLY-NILLY	having no choice in the matter

WILLIEWAUGHT *(WILLIE-wahkt)*	an Old Scot word for a draft of liquor
WILLIWAW	a sudden gust of wind that moves towards the sea, down the slope of a coastal mountain range
WILL-O'-THE-WISP	something that is misleading or is not what it seems to be; something that is here-and-gone (elusive)
WILLOWER	a person that weaves baskets out of willow splits; one that "willows"
WILLOW or WILLOWS or WILLOWAY	names given to girls that are founded in the Cherokee Indian language; they are nature names for of the willow or freedom
WILLOWWARE	fancy china that is painted with a willow motif
WIND-BORNE	something that is carried on the winds
WIND-BOUND	when an airplane, or sailing ship is delayed by contrary winds
WINDBREAKER	a trade name for the light, yet warm, jacket that serves as a barrier against winds
WIND CHIMES or WIND BELLS	a cluster of chimes that are suspended so that a breeze causes them to bump into one another to produce a tinkling sound
WINDFALL	something that is knocked down by a strong wind (a tree, or ripe fruit usually)
WINDIGO *(WIN-dee-goh)*	the Algonquian Indian word for the evil demon
WINDJAMMER	a sailing ship that is most often a merchant ship
WINDLING	an English word for something torn off by winds (tree branch)
WINDOW-SHOP	to look at goods displayed in store windows without buying
WINGBOW	a mark of color found on the bend of a bird's wing
WINGED WOLF	(same as a Harpy); a Greek mythological creature that was a hideous monster; sometimes used to refer to a greedy person
WINGLET	a baby bird that is just learning to fly; someone who is just beginning to learn something
WINKEN *(VING-ken)*	the German word for to wave
WINKER	a person who winks; often said of a flirtatious young lady

WINKLE	a nickname for the periwinkle flower
WINNOW	when someone goes about separating grain from the husks (rice, wheat)
WIRE DANCER	one who balances on a wire strung in mid-air (another name for a high-wire artist)
WIRETAP	to illegally tap into someone's telephone for the purpose of gaining information on their activities
WISHTONWISH (*WISH-ten-WISH*)	an Indian boy's name it means prairie dog
WITCHCRAFT	the witch's art; black magic
WITCH DOCTOR	someone who practices medicine and healing through magic
WITCHES' BROOM	a broomlike growth on certain shrubs and trees
WITCHGRASS	hairy tufts of spiked grass growing in sandy soils, it is sometimes referred to as "panic grass"
WITCH HUNT and WITCH HUNTER	cruel harassment (as was practiced during the Salem Witch Hunts)
WITCHING	acting in the witch's art
WITH BELLS ON	a phrase that means enthusiasm for a project
WITHERSHINS	an Old Scot term for going in an opposite direction or going in reverse
WIVERN (*WHY-vurn*)	refers to the heraldic winged dragon with a barbed tail
WOEBEGONE	looking extremely sad, woeful, or pitiful
WOLVER	a person who hunts wolves
WOMBAT	an Australian animal that looks like a little bear, but possesses a nasty temperament
WOMENFOLK	a description of women as a whole
WONDERWORK	a work that is an inspiring wonder; a miracle
WOODNOTE	a simple, natural song, as if made by a bird in the woods
WOODS WITCH	a nickname for the Great Horned Owl
WUNDERKIND (*VOOHN-duhr-kint*)	a German word meaning wonder child (referring to a child prodigy)
WYANDOTTE (*WHY-uhn-daht*)	the Iroquoian name for the Huron Indians
WYANET (*wee-AH-net*)	an Indian girl's name, it means beautiful

X

XEBEC *(ZEE-beck)*	a small, three-masted ship (at one time it was very common in the Mediterranean)
XINGU *(SHINJ-goo)*	a river in northern Brazil

Y

YACHT CLUB	a club for yachtsmen, usually with docks and moorings, fancy club buildings and restaurant
YAKECHEN *(YAH-keh-shen)*	an Indian boy's name, it means sky
YAKOV *(YAH-kovv)*	the Yiddish form of Jacob
YANKEEDOM	where the Yankees live; the northern US as opposed to the southern US
YANKEELAND	the United States (sometimes used specifically for the New England area)
YAQUI *(YAH-kee)*	a tribe of Indians living in Mexico (of Aztec descent)
YASHMAK	the double veil that Moslem women wear in public
YASMEEN *(YAS-meen)*	a very popular Middle Eastern girl's name, it means jasmine flower
YEASAYER *(YAY-say-ehr)*	someone who is confident and optimistic and has a very good attitude about life
YELLOWBIRD	a nickname for the American Goldfinch
YELLOWHAMMER	another nickname for the Gilded Flicker (a gilt-winged member of the woodpecker family)
YELLOW-JACKET	a nasty-tempered wasp that hives underground
YELLOWKNIFE	a great Indian chief; a town in northwestern Canada

YELLOWLEGS	what the Indians called the US Cavalry officers, since their blue riding britches had bold yellow stripes
YELLOWTAIL	the California rockfish
YENGEESE *(YENG-geez)*	what the early American Indians called the New England settlers (it means "white man," and is their "corruption" of the word *Yankee*)
YENTA *(YEHN-tuh)*	the Yiddish for a busybody; a gossipy woman who gives freely of her unsolicited opinions/advice
YEOMAN *(YOH-man)*	in the US Navy this is a Petty Officer
YLANG-YLANG *(ee-LAHNG ee-LAHNG)*	a perfume that comes from the flowers of the Malayan custard-apple
YODELER	a person who yodels
YOICKS	a traditional cry given when foxhunting to urge the hounds on
YOKI *(YOH-kee)*	an Indian girl's name meaning little bird
YONKERS	a city in New York State (on the Hudson)
YOUNGBLOOD	young people; new vigor; the up-and-coming generation
YOUNGEST SON	a tendency seen in folklore to use a "youngest son" as the main character (he was the smart one in some stories, the simpleton who made it rich in other stories, or he was the one who was mistreated by his older siblings only to eventually achieve success)
YQUEM *(ee-KEM)*	an excellent Sauterne wine from the estate "Chateau Yquem" in southern France

Z

ZAFFER	a blue pigment (cobalt) used to paint glass and porcelain
ZAHARA *(ZAH-rah)*	an African girl's name meaning flower
ZALTANA *(zahl-TAH-nuh)*	an Indian girl's/boy's name meaning mountain

ZAMBEZI *(zam-BEE-zee)*	a river in central and southeastern Africa
ZAMPA *(TSAHM-pah)*	the Italian word for paw
ZANZIBAR	a Sultanate in east Africa (it combined the protectorates of Kenya and Zanzibar)
ZAPATILLA *(sah-pah-TEE-lyah)*	the Spanish word for slipper
ZARIFA *(zah-REE-fah)*	an Arabic girl's name, it means graceful
ZARZAMORA *(sahr-sah-MOH-rah)*	the Spanish for blackberry
ZASTRUGA *(zuh-STROO-guh)*	the Russian word for the long ridges of snow that are wind-built on the Russian plains
ZEITGEIST *(TZIET-geist)*	the literal in German is "time spirit" and it means the general ideas/ideals of any given time period (the morals, tastes, etc.)
ZIGANA *(ZEE-gaw-nah)*	a Hungarian word for gypsy girl
ZIGGURAT *(ZIG-oo-rat)*	the ancient Babylonian temple that was built in the shape of a deeply-stepped pyramid
ZINGARO	the Italian word for gypsy
ZIGUENER *(tsee-GOY-nehr)*	the German word for gypsy
ZIZI *(ZEE-zee)*	the Hungarian form of the girl's name Elizabeth
ZODIAC	word for the plotting of the heavens (stars) that is employed in astrological predicting
ZOHERET *(zoh-HAIR-et)*	an Israeli girl's name, it means glowing
ZORA *(SAW-ruh)*	a Slavic girl's name meaning dawn
ZORRA *(SOR-rah)*	the Spanish word for fox
ZUCCHERO *(TSOOK-keh-roh)*	the Italian for sugar
ZUCKER *(TSOOCK-ehr)*	the German for sugar
ZULU EXPRESS	an afternoon express train

ZULULAND　territory in northeastern Natal and East Union in South Africa; it came into the public eye when this Bantu Nation became involved in the Boer Wars and fought cruelly (but effectively)

ZUZA　the Czech form of Susan
(ZOO-zah)

PART II

GIRL'S NAMES/BOY'S NAMES

GIRL'S NAMES/BOY'S NAMES

From pet owner to show breeder, the favorite choice of a dog name is a name-name. They are, by far, the most popular "call names" and are commonly used as the base on which registration names are developed. Whether you call them name-names, baby names, first names, given names, or Christian names, there are more Heidis, Jamies, Nicoles, Erics, and Kellys in the American Kennel Club books than there are on file with the United States Census Bureau.

The following chapter on Girl's Names/Boy's Names offers an extraordinary collection of common, to very uncommon, name-names. Beginning with what is generally accepted as their "roots," the areas of origin and the original meanings are included. Generations of migration and mutation have resulted in taking the "root" and creating the loveliest, most interesting, ususual and usable forms imaginable. However, along with these delightful and lyrical variations, you may often find that the original meanings are either abrasive, or unfit for your purpose. Do not allow unflattering or irrelevant meanings to dissuade you from using a name. (And honestly, when is the last time someone asked you what your own name meant?) The "root" meanings were given as a source of interest, not as a working tool for selecting names.

GIRLS' NAMES

A

ABIGAIL   Hebrew: a source of joy
ABBY, ABBEY, ABBIE, GAIL, GALE, ABBA

ABRA   Hebrew: (the feminine of Abraham)

ACACIA   Greek: thorny (the acacia symbolizes immortality)
AKAKIA

ADA   Old English/Teutonic: prosperous, happy
ADDA, AIDA, ADABELLE, ADABEL

ADAH   Old Hebrew: crown, beauty, or ornament

ADAR   Hebrew: fire, very eminent

ADELAIDE   Old German: noble
ADELE, ADEL, ADDIE, ADDY, DEL, DELLA, ADELINE, ADELINA, ALINE, EDELINE, ADALINE, ADELYNNE, ARLISSE, ADELAIS, ADELICIA

ADELIZA   (combination of Adele & Liza)

ADINA   Hebrew: delicate, voluptuous (feminine of Adin)
ADINE, ADENA, DINA

ADOLPHA   Old German: noble wolf (also ADAL-WOLF)

ADONIA   Greek: beautiful or goddess come to life (feminine of Adonis)
ADONICA

ADORA   Latin-French: beautiful gift, glory and renown
ADORIA, ADORABELLE

ADOREE   French: adored one

ADORNA   Latin: adorned one

ADRIA   Latin: dark one (feminine of Adrian)
HADRIA, ADRIENNE, ADRIANA, ADRIANE, ADREA, ADRINI

AGATHA   Greek: good, kind
AGATHE, AGATA, AGGIE, AGGY, AGNA, AGNELLA, HAGGY, AGAFIA

AGNES   Greek: pure one, gentle meek lamb
AGGIE, ANNICE, ANNIS, ANIS, AGNA, NEYSA, NESSA, NESSI, AGNOLA, NESSIE, NESTA, INES, INEZ, YNES, YNEZ, AGNESSA, ANEZKA, AGNESCA

144

AILEEN Anglo-Irish: light
AYLEEN, ALEEN, ALENE, ELEEN, ELENE, EILEEN,
ILENE, ILEANA

AIMEE French version of Amy: beloved (also,
AMORET and AMORETTE)

AISHA Arabic: common name of Muslim people
AYESHA, AESHA, AIESHA, AYEISHA, AISIA,
IEESHA

AISLINN Irish Gaelic: vision, dream
ISLEEN

ALANNA Irish Gaelic: comely, fair, beautiful
(feminine of Alan)
ALAINNE, ALAYNE, ALLENE, ALLYN, ALINA,
ALLINA, LANNA, LANA, ALANAH

ALBERTA German/Old English: noble, brilliant
(feminine of Albert)
ALBERTINE, ALBERTINA, ELBERTA, ELBERTINE,
ALLIE, BERTA, BERTIE

ALBINA Latin: white, blonde
ALBA, ALVINA, ALBINIA, ELVIRA, ALVIRA

ALDORA Greek: winged gift

ALERIA Middle English: eaglelike

ALETHEA Greek: truth
ALETA, ALETTA, ALETTE

ALEXANDRA Russian/Greek: helper, defender (feminine
of Alexander)
ALEXANDRINE, ALESSANDRA, ALEJANDRA,
ALEXANDRIA, ALEXANDERINA, ALEXANDERINE,
ALEXANDRAENA, ALEXANDERIA, ALEX, ALEXA,
ALEXINE, ALEXIS, ALEXANA, ALEXIA, ALLA,
LEXA, LEXIE, LEXINE, SANDI, SANDIE, SANDY,
SANDRA, ZANDRA

ALFREDA Old English: elf counselor (wise) (feminine
of Alfred)
ELFREDA, ELFRIEDA, ELFRIDA, ELVA, ALFIE,
FREDA

ALICE Old German: noble, kind (the ancient title
for a German princess)
ALICEA, ALICIA, ALISSA, ALITHIA, ALLYS, ALYCE,
ALYS, ALIX, ALISON, AILIS, ALLIE, ELLIE, ELCIE,
ELSIE, ELSA, ALLA, ALLEY

ALIDA Latin: little winged one (little bird)
ALEDA, ALETA, ALITA, ALETTA, ALETTE,
ALLENA, ALLENE, ALLEYNE, LEDA, LITA

ALISON Irish Gaelic: little truthful one (combining
Alice & Louise)
ALLYSON, ALISANNE, ALYSANNE, ALLISON, ALIE,
ALLIE, ALLEY, LISSIE, LISSY

ALLEGRA Italian: cheerful, gay

ALMA Latin: fair, kind   Arabic: exalted princess
ALMIRA, ELMIRA, ALMENA, ELMINA

ALOHA Hawaiian: greetings or farewell

ALPHA Greek: first one; the first letter in the Greek alphabet
ALFA

ALTHEA Greek: healer, healthy and wholesome
THEA

ALULA Latin: winged one

ALURA Old English: divine counselor
ALLURA

ALVA Latin: blonde one   Old English: elf-friend (the feminine of Alvin)
ALVINA, ALVENA, ALVERDINE, ALWYNA, ALWYNNE

ALZENA Arabic-Persian: the woman
ALZAN

AMABEL Latin: lovely, beautiful
AMABELLE

AMANDA Latin: worthy of love
MANDA, MANDY, MANDIE, MANDALINE, AMADEE, AMANDINE

AMARIS Hebrew: God has promised
MARY, MARYA, AMARIAH

AMARYLLIS Greek: fresh, sparkling; also, the Amaryllis Lily
RYLLIS, RILLA

AMBER Old French/Arabic: a jewel name (the red amber, an ancient tree sap made solid by nature)
AMBRA, AMBREE, AMBERETTE

AMBROSIA Greek: immortal (the feminine of Ambrose)
AMBROSINE, AMBROZINE, AMBROSINA

AMELIA Gothic/Old German: work and industrious
AMALEA, AMALIA, AMILIA, EMILIA, AMELINE, EMELINA, EMELINE, AMELITA, EMELITA, EMMELINE, EMELIE, AMALIE, AMY, EM, EMMIE, EMMY

AMELINDA Latin: beloved, pretty

AMETHYST Greek: wine-colored; a precious purple stone

AMITY Latin/Old French: friendly

AMY Old French/Latin: beloved
AIMEE, AME, AMIE, AMICIA, AMELITA

ANASTASIA Greek: resurrection
NASTASYA, ANSTICE, ANASTASIE, ANASTACE, ANSTIS, STACIE, STACIA, STACY, STACEY

ANCELIN French: handmaiden (the feminine of Lancelot)
ANCELOT, ANCILEE, ANSELOTE, ANCELOTE

ANCHORET Old Welsh: much loved
INGARET

ANDREA Latin: womanly (the feminine of Andrew or Andreas)
ANDREE, ANDRIA, ANDREANA, ANDRIANA, ANDRA, ANDREWINA, RENA, ANDRINE, ANDRETTE, ANDREENA, ANDRIETTE, ANDY, ANDIE, DREENA

ANDROMEDA Greek mythological maiden rescued from a sea monster by Perseus

ANEMONE Greek: wind flower
ANEMONA

ANGELA Old French: angel   Latin: angelic one
ANGELICA, ANGELIKA, ANGELIQUE, ANGELITA, ANGELINA, ANGELOT, ANGELINE, ANGELE, ANGEL, ANGIE, ANGY, ANGIOLETTA, ANZIOLINA

ANIKA Czech: graceful
ANAKA, ANIKEE, ANNIKA

ANITA Hebrew: grace; also, the Spanish form of Ann
ANITRA, NITA

ANNABELLE Hebrew/Latin: fair Anne, graceful, beautiful
ANNABELLA, ANNABEL, HANNAH-BELLA, ANNIE, BELLE

ANNE Hebrew: graceful one
ANN, ANNIE, ANNY, ANNA, ANNALIE, ANNALISA, ANNALIESE, HANNAH, ANNA-LISA, ANNELIE, ANNAMARIE, ANA, ANITA, ANNETTE, HANNETTE, ANETTE, ANNETTA, ANNICE, ANNORA, ANORA, NAN, NANCY, NINA, ANNOR, NITA, NINON, NANA, NANON, NANINE, NANNY, NANCE, HANITA, ANNAH

ANTONIA Latin: priceless, beyond praise (feminine of Anthony)
ANTONIA, ANTONIE, ANTOINETTE, ANTONETTA, ANTOINETTA, TOINETTE, TONIE, TONI, TONY, TONIA, TONYA, NETTA, NETTIE, NETTY, TONNELI

APOLLINE Greek: sunlight (feminine of Apollo)
APOLLON, APOLLONIA

APRIL Latin: open (born in April, when the earth "opens" up to spring)
APRILLI, APRILETTE

ARABELLA Latin: beautiful altar
ARABELLE, BELLE, BELLA

ARDELLE   Latin: warmth, enthusiasm
ARDA, ARDELIA, ARDIS, ARDEEN, ARDENE,
ARDELLA, ARDELIS

ARGENTA   Latin: silvery one

ARTHURETTA   Welsh: bear   Celtic: rock (feminine of Arthur)
ARTHURINA

ARIA   Italian: melody
ARIETTA, ARIETTE

ARIANA   Latin: very holy, pleasing   Welsh: silvery

ARIELLA   Hebrew: lioness of God

ARLENE   Irish Gaelic: a pledge
ARLEEN, ARLENA, ARLETA, ARLETTE, ARLINE,
ARLYNE, ARLIE, LENA

ASGARD   Old German: the divinely guarded
ASGAR

ASHLEY   Anglo-Saxon: literally "ashfield" (a common surname - now popular as a trendy, "new" Christian name)
ASHLEA, ASHLEE, ASHLEIGH, ASHLIE, ASHLYN

ASTA   Greek: starlike (also, the constellation Virgo and the Greek goddess of justice)
ASTRA, ESTHER, STELLA, ESTELLE, ASTREA,
ASTRED, ASTRELLITA

ASTRID   Old Norse: divine strength (also, much used as a name for Scandinavian queens and princesses)
ASTRI, ESTRID

ATALANTA   Greek; the mythological huntress known for her beauty and swiftness
ATLANTA

ATHENA   Greek: wisdom
ATHENE, ATTIE

AUDREY   Old English: noble strength
AUDRIE, AUDRY, AUDRA, AUDREE, AUDREEN,
AUDREA

AUGUSTA   Latin: sacred, majestic
AUGUSTINE, AUGUSTINA, AUGUSTIA, AUGGIE,
GUS, GUSSIE, TINA, TEENE, GUSTA, GUSTAVA,
GUSTINE, GUSTEL, AUSTINE

AURA   Latin: gentle breeze
AUREA, AURIA, AURAL

AURELIA   Latin: golden (also, the Roman goddess of dawn)
AURIOL, AURELIE, ORALIA, ORELIA, ORLENA,
ORIANDA, AURONETTE

AURORA	Latin: daybreak
	AURORE, ZORA, ZORAH, ZORANA, ZORINA, ZORICA, ZORAY
AUTUMN	recently popularized, trendy, New-Age name for its seasonal quality
AVA	Latin: graceful
AVIS	Latin: birdlike Old French: warlike
	AVICE
AXAH	Hebrew: a tinkling anklet (Caleb's daughter in the bible)
	AXA
AZIZA	Swahili: precious
AZIZE	Turkish: dear, rare
AZURA	Old French: blue sky
	AZUR

B

BAMBI	Old Italian: little baby (through Bambino)
	BAMBALINA, BIMMI
BAPTISTA	Greek: the baptizer
	BATTISTA, BATISTA, BAPTISTE
BARBARA	Greek/Latin: stranger (one who doesn't speak the language)
	BARBARY, BARBETTE, BABETTE, BARBA, BARBRA, BARBIE, BARBY, BAB, BABS, BABE, BOBBIE, BARBE, BARBELI, BARBICA
BARRIE	Irish Gaelic: spearlike (a trendy feminine of Barrie)
	BARRI, BARRI-JANE, BARRIE-ANN
BASILIA	Greek: queenly, regal (the feminine of Basil)
	BASILIE, BAS, BASIE, BASILDA
BATHILDA	Old German: bright battle-maiden
	BATHILDE
BATHSHEBA	Hebrew: daughter of the oath
	SHEBA
BEATRICE	Latin: she that makes happy
	BEATRIX, BEATRISSA, BETRIX, TRIXY, TRIXIE, TRIX, TRICKS, TRICKSIE, TRISSIE, BEA, BEE
BEDELIA	Anglo Saxon: the well arrayed
BELINDA	Old Spanish: beautiful, pretty
	BELLA-LINDA, BELYNDA, BEL, BELLE, LINDA

BELLANCA Italian: blonde one

BELLE French/Spanish/Latin: beautiful
BELL, BELLA, BELVA, BELVIA, ABELLA, ABELLONA

BENEDICTA Latin: the blessed (the feminine of Benedict)
BENEDETTA, BENETTA, BENEDIKTA, BENITA, BINNIE, DIXIE

BERENGARIA Old German: bear spear
BERNGARD

BERENICE Greek: bringer of victory
BERNICE, BERRY, NICIE, NIKKI, NIXIE

BERNADETTE French: brave as a bear (the feminine of Bernard)
BERNADINE, BERNADENE, BERNARDINA, BERNETA, BERNETTA

BERTHA Old German: victorious, glorious (feminine of Albert/Bertram)
BERTA, BERTINA, BERTIE

BERYL Greek: precious stone, jewel
BERYLE, BERYLEE

BESS Hebrew: consecrated to God (the contraction of Elizabeth)
BESSIE, BESSY, BESSEY

BETH Hebrew: home
BETHEL, BETA, BETHANY, BETHAN, BETHANNE, BETHELL, BETHIA, BETHESDA

BETTY Hebrew: consecrated to God (another variation of Elizabeth)
BETINA, BETTINA, BETSY, BETSEY, BETTI, BETTE, BETTY ANN, BETTY JO, BETTY LOU, BETTY SUE, BETTY MAE

BEULAH Hebrew: she who is to be married
BEULA

BEVERLY Old English: literally "dweller of the beaver-meadow" (a surname popularized into a Christian name)
BEVERLEY, BEV

BIANCA Spanish: the fair one
BELLANCA

BILLIE Old English: resolution, will-power (feminine of William through Wilhelmina)
BILLIE-JEAN, BILLY

BINGA Old German: from the kettle-shaped hollow

BIRDIE English: little birdlike one

BLAIR Gaelic: marshy plain

BLAISE Old German: firebrand
BLASIA, BLAZE, BLAZIA, BLASE

BLANCHE French/Latin: white, fair one
BLANCH, BLANKA, BLANCA, BLINNIE

BLANCHEFLEUR French: white flower

BLESSING Old English: consecrated one

BLISS Old English: gladness, joy

BLITHE Old English: gladness, joy
BLYTHE

BLOSSOM Old English: fresh, lovely (modern "flower" suggestive)

BONITA Spanish: pretty
BONNIE, NITA

BONNIE French/Latin: sweet, fair
BONNY, BUNNI, BUNNIE, BUNNY, BONNIBEL, BONNIBELLE, BONBON

BRANDY alcoholic liquor fermented from fruit juice (a trendy, New-Age name of recent popularity)
BRANDI, BRANDEE, BRANDIE

BRENDA Old Norse: sword Irish Gaelic: little raven (feminine of Brendan)
BRENNA

BRIANN Celtic: hill, strength (the feminine of Brian)
BRIANA, BRIANNE, BRIANNA, BRYAN, BRYNA

BRIDGET Celtic: Strong
BRIGITTE, BRIGITTA, BRIGIT, BRIGID, BRIGIDA, BRITA, BRYDIE, BRIDIE, BIDDIE, BIDDY, BRIETTA, BRITT, BRITTA, BRITTANY, BRIGANTI, BRYDE, BRIDE

BRITANNIA English: maid of Britain
BRITANIA, BRITT

BRONWYN Welsh: white bosomed (girl with lovely white skin)
BRONWEN, BRONYA, RONWEN, ROWENA

BROOK a small stream (a trendy, New-Age feminine name)
BROOKE, BROOKES

BRUNHILDA Old German: armored battle-maiden
BRUNHILDE

c

CADENCE   Latin: rhythmic
         CADENA, CADENZA

CALANDRA   Greek: the lark
         CALANDRE, CALANDRIA, CAL, CALLIE, CALLY

CALEDONIA   Latin: from Scotland

CALIDA   Spanish: warm, ardent
         CALLIDA

CALISTA   Greek: most beautiful one
         CALLISTA, CALLISTO, CALIXTA, CALLIE

CALLA   Greek: beautiful

CALLULA   Latin: little beautiful one

CALYPSO   Greek: concealor
         KALYPSO

CAMEO   Italian: a sculptured jewel

CAMILLE   Latin: young ceremonial attendant
         CAMILLA, CAMELIA, CAMMIE, CAMMY, CAM,
         MILLIE, MILLY

CANDACE   Greek: glittering, flowing white
         CANDICE, CANDIDA, CANDIDE, CANDEE,
         CANDIE, CANDY, CANDANCE

CAPRICE   Italian: Capriccio fanciful
         CAPPY

CARA   Latin: dear   Irish Gaelic: friend
         KARA, CARINA, CARINE, CARALYN, CARALYNE,
         CORALINE

CARESSE   French: endearing one
         CARISSA, CARITA

CAREY   Old Welsh: dweller of castles, dark
         CARY, CARRIE, CARI, CARRIE-LEE

CARIN   Latin: the keel (one of the 5 stars in the
Orion constellation)
         CARYN, CARINA, KARINA, KARENA, KERRIE,
         KERRY

CARISSA   Latin: dear one
         CARISA, CHARISSA, CARITA

CARLA   Old German: strong (the feminine of
Charles)
         KARLA, CARLEEN, CARLENE, CARLINE, CARLIE,
         CARLI, CARLEY, KARLEEN, KARLENE, KARLINE,
         KARLI, KARLIE, CARLETTA, CARLINA, CARLOTTA,
         CARLITA

CARMA   Sanskrit: fate, destiny
         KARMA

CARMEL Hebrew: God's vineyard   Spanish: a song and rosy
CARMELA, CARMELITA, CARMELINA, CARMELLE, CARMEN, CARMIA, CARMILA, CARMINA, CARMINE, CARMITA, CARMENCITA, CARMELINDA, CARMIE, LITA

CAROL Old French/Latin: strong, womanly (the feminine of Charles)
CAROLE, CARYL, CAREL, CARO, CAROLINE, CAROLINA, CAROLEEN, CAROLEE, CAROLINDA, CAROLYNN, CARLINE, KAROLINE, CARY, CAROL LEE, CAROL SUE, CAROL-ANNE, CAROLA, CARRIE, CAREY

CASILDA Spanish: a "place" name

CASSANDRA Greek: a snarer of men
CASSANDRE, CASANDREY, CASANDRA, CASS, CASSIE, CASSY, KASSANDRA

CATHERINE Greek: pure
CATALINA, CATERINA, CATHARINE, CATERINE, CATHERIN, CATHRENE, CAITRIN, CATRIONA, CATHRIN, CATRINE, CATHERINA, CATELINE, CATHLEEN, CATHIE, CATHY, CAITRIONA, CAITLIN, KATHERIN, KATHERINE, KATHERYN, KATINKA, KATHRYN, KATRINE, KATRINA, CATTRINA, KATHERINA, KATHLEEN, KATHLYNN, KATLEEN, KATRYNA, KETTI, KATARINA, KATINKA, KATTI, KITTY, KATE, KATYA, KATEY, KATIE, KATY, KATHIE, KATHY, KIT, TRINE, TRINA, TRINETTE, EKATERINA, TINKA, TEEKA, KATCHEN, KATS, KATRA, KATRI, KATLA

CECILIA Latin: dim-sited one (the feminine of Cecil)
CECILE, CECILY, CELIA, CICELY, CELIE, SISELY, CISSY, CIS, SISILE, SISSIE, SILEAS, CELE, CIEL, CICELIE, SICLEY

CELIA Latin: heaven
CELESTE, CELESTINE, CELESTINA, CELESTA

CERELIA Italian: fruitfulness (also, the Roman goddess of Harvest)
CERES, CERI, CERYS, CERIS, CERRIS, CERISE

CESARINA Latin: a queen (the feminine of Caesar)

CHANCELLA Latin: the place of the altar

CHANDRA Sanskrit: moonlike

CHANEL trendy, New-Age name (re: Coco Chanel the French designer)
SHANEL, SHANELLE, SHANELL

CHANTAL French: a common girl's name of uncertain origin
CHANTELLE, CHANTELE, SHANTELLE

CHARA Greek: joy

CHARITY Latin/Greek: loving, benevolent, charitable
CHARIS, CHARISSA, CHARITA, CHARRY, CHERRY

CHARLOTTE   French: little womanly one (the feminine of Charles)

SHARLEEN, SHARLENE, CHARLEEN, CHARLENE, CHARLINE, CHARLOT, CHARLOTTA, CHARLOTTY, CHARLESINA, CHARLZINA, CHARLETTA, CHARLINNA, CHARLISA, CHARLIE, CHARLEY, CHARLESENA, CHATTY, LOTTY, LOTTIE, CHARLET, CHARLETTE, CHARLIZE, SHARLET, LOTTA

CHARMAIN   Latin/Greek/French: a little joy, singer

CHARMAINE, SHARMAINE, SHARMANE, CHARMION, CHARM, CHARMIE

CHELSEA   English: a "place" name of recent trendy popularity

CHELSIE, KELSIE

CHER   French: dear   Welsh: love

CHERIE, CHERE, CHERALYN, CHEREEN, SHEREEN, CHERILYN, SHERILYN, SHEREE, SHERI, SHERRY, SHERIE, SHERREE, CHERILYNN, CHERRYLYN, SHERILYN, CHERRIE, CHERRY, CHERYL, CHERRYLL, SHERYL, SHERRELL, CHERALYN, SHERRLYN

CHIARA   Latin: bright, clear (Italian form of Clara)

CHIQUITA   Spanish: little one

CHLOE   Greek: young, verdant

CHRISTA   Latin/French/Greek: Christian

CHRISTINE, CHRISTINA, CHRISANDA, CHERISTINA, CHRISTA, CHRISTIANE, CHRISTABLE, CHRISTABELLA, CHRISTABELLE, CHRISTELLA, CHRISTOBEL, CHRISTAL, CHRISTEN, KRISTEN, CHRISTIANA, KIRSTIE, KIRSTY, KRISTINA, CHRISTEEN, CHRISTIEN, KRISTEEN, KRISTEL, CRISTIONA, CRISTIN, CAIRISTIONA, CHRIS, CHRISSIE, CHRISSY, CHRISTIE, TINA, TEEN, TINE, TINY

CINDERELLA   French: little one of the ashes

CINDIE, CINDY, ELLA, CINDERS

CLANCY   English: a popular, trendy, New-Age name

CLANCIE

CLARA   Latin: clear, bright, illustrious

CLARE, CLAIRE, KLARA, CHIARA, CLARETA, CLARITA, CLARABELLE, CLARIBEL, CLARETTE, CLARINDA, CLARINE, CLARAMAE, CLARISSA, CLARRISSE, CLARICE, CLARIS, CLARESTA, CLERISSA, CLARIMOND, CLAREY, CLARI, CLARIE, CLARY, CLAIRETTE, KLARISSA, CLARIN

CLAUDIA   Latin: lame (the feminine of Claudius)

CLAUDIANNA, CLAUDIE, CLAUDELLE, CLAUDETTE, CLAUDINE, CLAUDEEN, CLAUDINA

CLEMENCY   Latin: mild, merciful

CLEMENCE, CLEMENTINE, CLEMENTINA, CLEMENTIA, KLEMENTINE, CLEM, CLEMMIE, CLEMMY, CLEMENZA

CLEOPATRA Greek: fame of her father
CLEO

CLEVA Middle English: dweller at the cliff

CLIANTHA Greek: glory flower
CLEANTHA, CLEANTHE

CLOTILDA Old German: loud battle, famous in battle
CLOTHILDE, KLOTHILDE, TILDY, CLO

CLOVER Anglo-Saxon: clover blossom

COLEEN Irish: girl
COLINE, COLLEEN, COLENE, COLINA, COLENA,
COLLIE, COLLY

COLETTE French/Latin: a necklace
COLLETTE, COLETTA, NICOLETTE

COLUMBA Latin: the dove
COLUMBINE, COLUMBIA, COLLIE, COLLY

COMFORT French: to give aid or comfort

CONCHA Latin: beginning
CONCHITA, CONCETTA, CONCHETTA,
CONCHETTE

CONCORDIA Latin: harmony

CONSTANCE Latin: constant, firm of purpose
CONSTANCY, CONSTANT, CONSTANTA,
CONSTANTINA, KONSTANZE, STANZE, CONNIE,
CONNY, CUSTANCE

CONSUELA Spanish: consolation
CONSOLATA

CORA Greek: the maiden
CORRINE, CORINA, CORRINA, CORELLA,
CORRIN, CORETTE, CORREEN, CORRIENNE,
CORY ANNE, CORY LEE, CORRIE, CORY, COREY

CORAL Latin: coral from the sea   Old French:
cordial, sincere
CORALINE, CORALIE

CORDELIA Old Celtic: jewel of the sea
CORDELIE, KORDULA, CORDIE, DELIA, DELLA

CORNELIA Latin: yellowish, horn-colored
CORNELLE, CORNELA, CORNELIE, CORNIE,
NELIA, NELLIE

CORONA Spanish: crown, crowned one
CORONETTA

COSETTE French: victorious army
COSETTA, COZETTE

COSIMA Greek: order, harmony of the world
(feminine of Cosmo)
COSIMO

COURTNEY French: a place/surname; recently popularized as a girl's/boy's Christian name
COURT, CORT

CRESCENT Old French: to increase, to create
CRESCENTIA, CRESCENCE

CRISPINA Latin: curly haired (the feminine of Crispin)
CRISPETTE

CRYSTAL Latin/Greek: clear as crystal, brilliantly pure
CRISTA, CHRISTIE, CHRYSTAL, CHRISTY

CYMBELINE Greek: melody

CYNARA Greek: thistle

CYNTHIA Greek: the moon (one of the titles of the moon-goddess)
CYNTHIE, CYNTH, CINDY, SINDY, CINDY-ROSE

CYPRIS Greek: from the Island of Cyprus

CYRENA Greek: from Cyrene (also, the mythological Greek water nymph loved by Apollo)
KYRENE

CYTHEREA Greek: one of the titles of Aphrodite
CYTHERIA

D

DACIA Ancient Latin: from Dacia (a Roman province)
DAKOI

DAFFODIL Old French: the daffodil flower
AFRODILLE

DAGMAR Old German: day glorious   Danish: joy of the Danes
DAGOMAR, DRAGOMIRA, DAGNA

DAHLIA Old Norse: from the valley
DALIA

DAISY Old English: eye-of-the-day (a flower name)
DAISEY, DASEY, DASIE, DAISY BELLE, DAISIE

DALE Old English: from the valley
DAILE, DAYLE, DALE LEE, DALE LYNN

DALLAS Anglo-Saxon: dweller in the dale

DAMARIS Greek: the gentle
DAMARA, DAMERIS, DAMPRIS, DAMARAS, DAMARESS, TAMARIS

DANA	Anglo-Saxon: Dane Celtic: goddess of fertility DANNA, DANA ANN, DANA LYNN, DANA LEE, DAYNA, DANICA
DANIELA	Hebrew: God is my judge (the feminine of Daniel) DANELLE, DANELLA, DANIELLE, DANIELLA, DANYELLE, DANETTE, DANITA, DANETTA, DANICE, DANIKA, DANISE, DANNE, DANI, DANNIE, DANY, DANNY
DAPHNE	Greek: the laurel or bay tree DAPHNEY, DAFFY, DAPHNA, DAPH
DARA	Hebrew: heart of wisdom
DARALIS	Old English: beloved, dear DARALICE
DARCY	Old French: from the fortress D'ARCY, DARCEE, DARCI
DAREA	Persian: queenly (the feminine of Darius) DARYA, DARYN, DARIA
DARLENE	Old Anglo-French: little dear one DARLINE, DARLEEN, DARLA, DARLA ANN, DARLA SUE
DAVIDA	Hebrew: beloved one (the feminine of David) DAVINA, DAVEEN, DAVINIA, DAVELLE, DAVINE, DAVENA
DAWN	Anglo-Saxon: break of day DAWNA, DAWNE, DAWNETTA, DAWNIELLE, DAWNYSIA, DAWNN
DEBORAH	Hebrew: the bee (the who seeks the sweetness of life) DEBBORA, DEBBRA, DEBORA, DEBRA, DEB, DEBBY, DEBBIE
DEIRDRE	Old Celtic: the raging one DEIDRIE, DEIDRE, DEE, DEE DEE, DEE-ANN
DELFINE	Greek: the delphinium flower DELFINA, DELPHINE, DELPHINA, DELL
DELICIA	Latin: delicate, delightful one DELISE, DELISHA, DELESHA, DELYS, DELYSE
DELIGHT	Old French: delight, precious
DELILA	Hebrew: pining with desire, temptress DELILAH, DALILA, LILAH
DELPHA	Greek: from the Delphic Oracle of Apollo DELPHIA, DELL, DELLA
DELTA	Greek: fourth letter of the Greek alphabet
DEMETRIA	Greek: Greek goddess of fertility and harvests (the feminine of Demetrius) DEMETER, DEMITRICE

DENISE French: the feminine of Dennis (Greek god of wine)
DENNICE, DENYSE, DENIZE, DENYCE, DENNIE, DENVA, DENIS

DERON Irish Gaelic: great one, red one
DERREN, DERRYN

DESIREE French: desired, longed for
DESIRE, DESIDERIA, DESIRATA

DESMONA Greek: ill-starred
DESDEMONA, DESDEMONIA

DEXTRA Latin: skillful
DECK, DEX

DIANA Latin: goddess, divine one
DYANA, DIANNA, DIANNE, DYANE, DEANN, DEANNE, DEANA

DILYS Welsh: genuine
DYLLIS

DINAH Hebrew: judged
DINA, DINORAH, DI

DIVINA Latin: devoted to God
DIVINIA

DIXIE French: tenth (dix); also girl from the South
DIXEE

DOCILA Latin: gentle
DOCILLA

DOLLY Greek: divine gift
DOLL, DOLLIE

DOLORES Spanish: sorrows
DELORES, DELORIS, DELORA, DELORITA

DOMINA Latin: lady

DOMINICA Latin: the Lord's
DOMINIQUE, DOMINELLA, DOMINGA

DONIA Scotch: world ruler (the feminine of Donald)
DONALDA, DONELDA, DONELLA, DONALEEN, DONETTE, DONALDINE

DONNA Italian: lady, mistress
DONA, DONNA-MARIE, DONNA-MICHELLE

DORA Greek: gift
DOROTHY, DORI, DORRIE, DORIA, DORAH, DORCAS, DORALIN, DORALYNNE, DORETTE, DOREEN, DOIREANN, DOROTHEA, DORIAN, DORIE-ANN, DORICE, DORALICE, DORINDA, DORTHY, DOT, DOTTY, DOTTIE, DOLLY, DOLLIE, DOL, DODO, DASHA, DORTHEE

DORCAS Greek: a gazelle
DORCEA, DORCIA

DORE	French: golden one
DORIS	Greek: from the ocean
	DORIA, DORICE, DORISE, DORRIS
DOUGLASINA	Scotch-Gaelic: from the dark water (feminine of Douglas)
	DREENA
DOVA	Middle English: a dove
	DOVIE
DRUSILLA	Latin: the strong one
	DRUSA, DRUCIE, DRUSIE, DRUCILLA, DRUCELLA, DREWSILA, DRUZELLA, DRU, DREW, DRUZELLE
DULCIE	Latin: sweet one
	DELCINE, DULCEA, DULCIBELLA, DULCY, DULCIBEL, DOWSABLE, DULCE, DULSIE, DULCINEA, DULCE, DULCIANA
DUNCANNE	Celtic: brown chieftainess (the feminine of Duncan)

E

EARLENE	Old English: noble woman
	EARLEEN, ERLENE, ERLINE, EARLINDA, EARLIE, EARLEY
EARTHA	Old English: the earth
	ERDA, ERTHA, HERTA, HERTHA
EASTER	Old English: born at Easter time Anglo-Saxon: the goddess of spring
EBONY	English: black, dark
	EBONIE, EBONYI
ECHO	Greek: reflected sound (from Echo - the Greek nymph who pined away for the love of Narcissus, until all that remained was her voice)
EDEN	Hebrew: delight
EDITH	German: rich gift
	EDIVA, EDYTHE, EYDIE, EDIE, EDITHA, EDA, EDITA
EDLYN	Old English: noble little one
	EDLA, EDMEE
EDWINA	Old English: prosperous little one (feminine of Edward)
	EDWARDINA, EDINA, EDWEENA, EDWENA, EDWINE, EDWINETTE, WINNIE

EGLANTINE	Old French: sweetbrier rose AIGLENTINE
EILEEN	Greek: light Irish: pleasant EILLEEN, ILEAN, ILEENE, AILEEN
ELAINE	Greek: light ELANE, ELAYNE, ELAINA
ELATA	Latin: lofty
ELEANORE	Old French/Greek: light ELEANOR, ELINOR, ELINORE, ELEONORE, ELEONORA, ELNORE, ELLIE, NELDA, NELLY, NELLIE, LEONORA, LEONORE, ELLA
ELECTRA	Greek: bright, shining ELEKTRA
ELFLEDA	Anglo-Saxon: elf beautiful
ELFREDA	Old German: supernaturally wise ELFRIDA, ELFRIEDA
ELGA	Gothic: holy
ELINDA	Spanish: light
ELIZABETH	Hebrew: consecrated to God ELISABETTA, ELSBETH, ELSPETH, ELSABET, ELISABETH, ELISHEBA, ELISSA, ELITA, ELIZA, ELIZAH, LISETTE, ELYSE, LISBETH, LIZZIE, ELSE, ELSIE, LIZABETH, BESS, BESSIE, BESSY, BETH, BETSEY, BETSY, BETT, BETTA, BETTE, BETTINA, LIBBY, LISA, LISE, LIZA, LIZZY
ELKE	Old German: elf ELKA, ELKEE, ELKEY
ELLA	Old English: elf ELLAMAY, ELLIE, ELLY, ELLADINE, ELLAMAE, ELLETTE, ELLADINE, ELETTE
ELLEN	Greek: light ELENA, ELON, ELLAN, ELYN, ELLYN
ELLICE	Hebrew: Jehovah is God (feminine of Elias)
ELOISE	German: famous in battle ELOUISE, ELOISA
ELRICA	Old German: ruler of all
ELSA	Old German: noble one ELSIE, ELSEY, ELSE, HELSA, ELZE
ELVA	Anglo-Saxon/Old English: the elfin ELVIA, ELVIE, ELFIE, ELVINA
ELVIRA	Latin: white, blonde Old German: elf counsel ELVERA, ELVIRE
ELYSIA	Latin: sweetly blissful
EMERAUDE	French: emerald EMERANT, EMBERLY, EM, EMMIE

EMMA German: industrious
EMELINE, EMELINA, EMELIN, EMERA, EMLYN,
EMMYLOU, EMMALINE, EMELDA, EMILY, EMILIE,
EMLYN, EMLYNNE, EMERA, EMMALINDA, EMMA-
JANE, EMMA-LOUISE, EMMA-MARIA, EM, EMMIE,
EMMY, EMBLEN, EMBLYN, EMBLA, EMERENCE

ENID Celtic/Latin: soul, spirit

ENRICA German: ruler of the home
ENRIKA

ERICA Old Norse: over powerful (feminine of
Eric)
ERIKA, RICA, RIKA, RIKKI, RICKY, RICKIE

ERIN Irish Gaelic: from Ireland
ERINA, ERRIN, ERYN

ERMA Latin: noble
ERMINA, ERMINIA, ERMINIE, HERMINE,
HERMINIE, HERMIONE

ERMENGARDE Old German: people's guard
IRMINGARDE

ERRYL Irish Gaelic: a pledge (feminine of
Errol/Earl)
ERYL

ESME Spanish/Greek: the emerald
ESMERALDA, ESMA, ESMIRALDA

ESTELLE Latin: a star
ESTELLA, ESTRELITA, ESSIE, STELLA, STELLE,
ESTRELLA

ESTHER Hebrew: a star
STARETT, STARETTE, TRELLA, STELLITA, ESTER,
HESTER, HESTHER, ESSIE, HETTY, ETTIE, ETTY,
ESTA

ETHEL Old English: noble one
ETHELDA, ETHELINDA, ETHELINE, ETHELYN,
ETHYL, ETHELJEAN, ETHELEEN

EUDOCIA Greek: of good repute
EUDOSIA, EUDOXIA, DOCIE, DOXIE, DOXY

EUDORA Greek: generous
EUDORE, DORA

EUGENIA Greek: well-born (the feminine of Eugene)
EUGENIE, GENE, GENIE, LUGENE

EULA Greek: soft-spoken one
EULALIA, EULALIE, LALLIE, ULA

EUNICE Greek: happy, victorious

EUPHEMIA Greek: good repute
EUPHEMIE, EFFIE, EFFY, EPHIE, EUPHEME

EVANGELINE   Greek: bearer of glad tidings
VANGIE, VANGY, EVANGELIA

EVE   Hebrew: life-giving
EVA, EBA, EBBA, EVELINE, EVELINA, EVELYN, EVLYN, EVALEEN, EVELYNN, EVETTE

EZRELA   Hebrew: God is my strength
EZRAELA, EZRAELLA

F

FABIA   Latin: bean grower (feminine of Fabian)

FABRIENNE   Latin: mechanic (feminine of Fabron)

FAITH   Middle English: belief in God
FAITHFUL, FAYTH, FAY, FAYE

FALDA   Icelandic: folded wings

FANCHON   French: free (the feminine of François)

FANCY   capricious, extravagant (trendy, modern usage/popularity)
FANCIE, FANCEE

FANNY   German: free
FANNIE, FANIA, FRANCHETTE

FAUSTINE   French: the fortunate
FAUSTA, FAUSTINA

FAVOR   Old French: help
FAVOUR

FAWN   Old French: young deer
FAWNIE, FAWNA, FAWNIA, FAUNIA

FAY   Old French: a fairy or elf
FAYE, FAE, FAYETTE, FAYANNE

FAYME   Old French: lofty reputation
FAME, FAMIE, FAYMEE

FEDORA   Greek: divine gift

FELICE   Latin: happy one
FELICITY, FELICIA, PHELICIA, PHILICIA, FELISE, FELITA

FENELLA   Irish Gaelic: white-shouldered one
FYNOLA

FERN   Old English: a fern, fernlike

FERNANDA   Gothic: life-adventuring
FERDINANDA, FERNANDINA, FERNANDE

FIFI   Hebrew: He shall add
FIFINE

FIONA   Celtic: white, fair

FLANNA   Irish Gaelic: red-haired

FLAVIA   Old English: yellow-haired one

FLETA   Old English: swift, fleet one

FLEUR   French: a flower
FLEURETTE

FLORA   Latin: flowering, blooming
FLORELLA, FLORENCE, FLORIA, FLORIDA,
FLORINDA, FLORIS, FLORRIE, FLORRY, FLORE,
FLO, FLOSSIE, FLORINE, FLORENCIA, FLOSS,
FLORELLE, FLORANNE

FLOWER   Old French: a blossom

FLURRY   a sudden commotion (trendy, New-Age
name of increasing popularity)

FORTUNE   Latin: the fortunate
FORTUNA

FRANCES   Latin: free one, from France
FRANKLYN, FRANKIE, FRANCYNE, FRANCY,
FRANCIE, FRANNIE, FRAN, FRANCETTA,
FRANCESCA, FRANCENE, FRANCISCA, FRANCINE,
FRANCYNE, FRANNY, FRANCOISE, FRANZISKA,
FRANCISCA

FREDA   German: peaceful
FRIDA, FRIEDA, FREEDA, FREDERIQUE, FREDI,
FREDERICKINA, FREDIKA, FREDALENA, FREDDIE,
FREDERIKE, FRERIKA, FRITZE, FRITZI, FRITZINN,
FRYDA

FREYA   Old Norse: noble lady (goddess of love
and beauty)

G

GABRIELLE   Hebrew: God is my strength
GABRIELLA, GABRIELA, GABIE, GABY, GABBY

GAIL   Old English: gay, lively one
GALE, GAYLE, GAYLENE, GAYLEEN, GAILA

GALA   Old Norse: singer

GALINA   Russian: light (through the Greek - Helene)

GARDENIA   New Latin: the fragrant white gardenia
flower

GARNET Middle English: the garnet gem
GARNETTA, GARNETTE

GAZELLA New Latin: gazelle, antelope

GEMMA Italian: a gem, precious stone

GENEVA Old French: juniper tree

GENEVIEVE Old German: white wave
GENEVRA, GINETTE

GEORGIA Latin: farmer
GEORGETTE, GEORGIANA, GEORGINA,
GEORGENE, GEORGIENNE, GEORGY,
GEORGEANNE

GIANETTA Italian: God is gracious (the feminine of
Giovanni)
GIANINA

GILBERTA Old German: brilliant pledge
GILBERTINE, GILBERTE, GILLIE, GILLY

GILLIAN Latin: youthful, downy-haired one
GILL, GILLIE, GILLY, JILL

GINA Latin: queen (from Regina)

GINGER Latin: maidenly (from Virginia)
GINNY

GISELLE Old German: pledge
GISELE, GISELA, GISELLA, GIZELLA

GLADYS Old Welsh: ruler over territory
GLADIS, GLAD

GLENNA Old Welsh: dweller in a valley or glen
GLENDA, GLYNIS, GLYNNIE, GLENNIS, GLENYS,
GLENDENE, GLENDORA

GLORIA Latin: glory, glorious one
GLORI, GLORIANA, GLORIANE, GLORY,
GLORIOSA, GLORIE, GLORIS, GLORIANNE,
GLOREE

GODIVA Old English: gift of God

GRACE Latin: grace, graceful one
GRACEY, GRACIE, GRAZIA, ENGRACIA, GRACIA,
GRATIANA, GRATIA

GREGORIA Greek: watchman (feminine of Gregory)
GREER

GRETA Greek: a pearl
GRETCHEN, GRETEL, GREDEL, GRETHEL, GRETE,
GRETTAMAE

GRISELDA Old German: gray battle-maiden
GRIZELDA, GRISHILDA, CHRISELDA, GRIZZEL,
GRIZEL, GRISELDIS, GRISSEL, ZELDA, SELDA,
GRISHILD, GRIZE, GRITTY

GUINEVERE	Old Welsh: white phantom
	GWENDOLYN, GENVIEVE, GWENORE, VANORA, GWEN, GWENDA, GWENDOLINE, GWENNIE, GWENETH, GWYNNE; GWYN, GWYNETH, GWINNY
GUSTAVA	Swedish: staff of the Goths
	GUSSIE, GUSSY
GYPSY	Old English: a gypsy, a wanderer
	GIPSY, GYP, GIP

H

HAIDEE	Greek: modest, honored, to caress
HAILEY	A surname that was adopted as a Christian name by it's popularity over the past decade
	HAYLEY, HALEY, HAYLEE, HALIE, HALLIE, HALLY
HANNAH	Hebrew: graceful one
	HANNIE, HANNY, HANA, ANNIE, NAN, NANNY, HANNELE, HANNI, HANNE
HAPPY	lucky, fortunate (a modern pet name)
HARMONY	Latin: concord, harmony
	HARMONIA, HARMONIE, HARMONEE
HARRIET	Gernam: mistress of the home
	HARRIETTE, HARRIETTA, HARRIOTT, HATTIE, HATTY
HAZEL	German: commander
	HAZELLE, HAZELINE, HAZELGROVE
HEATHER	Middle English: the heather flower
HEDDA	Old German: strife
	HEDY, HEDDI, HEDDY, HEDVICK
HEIDI	German: nobility
HELEN	Greek: the bright one
	HELENA, HELENE, HELLEN, HELENOR, HELLENOR, HELLI, ELENI, ELETTE, NELLETTE, NELLIANA, HELENKA, HELAINE, HELLA
HELGA	Old German: pious, religious
HELOISE	German: famous in battle
HENRIETTA	French: home ruler
	HENRYETTA, HETTY, HENNY, HENDRIKA, HENRIKA, HATTIE, HATTY

HEPHZIBAH   Hebrew: my delight is to her
HEPZIBETH, HEPSIBA, HEPZIBAH, HEPSEY,
HEPSIE, HEPSY

HIBERNIA   Latin: Ireland

HIBISCUS   Latin: the marshmallow plant and flower

HILARY   Latin: cheerful one
HILLARY, HILLARIE, HILARIA

HILDA   Old German: battle maid
HILDE, HILDIE, HILDY, HULDA, HULDIE,
HULDAH, HILDEGARDE, HILDEMAR, HILDRETH,
HILMA, HILDAGARDE, HELMA, HELMI, HYLDA

HOLLY   Old English: holly tree
HOLLIE, HOLLEE, HOLLEY, HOLLY-ANN

HONEY   Old English: honey
HANNEY, HANNY, HONEYBALL, HONEYBUN,
HONEYCHILD, HONEYCOMB

HONORIA   Latin: honor
HONOR, HONORA, HONOURE, NORAH, NORIE,
HONEY, NORRY

HOPE   Old English: hope, expectation, desire

HORTENSE   Latin: worker in a garden

HUGHINA   German: small, intelligent girl
HUGETTE, HUGHETTE, HUGUETTE, HUETTA

HYACINTH   Greek: hyacinth flower or purple hyacinth
color
HYACINTHA, HYACINTHINE, HYACINTHIA,
JACINTHE, JACKIE, JACKY, HYACINTHIE,
JACINTA, SINTY

I

IANTHE   Greek: violet-flowered
IANTHINA, IANTHA, JANTHINA

IDA   Old German: industrious
IDALIA, IDALINE, IDELLE, IDETTE, IDORA

IDONA   Latin: the appropriate
IDONEA, IDONIA

ILA   French: from the island
ISLA

ILEANA   Greek: from the Island of Troy
ILEANE

ILKA   Slavic: flattering

IMPERIA   Latin: imperial one

INDIA	the region of South Asia that lies in the foothills of the Himalayas (recently popularized New-Age name) INDIE, INDY
INEZ	Greek: pure, gentle, mild INES, INESSA, INESITA
INGRID	Old Norse: hero's daughter INGA, INGER, INGABERG, INGEBORG
IRENE	Greek: peace IRENA, IRINA, EIRENA, EIRENE, RENA, RENIE
IRIS	Greek: the rainbow
ISABELLE	Old Spanish: consecrated to God ISABEL, ISABEAU, ISSIE, ISSY, BELLE, ISHBEL, YSABEL, ISABELITA, BELICIA, IZABEL
ISADORA	Greek: gift of Isis ISIDORA, ISMAY, ESMEE, ISADORE
ISIS	Egyptian: supreme goddess
ISOLDE	Old Welsh: the fair one YSOLDE, ISOLDA, IZOT, IZOLDA
IVORY	creamy-white (trendy, New-Age name) IVORINE
IVY	Old English: ivy vine IVAH, IVIE, IVEY, IVENE, IVIS
IZETTA	Latin: of the little house

J

JACINTA	Greek: lovely, beautiful JACINTH, JACINDA, JACINTHA, JACINTHE
JACOBA	Hebrew: the supplanter (the feminine of Jacob) JAKOBA, JACOBINA, JACOBINE, BINA, JACOBEE, JAKOBINE, JACOMINA
JACQUELINE	Old French: the supplanter (the feminine of James) JACQUETTA, JACALYN, JACKALIN, JACALINE, JACLYN, JACLYNN, JACQUALYN, JACQUELEAN, JACQUELIN, JACQUELYN, JACQUILINE, JAKELYN, JACKELYN, JACQUELLIN, JACKEY, JACKI, JACKIE, JACKY, JACQUERY, JACQUI, JACQUENELLE, JACQUENETTE, JACKQUIMINOT

JADE Spanish: jade stone
JAYDE, JADA, JADDA

JAEL Hebrew: wild she-goat

JAIME Old Spanish: the supplanter (feminine of James)
JAMIE, JAYMEE, JAMESINA, JEM, JEMMY

JANE Hebrew: God is gracious
JANEL, JANELLA, JANET, JANETTE, JANETTA, JANA, JANICE, JAN, JANINA, JANNA, JAYNE, JAINE, JANIE, JANEY, JANETTA, JANENE, JANIS, JAYNIE, SHEENA, SHEONA, SHEENAH, JEAN, JEANNETTE, JEANIE, JEANEY, JOAN, JOANNE, JOHANNA, GIANINA, GIOVANNA, JUANA, JUANITA, JENNETTE, JENNET, JENNETTE, JENETTA, JONET

JARITA Hindu: legendary bird that was so devoted to her young that she was given a human soul

JASMINE Persian: the Jasmine flower
JASMINA, JASMIN, YASMIN, JESSAMINE, JESSAMYN, JESS, JESSIE, JESSY, JESSAMY

JEMIMA Hebrew: a dove
JEMIMAH, JEMMY, JEMMA, MIMA, JEMIE, MIMI

JENNIFER Celtic: white wave
JENNY, JENNIE, JEN

JESSICA Hebrew: wealthy one
JESSALYNN, JESS, JESSIE, JESSY

JEWEL Old French: a precious thing, gem
JEWELLE, GEMMIE, GEMSIE, JEWELE

JEZEBEL Hebrew: an evil woman

JILL English: girl
JILLY, JILLIAN, JILLIANNE

JINX Latin: a charm, a spell
JINKS, JYNX

JOAN Hebrew: God's gracious gift
JOANNE, JOANNA, JOANIE, JOHANNA, JO, JO-ANN, JO-ANNA

JOCELYN Old English: the just one
JOCELYNE, JOCELINE, JOSELYN, JOSSLYN, JOSSE

JOELLA Hebrew: Jehovah is God (the feminine of Joel)
JOELA, JOELLEN

JOLIE Latin: youthful one (a modern and popular form of Julia)
JOLEY, JOLINE, JOLYNNE, JOLETTA, JOLEEN, JOLEAN

JONI Hebrew: gift of God (the feminine of John)
JONELLA, JOHNNIE, JONNIE

JONQUIL Latin: a flower name

JORDANA Hebrew: flowing down (the feminine of Jordan)
JORDIE, DANA

JOSEPHINE Hebrew: He shall increase (the feminine of Joseph)
JOSEPHINA, JOSEPHA, JOETTE, JOSETTE, FIFI, FIFINE, JOSEFA, JOSEFINA, JO, JOSIE, PHEENY, JOE, JOEY, JOSETTE, JOZEFA

JOY Latin: joyful one
JOYOUS, JOYCE, JOICE, JOVITA, JOI, JOYE, JOYA, JOIE, JOYAN

JUDITH Hebrew: praised
JUDI, JUDIE, JUDY, JODY, JODI, JODIE, JUDITHA

JULIA Latin: youthful one
JULIE, JULIET, JULIETTE, JULIETTA, JULIANA, JULI, ZULIA, JULINA, JULIANE, SULIA, SULIANE, JULITTE

JUNE Latin: youthful or born in June
JUNIA, JUNIATTA, JUNETTE, JUNELLA, JUNIE, JUNETH, JUNEE

JUSTINE Latin: the just one
JUSTINE, JUSTA

K

KANDI Greek: daughter of the wind (through Candace)
KANDY, CANDEE, CANDI, CANDY

KARA Greek: pure
KAREN, KARIN, KARYN, KARAN, KARANNE, CARYN, CARREN, CARON, CARRAN, CAREN, CARONNE, KARENZA, KERENZA, KARINA

KARLA Old German: tiller of the soil (another feminine version of Carl/Charles)
KARLEEN, KARLENE, KARLI, KARLIE, KAROL

KARRIE Latin/French: little womanly one (from Carol/Caroline)
KARIE, KARI, KARRY, KAREY

KASMIRA Old Slavic: commands peace

KASIA Greek: pure
KASSIA

KAYE Greek: rejoicing

KEIRA Old English: the queenly (from the word Kaiser)

KELDA Old Norse: a fountain, spring
KELLAH

KELLY Irish Gaelic: warrior maid
KELDA, KELLIE, KAYLEE, KAYLEY, KEELIE,
KELLIE, KELLEY, KILEY, KIELI, KEELY,
KEIGHLEY, KYLEE, KYLE, KELLY-ANN,
KELLY-ROSE

KELSEY Old Norse: dweller at ship-island
KELSI, KELCI, KELCIE, KELCY, KELSY

KENDRA Anglo-Saxon: understanding

KERRIE Celtic: dark one
KEREE, KERRY-ANN, KERRY, KERRI, KERRYANN,
KERRIANNE, KERRY-ANNE

KESAVA Hindu: having much hair

KETURA Hebrew: incense, perfume
KETURAH

KEZIAH Hebrew: Cassia (popular name with the
Puritans)
KEZIA, KAZIA, KETSY, KISSY, KITSY

KIKI Egyptian: the castor plant

KIMBERLY Old English: from the royal-fortress
meadow
KIMBERLEY, KIMBER, KIM, KIMBERLEE,
KIMBERLEA, KYM, KIMBA LEE, KIMBERLYN,
KIMARIE, KIMMIE

KINETA Greek: active one

KIRA Russian girl's name; unknown meaning

KIRSTEN Greek: Christian, annointed
KIRSTEEN, KIRSTY, KIRSTYN, KIRSTIE, KRISTA,
KRISTEN

KOLFINNA Old Norse; cool white one
KOL

KOREN Greek: the maiden
KORI, KORY, KORRIE

KYLA Gaelic: pretty

KYLIE Australian: boomerang
KYLY

KYNA Irish Gaelic: high, exalted (the feminine of
Conan)

L

LACEY Greek: rejoice   French/Latin: lace
LACY, LACIE, LACEE, LACYNDORA

LALLA Scottish: lowlands dweller
LALLY, LALLIE, LALAH

LARA Latin: famous
LARETTA

LARAINE Latin: seabird
LARINE, LARINA, LORAINE

LA REINA Spanish: the queen
LAREINA, LARENA

LARISSA Greek: cheerful maiden
LARISA

LARK Middle English: skylark, singing lark

LA ROUX French: red-haired

LATONIA Latin: the mother of the Greek god Apollo
LATONA, LATONYA, LATOYA

LAURA Latin: a crown of laurel leaves
LAURETTA, LAURENCIA, LAURANA, LAUREOLA,
LAURINDA, LORINDA, LORETTA, LORETTE,
LORA, LORITA, LAURITA, LAUREL, LAUREEN,
LAURI, LAUREN, LOLLY, LAURELLA, LAURENA,
LAURENE, LAURICE, LORIS, LOREN, LORI,
LAURIE, LORRIE, LOURETTE

LAVENDER Latin: a flower name

LA VERNE Old French: springlike

LAVINIA Latin: purified
LAVINA, VINNIE, VINNY, VINA, LAVINIE, LOVINA,
LOVENAH

LAYLA Persian: dark haired
LEILA, LELA, LILA, LILLA, LELAH

LAYNE Middle English: from the narrow road
LANE

LEE Old English: meadow
LEIGH, LEANDA, LEANNE, LEANNA, LEE-ANN,
LEAH, LEA

LEELANNEE North American Indian: delight of life

LEILA Latin: dark as night
LAYLA, LEILAH, LILA

LEONIE Latin-French: lion
LEONA, LEONELLE, LEOLINE, LEONI, LEONTINE,
LEONORA, LEONTYNE

LESLEY Celtic: from the gray fort
LESLIE, LESLEE, LESLI, LESLYE, LESLYN

171

LETITIA Latin: joy, gladness
LETA, LETTY, LETTIE, LETHA, LETTICE,
LAETITIA, LETICIA, TISH, LEITH, LITIZIAH

LEWANNA Hebrew: beaming, white one

LIANA Latin: to bind
LIANNA, LIANE, LIALETTE, LIA

LIBBY Hebrew: consecrated to God (diminutive of Elizabeth)
LIBBIE

LIBERTY Latin: freedom

LILAC Persian: bluish color, a lilac flower

LILITH Jewish: belonging to the night
LILIS, LILLIS

LILLIAN Latin: a lily flower
LILLA, LILA, LILAH, LILY, LILI, LILINORE,
LILYBELLE, LILIA, LILIANE, LILYAN, LILIAS,
LILIANA, LILLY, LILYANNE

LINDA Latin: beautiful
LYNDA, LINDY, LYNDY, LYNN, LYN, LYNNE,
LYNDI, LINDYLOU

LINDSAY Scottish: an ancient surname now a trendy, New-Age name
LINDSEY, LINZIE, LINSEY, LYNDSAY, LYNSAY,
LYNSEY, LINDSIE, LYN

LINNET Old French: the Linnet bird   Celtic: graceful
LINNETTE, LYNETTE, LINETTE, LYNETTA,
LYNNETTE, LYNNELL, LYNN, LYNET

LISA Hebrew: consecrated to God
LIZA, LISABETTA, LISABET, LISBETH, LISANNE,
LISA-MARIE, LISALOTTE

LISE French: consecrated to God (form of Elizabeth)
LIESE, LISEL, LISETTE, LISETTA, LIZETTE,
LIZETTA

LOLA Spanish form of Charlotte
LOLITA, LOLETA

LORELEI German: siren (one of the temptresses of folklore)

LORRAINE Old German: famous in war
LORAINE, LORAYNE, LORRAYNE

LOTUS Egyptian: sacred flower of the Nile

LOUISE Old German: famous warrior maid
LOUISA, ELOISA, ELOISE, LOIS, LOUISETTE,
LUWANNA, LOUANN, LUANNE, LOUANNE, LUAN,
LOUELLA, LULIE, LULU, LU, LULA, LUISA,
LOUANNA, LOUISINE, LOULOU, LOISELLE,
LOLLY, LUELLE

172

LOVE Old English: tender affection
LOVIE, LOVEY, LUV, LUVVY

LUCIE Latin: bringer of light
LUCILLE, LUCIANNA, LUCIA, LUCILLA, LUCETTE,
LUCIENNE, LUCY, LUCELLA, LUZIA, LUZETTE,
LUCINDA, CINDERS

LUCRESE Latin: to gain riches
LUCRECE, LUCRETIA, LUCREZIA

LUNA Italian: little moon
LUNETTA

LUPE Latin: wolf

LURLINE German: variant of Lorelei - one of the "sirens"
LURA, LURLEEN, LURLENE, LURETTE, LURANA,
LURAH, LURENA, LUREL

LYDIA Greek: woman of Lydia (province of Asia Minor)
LYDIE, LIDIA, LYDIANNE

LYRIS Greek: lyre, harp
LYRA

M

MAB Irish Gaelic: mirth, joy
MAVE, MEAVE, MAVIS, MABS, MAVISH

MABEL Latin: lovable one
MABELLE, MABLE, MAYBELLE

MADELINE Greek: elevated, magnificent
MAGDALA, MAGDALEN, MADALINE, MADELENA,
MADALYN, MADELEINE, MADELON, MADLEN,
MADELLE, MAGDA, MAGDALENE, MALINA,
MARLEEN, MADDALENA, MADA, MADDY

MAGNILDA Old German: powerful battle maiden

MAGNOLIA French: the magnolia tree

MAHALA Hebrew: tenderness
MAHALAH, MAHALIA, MEHALA

MAIDA Anglo Saxon: a maiden
MAYDA, MAYDE, MAIDIE

MAJESTA Latin: majestic one

MAISEY Greek: a pearl (through the name Margaret)
MAISIE, MAIZIE

MAKEPEACE Old English Puritan "virtue" name: to make peace

MALINDA Greek: mild, gentle one
MELINDA, MALENA, MELENA, MELLIE, LINDY,
MELINDER, MELYNDA

MANUELA Hebrew: God is with us (the feminine of
Manuel)
MANUELITA

MARA Hebrew: bitter
MARALINE, MARILYN, MARALYNN, MARALINE,
MARAH

MARCELLA Latin: little warlike one (the feminine of
Marcellus)
MARCELLE, MARCELLINA, MARCELLINE,
MARCILLE, MARCY, MARCIE, MARCIA,
MARCHITA, MARQUITA, MARSHA, MARSELLA,
MARCENE, MARCIANN, MARCY, MARZETTA,
MARKITA

MARELDA Old German: famous battle maiden
MARILDA

MARGARET Latin: a pearl
MARGARETA, MARGARITA, MARGERY,
MARGORY, MARGET, MARGETTE, MARGALO,
MARGUERITE, MARJORIE, MARJORY,
MARGHERITA, MARGOT, MARGARETHE,
MARGARETE, MARGRETT, MARGE, MARGIE,
MARGO, MEG, MADGE, MEGGY, PEG, PEGGY,
MARGERY, MARGARETTA, MARJERY

MARIGOLD English: the golden Marigold flower
MARYGOLD

MARINA Latin: maid of the sea
MARNA, MARNI, MARNIE, MARNY, MARNA, MARIS

MARLENE Greek: elevated, magnificent (through
Magdalene)
MARLEEN, MARLENA, MARLAINA, MARLANE,
MARLEE, MARLEA, MARLEENE

MARMARA Greek: flashing, glittering

MARTHA Armenian: lady
MARTHENA, MARTITA, MARTELLA, MARTA,
MARTIE, MARTHE, MARTH, MARTY, MART

MARTIBELLE Hebrew/Latin: beautiful mistress
MARTYBEL, MARTIBEL

MARTINA Latin: warlike one
MARTINE, MARTIE, MARTY

MARVEL Old French: a miracle
MARVA, MARVELA, MARVELLA, MARVELLE,
MARVELINE

174

MARY Hebrew: bitter, bitterness (as to it's interpretation — it is a name used in honor of the blessed Virgin Mary: "God has dealt me a bitter blow ... to take away my son")
MARAH, MARA, MARIA, MARIE, MARETTA, MARETTE, MARELLA, MARIETTA, MARILLA, MARILYN, MARLA, MARYA, MIRIAM, MURIEL, MARYSE, MANON, MANETTE, MARITA, MARIQUITA, MAIRE, MAURA, MAUREEN, MEARR, MOIRA, MOIRE, MAME, MOYA, MUIRE, MAIRI, MOLL, MOLLIE, MOLLY, MAMIE, POLLY, MARYANN, MARYLOU, MARYRUTH, MAREA, MINNIE, MARI, MARRIANNE, MARYLYN, MERRILYN, MERRILY, MERRILEE, MARALYAN, MAIRWEN, MAIR, MANYA, MAREE, MARIAH, MARILYNNE, MARIBEL

MATHILDA Old German: mighty battle-maiden
MATILDA, MATHILDE, MATILDE, MAT, MATTIE, MATTY, TILDA, TILLIE, TILLY, MAUD, MAUDE, MAUDIE

MATTEA Hebrew: gift of God (the feminine of Matthew)
MATTHEA, MATHIA, MATHEA, MAT, MATTIE

MAURA Greek: dark, black
MOIRA, MAIRE, MOURA, MAURE, MAVRA, MAURITA, MAURELLA

MAUVE Latin: lilac-colored

MAVIS Celtic: the song-thrush
MAVEN, MAVIA

MAXINE Latin: greatest
MAXIE, MAXY, MAXA, MAXI, MAXEEN, MAXIMA, MAXENA

MAY Latin: goddess of growth (MAIA)   Anglo-Saxon: kinswoman or maiden
MAE, MAIA, MAYE, MAYA, MAYDEE, MAYELLA, MAYETTA, MAYBELLE, MAYLEE, MAI, MAYETTE

MEARA Irish Gaelic: mirth

MEGAN Greek: great, mighty one
MEG, MEGHAN, MEGGIE, MEGGY, MEGALE

MELANIE Greek: black, dark
MELAINE, MELONIE, MELANY, MELLONEY, MEL, MELLIE

MELISSA Greek: honey, a bee
MELITTA, MELLY, MILLICENT, MILLIE, MELISENT, MISSY, MELICENT, MELISSE, MELLIE, MELESSA

MELODY uncertain origin; through "melodious"
MELODIA, MELODIE, MELONIE, MEL, MELLIE

MERCY Middle English: compassion, pity (an English Puritan "virtue" name)
MERCEDES

MEREDITH   Old Welsh: mortal day
     MERRY, MERIDITH

MERLE   Latin: thrush, blackbird
     MERL, MERLINA, MERLINE, MERYL, MYRLENA,
     MEROLA

MESSINA   Latin: middle

MIA   Italian/Spanish: mine

MICHAELA   Hebrew: who is like God? (the feminine of Michael)
     MICHELLE, MICHELE, MYKELA, MICKALA,
     MICKIE, MICHAELINA, MICHELINA, MIKAELA,
     MICHEL, MICHAELLA, MIGUELA, MIGUELITA

MIGNON   French: a dainty, graceful, darling
     MIGNONETTE, MINNIONETTE

MINERVA   Greek: force, purpose

MINNA   Old German: love
     MINETTA, MINETTE, MINNIE, MINA, MINDA,
     MINDY

MIRA   Spanish: beautiful one   Latin: wonderful one
     MIRABELLE, MIRABELLA, MYRA, MIRELLA,
     MYRILLA, MIRILLA, MIRRA

MIRANDA   Latin: one to be adored
     RANDIE, MANDY

MIRIAM   Hebrew: bitter (through Mary)
     MIMI, MINNIE, MITZY

MONA   Irish Gaelic: noble

MONICA   Latin: advisor
     MONIKA, MONIQUE

MORGANA   Old Welsh: shore of the sea

MOSELLE   Hebrew: taken out of the water (feminine of Moses)
     MOZELLE

MURIEL   Greek: bitter (through Mary)

MUSETTA   Old French: quiet, pastoral song

MUSIDORA   Greek: gift from one of the Greek goddesses (Muses) who presided over the arts

MYRRHA   Arabic: myrtle; a plant name

N

NADIA   Serbo-Croat: hope
NADA, NADINE, NADYA, NADJA, NADENE, NADEEN

NAN   Hebrew: grace
NANCY, NANCE, NANCIE, NANETTE, NANNY, NANNIE, NANA

NAOMI   Hebrew: the pleasant one
NAOMIE, NAOMA

NAPEA   Latin: she of the valleys

NARCISSA   Greek: daffodil

NARELLE   Australian: popular name

NATALIE   Latin: birthday, the Lord's birthday
NATHALIE, NATALYA, NATALEE, NATHALIA, NATALA, NATALINE, NAT, NATTIE, NATTY, NETTIE, NETTY, NATASHA, NATACHA, TASHA, NOEL, NOELLE, NOVELLA, NOELEEN, NOELLA

NATHANIA   Hebrew: gift, given of God (feminine of Nathaniel)
NATHENE

NATIVIDAD   Spanish: born at Christmas

NEALA   Irish Gaelic: champion (the feminine of Neal)
NEILA, NEILIE, NEELEY

NEBULA   Latin: mist, vapor, a cloud

NEDA   Slavic: born on Sunday
NEDDA

NELLIE   Greek: light (through Helen)
NELLIS, NELDA, NELLA, NELLY

NEVADA   Spanish: white as snow
NEVA

NICOLA   Greek: victorious army (the feminine of Nicholas)
NICHOLA, NICOLINE, NICOLETTE, NICOLENA, NICOLETTA, NICKIE, NICKY, NIKKI, NIKI

NIKE   Greek: victory

NILA   Latin: the River Nile of Egypt

NINA   Spanish: girl
NINETTE, NINETTA

NISSA   Scandinavian: a friendly elf

NIXIE   Old German: a little water-sprite

NOKOMIS   Chippewa Indian: grandmother

NOLA   Late Latin: a small bell

NONA Latin: ninth child
NONIE

NORDICA German: from the North

NORMA Latin: rule, model, pattern

NOVA Latin: newcomer
NOVIA, NOVELLA

NYDIA Latin: from the nest

NYREE New Zealand: a popular Christian name

NYX German: night

O

OCTAVIA Latin: the eighth
OTTAVIA, OCTAVIE, TAVY, TAVIE, TAVINE

ODELETTE French: a little ode, lyric song
ODELET

ODELIA Old Anglo-French: little wealthy one
ODELLA, ODELINDA, ODELYN, ODETTE, ODILIA, OTTILIE

ODESSA Greek: the Odyssey, a long journey

OLGA Old Norse/Russian: holy
OLVA, ELGA

OLINDA Latin: fragrant, perfume

OLIVIA Latin: olive branch
OLIVETTE, OLLIE, OLLY, LIVVIE, LIVIA, NOLA

OLYMPIA Greek: heavenly one
OLYMPIE

OONA Irish: unity
ONA, OONAGH

OPAL Sanscrit: a precious stone
OPALINE

OPHELIA Greek: help, usefulness
OFELIA, OPHELIE, OTHILIA

ORA Old English: shore, seacoast
ORABELLE, ORABEL

ORALIA Latin: golden
ORIEL, ORIELDA, ORIOLE, ORIELLE, ORLENA, ORLENE, ORLENES, ORALIE

ORIANA Latin: to rise

ORSINA Latin: bear

OUIDA	French: yes (through the French word "oui") OUIDETTE
OZORA	Hebrew: strength of the Lord

P

PAGE	Greek: child PAIGE, PAGET
PALLAS	Greek: virgin
PALOMA	Spanish: the dove PALOMITA
PAMELA	Anglo-Saxon: beloved elf PAMELLA, PAMELINE, PAM, PAMMIE
PANDORA	Greek: all gifted
PANSY	Old French: to think
PARNELLA	Old French: little rock (reckoning to Peter)
PARTHENIA	Greek: maidenly PATHINA
PASCHA	Latin: passover PASQUA, PASQUETTE
PATIENCE	French: patience (English Puritan "virtue" name) PATIENT
PATRICE	Latin: nobility PAT, PATRICIA, PATRIA, PATTI, PATSY, PATTY, TRISH, TRICIA
PAULA	Latin: little one PAULEEN, PALETTE, PAULINE, PAULYNE, POLLY
PEACE	Latin: peace PAX, PACIFICA
PEARL	Late Latin: a pearl PEARLA, PEARLEEN, PEARLIE, PEARLY, PEARLINE
PENELOPE	Greek: a weaver PENNY
PENTECOSTE	Greek: the fifth day
PEONY	Latin: a flower name
PERDITA	Latin: the lost
PERFECTA	Latin: the perfect
PERIZADA	Persian: elf-born

PERPETUA   Latin: the everlasting

PERSIS   Greek: a woman from Persia
        PERSIDA

PERT   Anglo-Saxon: pert, saucy

PETRA   Greek: the rock (feminine of Peter)
        PETRINA, PIERETTE, PETRONA, PETRONELLA,
        PARNEL, PARNELLA, PET, PETTY, PETRONIA

PETULA   Latin: seeker

PETUNIA   Tupi Indian: a flower name

PHEDRE   Greek: the shining
        PHEADRA

PHILIPPA   Greek: lover of horses
        PHILIPPE, PHIL, PHILLIE, FILIPPA, PIPPA

PHILOMENA   Greek: of loving mind, lover of the moon

PHOEBE   Greek: the bright

PHOENIX   Greek: heron, eagle

PHYLLIS   Greek: a green branch

PILAR   Latin: a pillar

PIPER   Old English: a pipe player

PLEASANCE   Latin: pleasant (English Puritan "virtue" name)

POLLYANNA   Hebrew: of bitter grace

POMPEIA   Latin: of Pompeii
        POMPIE

POPPY   Latin: the poppy

PRECIOUS   Latin: beloved

PRIDE   Anglo-Saxon: to be proud (Old English "virtue" name)

PRIMROSE   Latin: little first one

PRISCILLA   Latin: the primitive
        PRISSIE, PRIS

PRUDENCE   Latin: discretion (English Puritan "virtue" name)
        PRUE, PRU

PSYCHE   Greek: the soul

PYRENE   Greek: of the fire, the flaming-haired
        PYRENA

Q

QUEENA   Old English: a queen
QUEENIE, QUEENY, QUEENETTE

QUINTINA   Latin: the fifth
QUINNA, QUIANA, QUENNA, QUENTILLA

R

RACHEL   Hebrew: ewe
RACHAEL, RACHELE, RAQUEL, RAE, RAY, RAE
ANN, RAE LYNN, RAE LOUISE, RAELENE, RAINA,
RAYANN, RAYETTA, RAYLENE, RAYNETTE,
RAYONE, RAINELL, RAINELLE, RAINY, RAINE,
RAYE, RAYCENE, RAYMA, RAYNETTE, RAYNA,
RAYNELLE, RAYLEEN, RAYLENA, RAYONA,
RAYMONDA, RAYMONDE

RAISSA   Old French: thinker

RANDE   Old English: shield wolf
RANDEE, RANDY, RANDE, RANDIE

RANI   Hindu: a queen, royal
RANEE, RANIA, RANA

RAPHAELA   Hebrew: healed by God
RAFAELA

RAVEN   Latin: blackbird

REBECCA   Hebrew: to bind
REBA, REBEKAH, REBEKA, REBEKKA, BEKKI,
BECKIE

REGINA   Latin: a queen
RAINA, REYNA, REINA, REINETTE, REGAN, GINA,
RENIE, REENIE, REGINIA

RENATA   Latin: born again
RENE, RENEE, RENNIE, RENAY

REVA   Latin: to gain strength

REXANA   Latin: of royal grace

RHEA   Greek: a river
REA, RIVA, REVA, RIA, REBI, REBY

RICARDA   Old English: powerful ruler (feminine of Richard)
RICARDA, RICHELA, RICHENDA, RICKIE, RICKY, RICHIE, RICHENZA, RIKCHEN, RIKE, DICKIE, DICKSIE

RICCADONNA   Latin/German: rich lady

RILLA   Greek/German: a stream
RYLLA, RILLETTE

ROANNA   Old German: of contented grace
ROANNE

ROBERTA   Old German: bright in fame
ROBYN, ROBERTINA, ROBIN, ROBBIN, ROBINA, ROBENA, ROBINETTE, BOBBY, BOBBETTE, BOBBIE

ROCHELLE   French: little rock
ROCHELLA, ROCHETTE, SHELLY

RODERICA   Old German: famous ruler
RODDIE, RHODERICA, RODDY

ROMA   Latin: of Rome
ROMAINE, ROMAYNE, ROMY, ROMI, ROMELLA

RONELLE   Old Norse: mighty power (feminine of Ronald)
RONALDA, RONEE, RONETTE, RONI

ROSE   Greek/Latin: the rose
ROSA, ROSABELLA, ROSABEL, ROSALEE, ROSALIE, ROSALEEN, ROSALENE, ROSALINDA, ROSELLA, ROSELIA, ROSELEA, ROSELEE, ROSALINE, ROSALIND, ROSALYNNE, ROSALYN, ROZALYN, ROSANNE, ROSEHANNAH, ROSE ANNE, ROSEMARY, ROSETTA, ROSETTE, ROSEY, ROSIE, ROSHEEN, ROZA, ROSITA, ROSELLEN, ROZELLA, ROSEMONDE, ROSE MARIE, MARYROSE, ROSEBUD, ROSE CAROLINA, ROSEHELEN, ROSE HELENE, ROSELAINE, ROSE ELAINE

ROWENA   Celtic: the white-maned

ROXANNE   Persian: brilliant one
ROXANA, ROXY, ROXIE

ROYALE   French: a queen (through Roy/Roi)
ROYETTA, ROYCE

RUBY   Latin: the red (a "jewel" name)
RUBIE, RUBINA, RUBYE, RUBELET, RUBETTE, RUBIA

RUDOLPHINE   Old High German: famous wolf (feminine of Rudolph)

RUFINA   Latin: red-haired

RUTH   Hebrew: compassionate, beautiful
RUTHANNE, RUTHINA, RUTHIE, RUTHELLA

S

SABA   Greek: woman of Sheba

SABINA   Latin: woman of the Sabines
SAVINA, SABINE

SABRA   Hebrew: to rest
SABRAH, SABRE, SABBA, SABRINA, BREENA, ZABRINA, SAVA

SACHA   Greek: defender of men (through Alexander)
SASHA, SASCHA, SASHEE, SACHIE, SHASHEE

SADIRA   Persian: the lotus tree

SAFFRON   Indian: the saffron (yellow spice)

SALLY   Hebrew: princess
SAL, SALLIE, SALLIANNE, SALLYANN, SALLY-ANNE

SALOME   Hebrew: peace, completeness (through "shalom" and it is the feminine of Solomon)
SALOMA, SALOMI, SALAMAS, SALOMEE

SAMANTHA   Aramaic: the listener
SAMANTHY, SAMANNTHA, SYMANTHA, PANTHA, MANTHA, SAM, SAMMIE, SAMMY

SAMARA   Hebrew: a guardian
SAMARIA, SAMARIE

SAMUELA   Hebrew: His name is God (the feminine of Samuel)
SAMELLE, SAMUELLE

SANCHA   Latin: sacred
SANCHIA, SANCTITY

SANDI   Greek: helper (through Alexandra)
SANDY, SANDRA, SANDRIA, SANDRINA

SAPPHIRE   Sanscrit: dear to the planet Saturn, sapphire gem, sapphire-blue color
SAPHIRA, SAPPHIRA

SARAH   Hebrew: princess
SARA, SARI, SARINE, SARENE, SAREEN, SARETTE, SADYA, SADIE, SAIDEE, ZARA, ZARAH, SARAH-JANE, SARAJANE, SARAH-JAYNE, SARINA, SARITA, SARRA, SAYDE, SAYDIE, ZADAH, ZAIRA, ZADEE, ZAIDEE, ZARIA

SAVANNA   Spanish: a treeless plain; a United States "place" name
SAVANNAH, VANNY

SAVILLE   Spanish: a "place" name in Spain
SEVILLE, SEVILLA

SAXONA	Old German: a sword, knife of stone
SCARLETT	Middle English: a rich red SCARLET
SELENA	Greek: the moon SELENE, CELINA, SELINA, CELIE
SELBY	English: a surname in recent, trendy popularity SELBY-ANN, SELBEE
SERAPHINA	Hebrew: burning one SERAPHINE, SERAFINE, SERAFINA
SERENA	Latin: fair, bright, serene one (an English Puritan "virtue" name) SERENE, SERENITY
SHAN	Gaelic form of John Hebrew: God is gracious Celtic: slow waters SHANE, SHAÑNON, SHANNA, SHAYNE, SHAWN, SHANNAH, SHANA, SHANEEN, SHAUNA, SHAUNETTE, SHAVON, CHEVON
SHARON	Hebrew: a princess SHARI, SHARRY, SHERRY, SHARA, SHARAN, SHARIE, SHARYN, SHARRONNE
SHEENA	Hebrew: God is gracious (from John) SHEENAGH, SHIONA
SHEELAH	Arabic: a flame Hebrew: the asked for SHEELA, SHEILAH, SHEILA, SHEYA, SHEELAGH, SHEENA, SHAYA, SHEA
SHELLY	Old English: from the meadow on the ledge SHELLI, SHELLIE
SHEREE	Hebrew: the sweet Latin: a "place" name SHEREEN, CHEREEN, SHERALYN, SHERENE, SHERENA, SHERIDAWN, SHERIDA, SHERRYLYN, SHERICIA, SHERRITA, SHERRIS
SHIRLEY	Old English: from the bright meadow SHIRLEE, SHIRLIE, SHERYL, SHIRLEEN, SHIRLENE
SHONE	Hebrew: lily (through the Hebrew of Susan—Shoshannah) SHONA, SHONAH, SHOSHANA, SHOSHANNA, SHOSHANNAH
SIBYL	Greek: a prophetess SIBYLLA, SYBELLA, SYBILLA, SIBBELLA, SIBBY, SEVILLA, SEVILLE
SIDNEY	Latin: a "place" name (recently gaining in popularity) SYDNEY, SIDONIA
SIGNA	Latin: a signal, a sign SIGNALE
SIGRID	Old Norse: ruling counsel

SILVER	Anglo-Saxon: the white metal
SILVIA	Latin: of the forest (the feminine of Sylvester) SILVANA, SILVA, SYLVANNA, SYLVIE, ZILVIA
SIMONA	Hebrew: one who hears SIMONE, SIMONIA, SIMONETTE
SIRENA	Greek: a sweet singer or siren SIREN, SYREN, SYRENA
SISLEY	Latin: dim-sited one (through Cecile) SISSIE, SISSY, SIS, CISSIE
SOLANGE	French: sun angel
SOLITA	Latin: alone, solitary SOLA, SOLO
SOPHIE	Greek: the wise, the sensible SOPHIA, SOPHY, SOFIA, ZOFIA, SONIA, SONYA, SONJA
SORREL	French: a light reddish-brown color SORRELLE
SPRING	Old English: the springtime of the year
STACY	Greek: of the ressurection (springtime) STACEY, STACIA, STACIE, STACE
STAR	Old English: a star
STEPHANIE	Greek: crowned one STEPHANIA, STEPHANA, STEVANA, STEFA, STEFFIE, STEPHA, STEPANIE, STEPHANY, STEPHNEY, STEFANIA, STEFANIDA
STORM	Old English: a tempest or a storm STORMY, STORMEE
SUANNE	Hebrew: lily of grace (the combining of Susan & Anna) SUANNA
SUNNY	English: sunlike, cheerful SUNSHINE
SUSAN	Hebrew: lily or graceful lily SUSANNE, SUZIE, SUSIE, SUSANNA, SUKEY, SUZETTE, SUSY, SUKI, SUZANNA, ZSA ZSA, SOSANNA, SUSANNAH, SUSETTA, ZUZU, SUKE, SUSE, SUSCHEN, ZUZANE, ZUZI, SUE
SWANA	Old German: a swan
SWANHILD	Old German: swan battle-maiden SWANHILDA
SWANWHITE	Old Norse: white swan

T

TABITHA	Aramaic: a gazelle TABATHA, TABBIE, TABBY, TAB
TALITHA	Aramaic: a maiden TALETHA, TALISHA
TALLULAH	Choctaw Indian: leaping water TALLULA, TALLY, TALLIE
TAMAH	Hebrew: laughter
TAMAR	Hebrew: palm tree TAMARA, TAMMIE, TAMMY, TAMARAH, TAMMERA, TAMI, TAMIKA
TAMSEN	Greek: a twin (through Thomasina) TAMZEN, TAMASIN, TAMASINE
TANGERINE	English: girl from the city of Tangier, Morocco
TANKA	Teutonic: thanks (through Thankful)
TANSY	Middle Latin: tenacious one TANIS, TANIA, TANSEY, TANISHA, TANESHA, TANESHIA, TANISH, TENECIA, TENIESHA, TANYA, TANA, TANJA, TANNIS
TARA	Gaelic: the crag TARNYA, TARYN, TARRYN, TARAN
TATE	Anglo-Saxon: the cheerful TATTY, TATIANA
TEGAN	Celtic: a doe
TEMPERANCE	Latin: moderation (a Puritan "virtue" name)
TEMPEST	Old French: stormy one
TEMPLA	Latin: a temple, sanctuary TEMPLE
TERYL	Teutonic: pertaining to the Norse war god Thor TERRALL, TERRYLLE, TERRINA, TERELYN, TEREE, TERENA, TERI, TERRIE, TERRY
TERTIA	Latin: the third TERZILLA, TERZA
TESSA	Greek: the fourth TESS, TESSIE
THANKFUL	Anglo-Saxon: to give thanks (a Puritan "virtue" name)
THECLA	Greek: of divine fame THEKLA

THERESA	Latin: of the harvest
	TERESA, TERESSA, TERISE, TRESSA, TRISA, TEREZA, TREZA, THEREZA, TREASER, TERRI, TERRY, TERRIE, THERESE, TEREZIA, TRESCHA, TERESITA, TERESA
THIRZA	Hebrew: the pleasant
	TIRZAH
THOMASA	Greek: a twin
	THOMASINA, TOMASINA, THOMASENA, TOMASA, TOMMIE, TOMMY
THORA	the thunder (feminine of the Old Norse god Thor)
THORDIS	Old Norse: Thor's sprite
THORN	Anglo-Saxon: the thorn
	THORNIE, THORNY
THRINE	Greek: the pure
THYRA	Old Norse: the war borne
TIARA	English: a lady's bejeweled half-crown (recent trendy name)
	TIA
TIBERIA	Latin: from the River Tiber
TIFFANY	English: a trendy, New-Age name; reflecting the modern influence of labels and brand names, etc. (Tiffanys is known for it's precious gems, jewelry, lamps and stained glass)
	TIFANI, TIFFANI, TIFFANIE, TIFFANEY, TIFFNEY
TINA	Latin: the little one
	TINY, TEENIE, TEENA
TITANIA	Greek: great one
TOBY	Hebrew: the Lord is good
TOPAZ	Greek: the topaz (a "jewel" name)
	TOPAZA
TRACY	Anglo-Saxon: the brave
	TRACEE, TRACI, TRACIE
TRAVIATA	Latin: she who goes away
TRELLIS	Old French: of a bower
	TRELLIA
TRINA	Greek: pure one (through Catherine)
	TREENA, TREINA, TRINETTE
TRISTA	Latin: sad, secret sorrow
TULLIA	Irish Gaelic: truthful, quiet one

U

ULRICA	Old German: all-ruler
ULTIMA	Latin: the ultimate
UNA	Latin: the one, one, together UNITY
URANIA	Greek: the heavenly URANIE
URSULA	Latin: little she-bear URSA, URSE, URSEL, URSULINE

V

VALA	Gothic: the chosen one
VALBORG	Old German: protecting ruler VALBORGA
VALDA	Old Norse: destructive in battle
VALERIA	Italian: strength (valorous), feminine names that honor St. Valentine (the beloved third century martyr) VALENTINE, VALERIA, VALERY, VALOREE, VALERIA, VALLIE, VALOR, VALENCIA, VAL, VALENCE
VALESKA	Slavic: ruling glory
VALONIA	Latin: of the valley VALLONIA, VALLIE
VANESSA	Greek: a butterfly VANNY, VAN, VANNA, VANNIE
VANORA	Old Welsh: white wave
VASHTI	Persian: beautiful one
VEDETTE	Italian: guardian
VEGA	Arabic: the falling one
VELVET	English: from the Latin "a fleece" VELVETTE
VENETIA	Latin: to dare to give VENICE, VENUS, VENEZIA, VENICIA, VENETTA, VENITIA
VENTURA	Latin: to venture VENTURE

VERA	Latin: true
	VERINA, VERITA, VERENA, VERITY, VERENE, VERLA, VERE
VERNE	Latin: springlike
	VIRIDIS, VERNA, VERNETTE
VERONICA	Greek: harbinger of victory
	VERONIQUE, VONNIE, VONNY
VESPERA	Greek: the evening star
VESTA	she who dwells or lingers
VEVAY	Celtic: a white wave
	VEVA
VICTORIA	Latin: victory
	VICTORINE, VITORIA, VICKIE, VICKY, VIKKI, VIC, VICKI, VICTOIRE, VICTORIAN
VIDONIA	Latin: a vine branch
VIGILIA	Latin: the vigilant
VILLETTE	French: from a country home
VIOLET	Old French: a violet flower
	VIOLA, VIOLETTA, VIOLETTE, VIOLETA
VIRGINIA	Latin: maidenly
	VIRGILIA, VIRGINIE, VIRGIE, GINNY, GINGER, JINNEY
VIVIAN	Latin: life
	VIVIEN, VIVIA, VIVIANA, VIVIENNE, VYVIAN
VOLANTE	Italian: the flying
	VOLANT

WALLIS	Old English: one from Wales
	WALLIE, WALLY
WANDIS	Old German: wanderer
	WANDA, WENDELIN, WENDY, WENDA, WENDIE, WENDELINE
WANNETTA	Anglo-Saxon: little pale one
	WANETA
WELCOME	Anglo-Saxon: welcome or welcome to the earth (a "practical" Puritan name)
WESLA	Old English: from the west meadow (feminine of Wesley)
WILDA	Teutonic: the untamed or the wild one
	WYLDA

WILHELMINA	Old High German: chosen protection
	WILHELMINE, WILHELMA, WILLAMINA, WILONE, WILLELLA, WILLETTA, WILLETTE, WILMETT, WILLMOT, WILLANN, WILMA, WYLMA, BILLIE, BILLI, WILLI, BILLEE, MINNA, MINNIE, MINCHEN, MINETTE, MINKA, MIMI, WILLA, WILLY
WILLABEL	German-Latin: the chosen, the beautiful
	WILLABELLE
WINEMA	Modoc Indian: woman chief
WINIFRED	Teutonic: friend of peace
	WINIFREDA, WINIFRID, WINIFRYDE, WINNIEFRED, WINNE, WINNIE, WIN, WENEFRIDE
WINOLA	Teutonic: noble friend
WINONA	Sioux Indian: first born daughter
	WINONAH, WENONA
WINSOME	Old English: sweetly attractive
WYNNE	Celtic: fair, white
	WYN, WYNA, WYNETTE, WYNETTA

X

XANTHE	Greek: yellow-haired
XANTIPPE	Greek: yellow horse
	XANTHIPPE
XAVERIE	Arabic: the bright
	XAVIERA
XENA	Greek: hospitable
	XENE, ZENIA, XENIA, CHIMENE, XIMENA
XYLONA	Greek: from the forest
	XYLOTA

#

YEDDA	Teutonic: a singer
	YETTA
YOLANDA	Greek: violet flower
	YOLA, YOLINDA, YOLLANDE, YOLETTE
YVETTE	French: the archer (through the Scandanavian name Yves)
	YVONNE, YEVETTE, EYVETTE, EYVONNE, IVONNE

Z

ZADA Arabic: lucky one
ZADAH

ZAMORA Spanish "place" name

ZEA Latin: a kind of grain

ZELIA Greek: a devoted one
ZELE, ZELIE, ZELINA, ZELLA, ZELOSA,
ZELATRICE

ZEMIRA Hebrew: a song
ZEMIRAH

ZENDA Persian: woman

ZENOBIA Latin: given life by Zeus (Jupiter)
ZENAB, ZENAIDA, ZIZI, ZENOVIA, ZENOBIE,
ZENDA

ZEPHYRA Greek: of the dark, of the west wind of
Zephyr
ZEPHA, ZEPHRYS, ZYPHRA

ZERA Hebrew: the seedling
ZERAH

ZERLINDA Hebrew/Spanish: dawn-beautiful (Zerah-
Linda)

ZILLA Hebrew: a shadow
ZILLAH

ZINNIA New Latin: the zinnia flower

ZIPPORA Hebrew: little bird
ZIPPORAH

ZOE Greek: life
ZOA, ZOELA, ZOLITA, ZOI

ZORA Slavic: aurora or dawn
ZORINE, ZORINA

ZULEIKA Arabic: the fair

BOYS' NAMES

A

AARON Hebrew: lofty, exalted
ARON, AERON

ABBOTT Old English: father
ABBA, ABBOT

ABEL Hebrew: breath
ABELL, ABLE

ABELARD Teutonic: nobly resolute

ABIEZAR Hebrew: my father is help

ABRAHAM Hebrew: father of the multitude
ABE, BRAM, ABRAM

ACE Latin: unity
ACE₁

ADAIR Old English: from the oak-ford

ADAM Hebrew: of the red dust
ADDAM, ADAMS, ADAMO

ADLER Old German: eagle
ADLAR

ADONIS Phoenician: lord, the Greek god Adonis, a young man of godlike beauty

ADRIAN Latin: black, dark one
HADRIAN, ADRIEN, ADRIANO, ANDREIAN, ADEN, AIDEN

ADRIEL Hebrew: of God's flock

AHERN Celtic: lord of the horses

AHREN Old Low German: eagle

AIDAN Gaelic Irish: little fiery one

AINSLEY Anglo-Saxon: from Ain's meadow
AINSLIE

AJAX Greek: eagle

ALADDIN Arabic: the height of religion

ALAN Celtic: the comely and fair
ALLAN, ALLEN, ALAYNE, ALLEYN, ALAIN

ALARIC Teutonic: ruler of all
ALARICK, ALERIC, ALRICK, ARIC, ARICK, ALARIK

ALCANDER Greek: the manly

ALDEN   Anglo-Saxon: old friend
    ALDIN, ALDWIN, ALDWYN, ELDEN

ALDER   Anglo-Saxon: the alder

ALDIS   Old English: from the old house

ALDO   Old German: old and wise

ALDRED   Anglo-Saxon: old counsel
    ELDRED, ELDRID, ELDRIDGE

ALDRICH   Middle English/German: old king
    ALDRIC, ALDRIDGE, ELDRIC

ALERON   Latin: winged, eagle

ALEXANDER   Greek: helper and defender of mankind
    ALEC, ALEX, ALECK, SAUNDERS, ALESSANDRO,
    ALEXIO, ALEJANDRO, SAWNIE, ALEXANDRO,
    ALEXEI, SASCHA

ALFRED   Anglo-Saxon: elf in counsel
    AL, ALF, ALFIE, ALFREDO

ALGERNON   Old French: man with a mustache or beard
    ALGIE

ALLARD   Teutonic: nobly strong

ALLISON   Teutonic: of holy fame
    ALISON, ALLIE, ALLEY

ALMO   Greek: river god

ALPHEGE   Teutonic: elf-tall

ALPHONSO   Old High German: of noble family
    ALFONSO, ALONZO, ALON, LONNY, LON,
    ALPHONSE, ALPHONZUS

ALPIN   Celtic: elf   Scotch: blonde one

ALROY   Latin: the regal   Irish-Gaelic: red-haired
youth

ALSTON   Old English: noble stone

ALVIN   Old German: noble friend
    ALVAN, ALVYN, AYLWIN, ELVIN, ELWIN, ALVIS

AMBROSE   Greek: immortal, divine
    AMBROGIO, AMBROSIO, BRUSH

AMERIGO   Old German: industrious ruler

AMERY   Latin: the loving
    AMORY, AMES

AMOS   Hebrew: borne by God

ANATOLE   Greek: man from the East
    ANATOL

ANDREW   Greek: strong, manly
    ANDREAS, ANDRE, ANDRES, ANDY, ANDERS,
    DREW, ANDIE, DANDY, DANDIE, ANDRIEN,
    ANDREU

ANGELO	Greek: an angel
ANGUS	Scotch-Gaelic: unique strength, the choice
ANICET	Greek: the unconquered
ANSEL	Old French: with divine protection
	ANSE, ANSELM, ANSON
ANSGAR	Teutonic: of divine guard
ANTHONY	Latin: priceless one
	ANTON, ANTONIE, ANTONIO, ANTONY, TONY,
	ANTOINE, TONI, ANTONI, TONIO, TONNIO
APOLLO	Greek: of the sun's power
	APOLLOS
ARAH	Hebrew: lion's whelp
ARCHER	Middle English: archer, bowman
ARCHIBALD	German: nobly bold
	ARCHBOLD, ARCHY, ARCHIE, ARCH, BALDIE
ARDEN	Old French: fiery, flashing
	ARDITH, ARDETH, ARDIN
ARDOLPH	Old English: home-loving wolf
ARGUS	Greek: watchful guardian
ARMAND	Old German: army man
ARNFINN	Norse: white eagle
ARNO	Teutonic: eagle or eagle-wolf
	ARNOT, ARNOUX
ARNOLD	Old High German: strong as an eagle
	ARENT, ARNAULT, ARNALDO, AHRENT, ARNIE,
	ARN, ARNEY
ARNOT	Old Franco-German: little eagle
ARNSTEIN	Teutonic: eagle stone
ARTEMAS	Greek: gift of Artimis
ARTHUR	Welsh: noble, high
	AURTHUR, ARTURUS, ART, ARTIE
ARVAL	Welsh: wept-over
	ARVEL
ASA	Hebrew: healer
ASCOT	Old English: dweller at the East cottage
	ASCOTT
ASGRIM	Icelandic: divine wrath
ASHE	Middle English/Danish: beech tree
ASHER	Hebrew: happy one
ASHLEY	Old English: from the ash tree meadow
	ASHELEY, ASHLIE
ASHTON	Old English: dweller at the ash-tree farm

ATILLA	Teutonic: fatherlike
AUGUST	Latin: majestic dignity AUGUSTIN, AUGUSTUS, AUGUSTYN, AUSTIN, GUS, GUSTUS
AVERIL	Anglo-Saxon: the open
AXEL	Teutonic: divine reward AXTEL, AXTELL, AKSEL
AZA	Hebrew: the noble AZEL
AZAM	Aramaic: greatest
AZAZEL	Hebrew: entire removal
AZRAEL	Hebrew: God hath helped AZARIAH, AZREEL, AZARIEL, AZARAEL, AZAREEL, AZAR

B

BAILEY	Old French: bailiff or a keeper BAYLEY, BAILIE, BAILLY
BAIRD	Irish Gaelic: ballad singer BARD, BART
BALBO	Latin: the stammerer
BALDEMAR	Teutonic: of princely fame BAUMER
BALDER	Old Norse: bold prince BALDUR
BALDRIC	Teutonic: ruling prince BAUDRIC, BALDERIK
BALDWIN	Old High German: bold friend BALDUIN, BAUDOIN
BALFOUR	Scottish: from the pasture place
BALTHASAR	form of the Babylonian BELSHAZZAR: may God protect the king BALTHAZAR, BELSHAZZAR, BALTASAR, BALTASAROS
BANDI	Greek: man
BANNING	Late Latin: forbidden
BANQUO	Celtic: white
BAPTIST	Greek: a baptizer BAPTISTE, BATISTE

BARAK   Hebrew: the lightning
BARAQ

BARBOUR   Old English: a barber

BARDOLF   Old English: axe-wolf or boar-fierce
BARDO, BARDOU, BARDOLPH

BARNABY   Aramaic: son of exhortation
BARNABAS, BARNEY

BARNUM   Old English: a nobleman's home

BARRIE   Celtic: looking straight at the mark
BARRY

BARRON   Old High German: nobleman
BARON

BARTHOLOMEW   Hebrew: a farmer, son of the furrows
BARTH, BART, BAT, BARDO, BARTHELEMIEU

BASIL   Greek: kingly, royal
BASILE, BAS, VASILY

BAYARD   Middle Anglo-Saxon: the ruddy-haired

BEACHER   Old English: dweller by the beech tree
BEECH, BEECHER, BEACH, BEACHY

BEAMER   Old English: trumpeter

BEAU   Latin: handsome

BEAUFORT   Old French: from the beautiful fort

BEAUMONT   Old French: from the beautiful mountain

BEAUREGARD   Old French: from the beautiful view

BELDEN   Old English: dweller of the beautiful glen

BELISARIUS   Slavic: white prince

BELLAMY   Old French: handsome friend

BENEDICT   Latin: blessed one
BICK, BENEDIKT, BEN, BENDIX, BENNET,
DIXON, DIXEY, DIX, BENITO, BENEDYKT

BENJAMIN   Hebrew: the son of the right hand
BENJIE, BENJY, BENNIE, BENNY, BEN

BENONI   Hebrew: son of my sorrows

BENTLEY   Anglo-Saxon: from the bent-grass meadow

BEORN   Teutonic: bear
BJORN

BEOWULF   Teutonic: harvest wolf

BERENGER   Teutonic: bear spear

BERLIN   German: from the bear waterfall
BERLYN

BERN   Old German: bear
BERNE, BERNIE, BERNY

BERNARD	German: bold as a bear
	BARNARD, BERNARR, BARNEY, BERNIE
BERTHOLD	Old German: ruling in splendor
	BERTOLD
BERTRAM	Old High German: bright raven
BEVAN	Welsh: son of the well-born
	BEVEN, BEVIN, BEAVEN, BEAVUS
BEVIS	Old French: fair view
	BEAUVAIS
BIDDULPH	Teutonic: commanding wolf
BINGHAM	Teutonic: from the grain heap hamlet
	BING
BINK	North English: dweller at the slope
BIRCH	Old English: at the birch tree
BLADE	Anglo-Saxon: a sword
BLAINE	Anglo-Saxon: to flame
	BLANE, BLAYNE, BLAINEY, BLAYNEY
BLAKE	Anglo-Saxon: to whiten
	BLAKEY, BLAKELY
BLANCO	Spanish: white
BLARNEY	Irish "place" name (Blarney Castle)
BLAZE	Teutonic: blaze, brand
	BLAYZE, BLAISE, BLASE, BLAS, BRAZ, BLAZ
BOAZ	Hebrew: in the Lord is my strength
BODEN	Old Norse: the ready
BOGART	Danish: a bowman
BONNER	Old French: kind, gentle, good
BOONE	Old French: a blessing
BOOTH	Teutonic: a hut
BORG	Old Norse: a castle
BORIS	Russian: a fighter
BORS	Celtic: the wild boar
BOSWELL	Anglo-Saxon: from the cow's well
BOSWORTH	Anglo-Saxon: from the cow's barn
BOTOLF	Old English: herald-wolf
BOURBON	French: the royal
BOWIE	Irish Gaelic: yellow-haired
BOYCE	Old French: from the forest
	BOY
BOYD	Celtic: the fair-haired
	BOYDEN, BOY

BOYNE   English: white cow
       BOYNTON

BOZIDAR   Slavic: God's gift

BRADEN   Old English: from the valley

BRADLEY   Old English: from the broad meadow
       BRADLEE, BRAD, LEE

BRADY   Irish Gaelic: spirited one

BRAND   Old English: a flaming sword
       BRANNON, BRANT

BRANDON   Teutonic: from the flaming hill
       BRENDON, BREDON

BRANT   Old English: proud one

BRAVEN   Teutonic: to be brave

BRAWLEY   Middle English: he who quarrels

BRAZIL   Old French: the glowing

BRENT   Old English: steep hill

BRETT   Celtic: a native of Brittany
       BRET, BRETTON

BRIAN   Irish: the strong
       BRYAN, BRYANT, BRION

BRICE   Anglo-Saxon: the swift moving
       BRYCE

BRIDGER   Old English: a builder of bridges

BRIER   Greek: the strong
       BRIAR

BRIGHT   Old English: the bright

BRISBANE   Gaelic: royal steed

BROCK   Old English: a badger
       BROC, BROK

BRODIE   Irish Gaelic: a ditch
       BRODY

BRON   English: the brown
       BURNET, BRUN, BRUNO

BRUTUS   Latin: the heavy
       BRUT

BUCK   Old English: buck deer

BURLEIGH   Middle English: dweller at the castle
meadow
       BURLEY, BURL

C

CADELL Celtic: war defense
    CADE

CADOC Celtic: warlike
    CADO, CADOGAN

CADWALLADER Celtic: war arranger

CAESAR Latin: king, long-haired
    CESARE, CESARIO

CAIN Hebrew: possession
    CAINE, KANE, KAYNE

CALEB Hebrew: a dog
    CAL, CALE, KALEB

CALHOUN Irish Gaelic: from the narrow forest
    CALLAHAN

CANUTE Latin: the white-haired
    CNUT, KNUTE, KNUT

CARADOC Latin: the beloved
    CRADOC, CRAY

CAREY Old Welsh: dweller of the castles
    CARY

CARMICHAEL Celtic: Michael's friend

CARMODY Manx: god-of-arms

CARVELL Old French: spearman's estate

CASEY Irish Gaelic: valorous, brave, watchful

CASH Latin: vain one
    CASS

CASIMIR Old Slavic: commands peace
    KAZIMIR, KASIMIR, CASIMIRO, CAS, KAZ

CASSIDY Celtic: the ingenius

CASTLE Middle Latin: of the castle
    CASTELL, CASSEL

CATO Latin: the cautious

CAVAN Irish Gaelic: handsome one
    KAVAN

CAVANAGH Celtic: the handsome

CEDRIC Anglo-Saxon: chieftain

CHAD Celtic: the martial

CHANCE Middle English: good fortune

CHANDLER Old French: a candle maker

CHANNING Latin: a singer

CHARLES	Old High German: strong, manly CHARLIE, CHARLEY, CHUCK, CHICK, CHAZ, CHAY
CHARLTON	Old French/German: from Charles' farm
CHASE	French: a hunter
CHAUNCEY	Middle English: Chancellor church official CHANCE, CHAUNCE
CHESLEIGH	Latin/English: from the camp meadow CHESLEY
CHESTER	Latin: from the walled camp CHESTON, CHES, CHET
CHRISTIAN	Greek: a Christian CHRIS, CHRISTOPHER, CHRISTIANO, KIT, CHRISTOPHE, CHRISTOFLE, TOPHIE, TOFFER, TOPHER, CRISTOFORO, KRISTIAN, KRISTO, KRIS, CHRISTOFFER
CICERO	Latin: chick pea
CLARK	Anglo-Saxon: a learned man
CLAUDE	Latin: the lame
CLAY	Anglo-Saxon: clay
CLAYBORNE	Anglo-Saxon: born of clay
CLEMENT	Latin: the mild, merciful CLEMENCE, CLEMENS, CLEMENTE, KLEMET
CLIFF	Old English: from the steep cliff
CLINTON	Danish: from the flint cliff farm CLINT
CLOVIS	Teutonic: of holy fame CLODOVEO
CLUNY	Irish Gaelic: from the meadow
CLYDE	Welsh: heard from afar
COLAN	Latin: the dove COLUMBUS, COLE, CULLEN, COLIN
COLIN	Irish Gaelic: child, cub COLTER, COLT
COLLIER	Old English: a coal miner COLLYER, COLYER, COLIER, COLLEY, COLLIE
CONAN	Celtic: chief
CONRAD	Old High German: giver of wise and bold counsel CON, KONRAD, KURT, CONNIE, KORT
CONROY	Celtic/French: king of kings and wise king
CONSTANTINE	Latin: firm, constant
COOPER	Old English: barrel maker COOP

CORBIN	Old French: the raven
	CORBETT, CORBY
COREY	Irish: dweller by a hollow
CORMICK	Irish Gaelic: charioteer
	CORMAC, CORMACK
CORNELIUS	Greek: horn-colored
	CORNEL, NEELEY, CORNELIO
CORT	Old Norse: short
CORYDON	Greek: the crested dark
	KORYDON, CORY
CORYELL	Greek: a warrior
COSIMO	Greek: order, harmony, the universe
	COSMO, KOSMOS
COURTLAND	Old English: dweller at the farmstead
	COURTENAY, COURTNEY
CRISPIN	Latin: having curly hair
	CRISPIAN, CRESPEN, CRES, CRISPUS
CUTLER	Latin: a knife maker
CYNVELIN	Celtic: war god
CYPRIAN	Greek: of Cyprus
	CIPRIANO, CYP, CIPRIEN
CYRANO	Latin: warrior
CYRIL	Greek: lordly one
CYRUS	Persian: a king
	CY, KYROS, KURUSH

D

DACEY	Irish Gaelic: southerner
	DACY, DACIEN
DAGAN	Assyrian-Babylonian: the earth
	DAGON
DAGDA	Gaelic: the good
DAGFINN	Old Norse: white as day
DAI	Celtic: fire
DAGWOOD	Old English: bright one's forest
DALE	Old English: dweller in the valley
	DAYLE
DALLAS	Teutonic: the playful

DALTON	Anglo-Saxon: from the valley estate
DAMON	Greek: the taming DAMIEN
DANA	Anglo-Saxon: a Dane DAIN, DANE, DAYN
DANIE	Greek: man DANDY
DANIEL	Hebrew: God is my judge DANIELL, DANNIE, DANNY, DANNEL
DANTE	Latin: the enduring DURANT, DURAN, DURANTE, DURANDARTE, DURAND
DARAH	Teutonic: the bold
DARBY	Celtic: a freeman DERBY
DARCY	Old French: from the fortress DARSY, DARSEY
DARE	Anglo-Saxon: to dare
DARIAN	Persian: possessing wealth DARIEN, DARIUS
DARRELL	Anglo-Saxon: darling DARREL, DARRYL, DARYL, DERREL
DAVID	Hebrew: beloved one DAVE, DAVIE, DAVY, DAVIDDE, DAVEED, DAKE
DAVIN	Old Scandinavian: bright Finn DAVEN
DAY	Anglo-Saxon: of the day DAG, DAEGEL
DEAN	Old English: dweller in the valley
DELANO	Old French: of the night DELANE, DELANEY, DE LA NOYE
DELLING	Old Norse: the very shining one DILLINGER
DEMAS	Greek: popular one DEMOS, DEEMS, DEMIE, DEMUS
DEMPSEY	Irish Gaelic: proud one
DENNIS	Greek: god of wine DEN, DENNEY, DENNY, DENIS, DENYS, DENSIL, DENZIL, TENNIS, DENNISON, TENNYSON, DINIZ, DENTON
DENVER	Old English: dweller at the valley edge
DERMOT	Celtic: a freeman
DERRICK	Old German: ruler of the people DEREK, DIRK

DESMOND	Celtic: man of the world
DEVIN	Celtic: a poet
DEWEY	Old Welsh: beloved one
DE WITT	Old Flemish: blonde one
DEXTER	Latin: dexterous one DECK, DEX, DAX
DIGBY	Old Norse: from the dike settlement
DIGGORY	French: almost lost
DILLON	Irish Gaelic: faithful one
DOANE	Celtic: from the dunes DUANE
DOLAN	Irish Gaelic: black-haired
DOMINIC	Latin: belonging to the Lord DOM, DOMMIE, NICK, DOMINICK, DOMINGO, DOMINIK, DOMINICO, DOMINICUS, DOMINIK, DINKO
DONAHUE	Irish Gaelic: great brown chief DONOGHAN, DONOHUGH, DON, DONN
DONALD	Scotch-Gaelic: from the black water DOUG, DUGGIE
DOYLE	Celtic: dark stranger DUGAL, DUGGAN, DUGAN
DRAGAN	Slavic: dear
DRAKE	Old High German: the male duck or swan
DRAPER	Old French: one who drapes or deals in cloth
DRED	Scottish: to endure
DREW	Old Welsh: wise one
DRUCE	Celtic: the wise
DRURY	Old French: sweetheart
DUARD	Teutonic: rich guard DUARTE
DUDLEY	Old English: from the people's meadow
DUFF	Celtic: dark faced one DUFFY, DUFFIE, DAR
DUGAN	Anglo Saxon: to be worthy
DUKE	Old French: leader
DUNCAN	Gaelic: brown warrior
DURYEA	Latin: enduring
DUTCH	German: the German
DYLAN	Old Welsh: from the sea

E

EARL	Anglo-Saxon: noble man ERL, ERROL, ERLE, EARLE, EARLY
EBENEZER	Hebrew: the stone of help EB, EBEN
EBERHARD	Old German: wild-boar brave
EDGAR	Old English: prosperous protector ED, EDDIE
EDMUND	Old English: defender of property EDMOND, EDMONT, EDDIE, NED, NEDDY
EDRIC	Old English: prosperous ruler ED, RIC
EDSEL	Old English: from the rich man's hall
EDWARD	Anglo-Saxon: rich guard EDUARDO, ED, NED, TED, TEDDY
EGBERT	Anglo-Saxon: bright, shining sword edge
ELEAZAR	Hebrew: God hath helped (through Lazarus) LAZARUS, LAZAR, LAZARO, LAZARE
ELIJAH	Hebrew: Jehovah is God ELIAS, ELLIOTT, ELI
ELISHA	Hebrew: God is salvation ELISHAH
ELKANAH	Hebrew: God hath created ELQUANAH
ELLERY	Middle English: from the elder tree
ELMER	Anglo-Saxon: of noble fame
ELMO	Italian/Greek: the amiable
ELROY	Old French: the king
ELSU	American Indian: flying falcon
ELVET	Old English: elfin friend ELVY
ELWOOD	Old English: from the old forest
EMERY	Old German: industrious ruler
EMIL	Gothic: industrious one EMILE
EMMANUEL	Hebrew: God with us IMMANUEL, MANUEL, MANNIE, MANNY
ENNIS	Greek: the ninth

ENOCH	Hebrew: the dedicated HONOKH, HANOCH
ENOS	Hebrew: man
EPHRAIM	Hebrew: very fruitful
ERASMUS	Greek: lovely, worthy of love ERASTUS, RASMUS, RASTUS, RAS, RAZ
ERIC	Scandinavian: the kingly ERICK, ARICK, AREK, RICKY, ERIK
ERNEST	German: the earnest ERNESTUS, ERN, ERNST, ERNIE, ERNY
ESAU	Hebrew: covered with hair
ESSEX	Old English: "place" name
ETHAN	Hebrew: strength
EUCHARY	Greek: to rejoice
EUGENE	Greek: of noble race EUGENIO, EUGENIUS, GENE
EUSTACE	Latin: stable, tranquil EUSTIS, STACEY, EUSTAZIO
EVAN	Irish Gaelic: a youth
EVERARD	German: strong as a wild boar EVERITT, EVERET, EVERETT
EYULF	Old Norse: island wolf
EZEKIEL	Hebrew: strength of God EZEKIAL, EZEKIAH, ZEKE
EZRA	Hebrew: help ESRA, EZ

F

FABIAN	Latin: belonging to Fabius FABYAN, FABIO, FABIANO, FABIEN
FABRON	South French: little blacksmith FABRE, FABRIANO, FABRIZIO, FABRICE
FAGAN	Celtic: a small voice FAGIN
FAIRLEY	Teutonic: the unexpected FAIRLEIGH, FARLEY, FAIRLIE
FALKNER	Teutonic: a trainer of falcons FALCONER, FAULKNER
FANE	Teutonic: joyful

FARAND	Teutonic: the fair
	FARRAND, FARRANT
FAROLD	German: power that travels far
FARQUHAR	Celtic: the manly
FARRELL	Celtic: the valorous
	FARREL, FERRELL
FAXON	Teutonic: the thick-haired
FELIX	Latin: fortunate, lucky
	FELIZ
FENRIS	Old Norse: the wolf
FERDINAND	Gothic: world-daring
FERGUS	Middle Gaelic: the choice
	FERGIE
FERRIS	Irish-Gaelic: the rock
	FARRIS
FINGAL	Old Irish: the fair-haired foreigner
	FINGALL
FINLEY	Irish Gaelic: fair-haired one
	FINDLAY, FIN, LEE
FINN	Irish Gaelic: fair-haired one, the white
	FIONN
FISK	Scandinavian: fish
	FISKE, FISHER
FITCH	Middle English: ermine
FITZ	Latin/Old French: son
	FITZALAN, FITZCLARENCE, FITZGERALD, FITZHERBERT, FITZHUGH, FITZPATRICK, FITZJOHN, FITZROY, FITZARTHUR
FLANN	Irish Gaelic: red-haired one
FLAVIUS	Latin: golden-yellow hair
	FLAVIO, FLAVIAN
FLETCHER	Old French: a maker of arrows
FLINT	Old English: a stream
FLYNN	Irish Gaelic: son of the red-haired man
FORREST	Old French: dweller at a forest
FORRESTER	Middle English: forest guardian
	FORRIE, FOSS, FORSTER
FORTESCUE	Teutonic/French: strong and powerful shield
FORTUNE	Latin: chance
	FORTUNATUS, FORTUNIO
FONTAINE	Latin: a spring
	FONTANA

FOWLER	Middle English: a keeper of birds
	VOGLER, VOGEL
FOX	Teutonic: a fox
	FOXE, FUCHS
FRANCIS	German: the free
	FRANK, FRANCOIS, FRANCHOT, FRANZ, FRANS, FRANCESCO, FRANKIE, FRANZISCUS, FRANCK, FRANCISCO, FRANZEN
FRASER	Old French: curly haired
	FRAZER
FRAYNE	Teutonic: the asked for
	FRAINE, FREYNE
FREDERICK	Old German: peaceful ruler
	FREDERIC, FRED, FREDDIE, FREDDY, FREDRIC, FRITZ, FREDRIK
FREY	Old Norse: lord
FRICK	Old English: bold man
FRIDOLD	Teutonic: peace power
FRIDOLF	Teutonic: peace wolf
FYFE	Old English: one who holds property
	FIFE

G

GABRIEL	Hebrew: man of God
	GABE, GABRIELE
GABLE	Old French: little Gabriel
GAGE	Old French: a pledge of security
GALAHAD	Celtic: the valorous
GALEN	Latin: sea calm
GALLAGHER	Celtic: eager helper
GALLOWAY	Old Gaelic: a Scottish Celt of the Highlands
GALUSHA	Hebrew: an exile
GALVIN	Celtic: bird
GANNON	Irish Gaelic: little fair-complexioned one
GARDELLE	Old High German: a guard
GARDENER	Teutonic: one who gardens
	GARDNER, GARTH, GARETH

GARRETT	Anglo-Saxon: firm spear
	GARRETT, GARRETH, GARY, JARETT, JARRATT
GARFIELD	Teutonic: war field
GARRICK	Teutonic: spear king
GARROWAY	Old English: spear warrior
GARY	Old English: spearman
	GARI, GARRY
GASPAR	Persian: treasure holder
	CASPAR, JASPER, KASPAR
GASTON	Teutonic: the hospitable
GAVIN	Old Welsh: from the hawk field
	GAWAIN
GEORGE	Latin: land worker
	JORGE, GEORGY, GEORDIE, GEORGIO
GERALD	Teutonic: of unerring spear
	JEROLD, JERRY, JERRALD, GARCIA, GERAUD, GIRALDO
GERARD	Old High German: spear hard
	GERHARDT
GIDEON	Hebrew: the feller of trees
GIFFORD	Old English: gift brave
GILBERT	Old High German: bright of will
	WILBERT, WILBUR, GIL, BERT, GIP, GYP, GILPIN
GILBY	Irish Gaelic: yellow-haired
GILDERSLEEVE	Anglo-Saxon: one who gilds
GILES	Latin: a shield bearer
	GIL
GILROY	Teutonic: servant of the king
GLADE	Old English: a clear space in the woods
GLADSTONE	Anglo-Saxon: the shining stone
GLEN	Celtic: of the glen
	GLENN, GLENNIE
GORDON	Old English: from the cornered hill
	GORDIE, GORDY
GOUVERNEUR	Latin: to govern
GRANGER	Old French: a farm steward
GRANT	Middle English: great one
GRANVILLE	Old French: from the great town
GRAYSON	Middle English: son of the reeve
GREELEY	Old English: from the gray meadow
	GRIDLEY

GREGORY	Greek: to awaken
	GREG, GREGOR
GRISWOLD	Teutonic: from the grizzle (gray) forest
GROSVENOR	French: great hunter
GROVER	Old English: from the grove of trees
GUNTHER	Teutonic: warrior
	GUNTHAR, GUNNER, GUNNAR, GUNTER
GUSTAVUS	Swedish: staff of the Goths
	GUS, GUSSIE, GUST, GUSTAF, GUSTAV, GUSTAAF, GUSTAVO
GUTHRIE	Danish: war serpent
GUY	Old French: to steady, guide
	GUI, GUIDO, WYATT, WIATT

H

HAAKON	Teutonic: high kin
	HACON, HACO, HAKON
HACKETT	Old Franco-German: little hacker
HADAR	Syrian: a god
HADDEN	Old English: from the heath place
HADLEY	Old English: from the heath medow
	HEDLEY, HEDLEIGH
HAGEN	Irish Gaelic: little young one
HALE	Old French: from the hall
HALLEM	Teutonic: of the threshhold
HALLEY	Anglo-Saxon: the hallowed, holy
	HALEY, HOLLIS
HALLIBURTON	Teutonic: the bright and holy
HALLIWELL	Teutonic: from the holy well
HALSEY	Anglo-Saxon: from Hal's place
	HALSTED, HALSTEAD
HAMAL	Arabic: a lamb
HAMLET	Teutonic: a small home
HANNIBAL	Pheonician: grace of Baal
	HANNO, HANEY
HARDEN	Teutonic: to make bold
	HARDEE, HARDIE, HARDY
HARGRAVE	Teutonic: a title of honor

HARLAN	Teutonic: from the frost land
HARLEY	Old English: from the stag's meadow
	HARLEIGH, ARLIE, ARLEY
HARLOW	Old English: from the hill fort
	ARLO
HAROLD	Old Norse: army-ruler
	HARRY, HAL
HASLETT	Old English: hazel tree headland
	HAZLETT
HASTING	Teutonic: the swift
	HASTY, HASTINGS
HAVELOCK	Teutonic: of the lake haven
HAVEN	Teutonic: a harbor
HAVER	Old Norse: the wild oat
HAWTHORNE	Anglo-Saxon: the hawthorn
	THORNE, THORNIE
HAZARD	Arabic: the die (as in a game of chance)
HAZEN	Old English: the hoar frost
HEATH	Middle English: from the heath
HEATHCLIFF	Middle English: from the heath by the cliff
HECTOR	Greek: holds fast
HELLER	Old High German: the bright
HENRY	Old High German: ruler of an estate
	HAGEN, HAMLYN, HAL, HANK, HEINRICH, HEINIE, ENRICO, ENZIO, HARRY, HENRI, HENDRIK
HERBERT	Anglo-Saxon: army bright
	HERB, HERBIE, BERT, BERTIE
HERCULES	Greek: glory of Hera
	HERACLES, HERCULE, HERAKLES
HERMAN	Old High German: army man
	ARMOND, ARMANDO
HEWETT	Old Franco-German: little Hugh
HEZEKIAH	Hebrew: God has strengthened
HIAWATHA	American Indian: maker of rivers
HILDEBRAND	German: battle sword
HILLIARD	Old German: battle-brave
	HILLIER, HILLYER
HIRAM	Phoenician: most noble
	HI, HY, HYRAM
HOBSON	Arabic: the goodly
	HOGAN, HUGGINS, HOB
HOGARTH	Old English: the gardener from the hill

HOLT	Teutonic: of the woods
HOMER	Greek: pledges security
HONON	North American Indian: a bear
HOPESTILL	Old English: to continue hoping (English Puritan "virtue" name)
HORACE	Latin: of the hours
HORNE	Middle English: a blower of horns HORNER, HORNBLOWER
HOWARD	Old English: guardian
HUBERT	Old High German: bright of mind HUBER, HOBART, HUBBARD, HOYT
HUGH	Old High German: mind HUGHIE, HUEY, HUTCH, HUGO
HUMPHREY	Anglo-Saxon: home protector HUMP, HUMPH, HUMFREY, ONOFREDO
HUNTER	Old English: hunter HUNT, HUNTLEY, HUNTINGTON, HUNTINGDON
HUXLEY	Old English: a huckster

I

IAN	Hebrew: God is gracious (through John)
ICHABOD	Hebrew: the inglorious
IGNATIUS	Latin: the inflammable, ardent, fiery IGNATZ, IGNACE, IGNAZIO, IGNAZ, IGOR
INDRA	Hindustani: the thunder
INGAR	Scandinavian: from the place of Ing INGVAR
INGOMAR	Teutonic: Ing's fame
INGRAM	Teutonic: Ing's raven
INGVALT	Teutonic: Ing's power
INNIS	Celtic: from the island INNESS
INTREPID	Latin: the fearless, valorous
IRA	Hebrew: the watchful IRAH
IRVIN	Anglo-Saxon: sea friend IRVING, IRWIN, MERVIN, MERV
ISA	Greek: the equal

ISAAC	Hebrew: laughter
	IZAAK, IKE, IKEY, ZAK
ISAIAH	Hebrew: salvation of the Lord
	ISSIAH, ISHAM
ISRAEL	Hebrew: contender with God
IVANDER	Hebrew: divine man
IVANHOE	Anglo-Saxon: from the ivy cliff
IVER	Old Scandinavian: an archer
	IVES, IVOR, YVES, IVAN, IVON

J

JABEZ	Hebrew: he will cause pain
	JABESH
JABRIEL	Hebrew: God buildeth
JAMES	Hebrew: the supplanter
	JAKOBOS, JACOB, JAKE, JAQUES, JACK, JOCKO, JAMIE, JAYMEE, JIMMIE, JIMMY, JIM, JIN, JACQUES, JACQUET, DIEGO, JAMESON, JAGO, JAIME, DIAZ, JAYME, JACKEL, JAKOB, BOPP, JOGG, JAKOV, JASCHA, HAMISH, JOCK, SHAMUS, JAKIE, COB, COBB
JAPHET	Hebrew: enlargement
JARMAN	Old German: the German
JARVIS	Teutonic: spear sharp
JASON	Greek: the healer
JAY	Old French: blue jay
	JAYSON
JEDEDIAH	Hebrew: beloved of the Lord
	JED, JEDIDIAH
JEFFREY	Old High German: district peace
	JEFF, JEFFY, JEFFEREY, GODFREY, GEOFFREY, GOTTFRIED, JEFFERS, JEFFRIES, JOFFRE, JEFFY
JEPTHAH	Hebrew: God sets free
	JEP, JEPHTHAH
JEREMY	Hebrew: exalted of the Lord
	JEREMIAH, JEREMIAS, JERRY
JEROME	Greek: the holy name
	GERONIMO, JERONIMO, JERROLD
JESSE	Hebrew: God's grace
	JESS, JESSIE, JESSEY, JESSY, JESSEE
JETHRO	Hebrew: excellent

JOB	Hebrew: the afflicted
	JOBEY, JOBY, JOBIE
JOEL	Hebrew: the Lord is God
JOHN	Hebrew: God is gracious
	JOHNNY, JOHNIË, JON, JONNY, JONNIE, JACK, JACKIE, JACKY, JEN, JENKIN, ZANE, JEAN, JEHAN, JOHANNOT, JANNIK, JOCK, IAN, SEAN, SHAN, SHANE, SHAWN, SHAMUS, GIOVANNI, JUAN, JUANITO, JOHANNES, JOHANN, HANS, HANSCHEN, JEHAN, HANNEKEN, HANKA, HANSEL, IVAN, JOVAN, JANIK, JENKS, JANTZEN, IVANOVITCH, JANSON, JANSEN, JANZEN, JOLYON
JONAS	Hebrew: dove
JONATHAN	Hebrew: God has given
JORAH	Hebrew: autumnal rain
JORAM	Hebrew: the Lord is exalted
JORDAN	Hebrew: to descend
	JOURDAIN, JARED, JARRED, JAROD, JARROD
JOSEPH	Hebrew: he shall add
	JOE, JOEY, YOSEPH, YUSSUF, JOSE, PEPE, PEPITO
JOSHUA	Hebrew: Jehovah is deliverance
	JOSH
JOSIAH	Hebrew: Jehovah supports
JUBAL	Hebrew: tent dweller
	JUBA, JUBE, JUBILEE
JUDAH	Hebrew: the praised
	JUDA, JUDE
JUDD	Hebrew: praised
JULIEN	Latin: belonging to Julius
	JULE, JULYAN, JULIO, JULIAN, JULES
JUNIUS	Latin: of June
	JUNIOR, JUNOT
JUSTIN	Latin: the just
	JUSTUS, JUSTIS

K

KALON	Greek: the beautiful
KANE	Celtic: tribute
	KAIN, KAYNE, KAINE
KEANE	Middle English: the bold
	KEAN, KEENE, KEENAN

KEDAR	Hebrew: the dark
KEEFE	Irish Gaelic: handsome, noble
KEEGAN	Irish Gaelic: little fiery one
KEELEY	Irish Gaelic: handsome KEELY, KEALY
KEITH	Gaelic: the wind
KELLY	Celtic: warrior KELL, KELLEY
KELSEY	Teutonic: from the sea KELCEY, KELSIE
KELVIN	Irish Gaelic: from the narrow river KELVAN, KELVEN, KELVYN
KEN	Scottish: champion KEMP, KEMPER, CAMP, KENT, KIM, KENN
KENDALL	Old English: chief of the dale
KENDRICK	Irish Gaelic: son of Henry KENRICK, KENRIC, KENERICK
KENLEY	Teutonic: from the king's meadow
KENMAN	Old English: a kingly man KINMAN
KENNARD	Teutonic: firm love
KENNETH	Celtic: chief KEN, KENNITH, KENN, KENNY, KENNIE
KENTON	Celtic: from the chief's headquarters
KENYON	Irish Gaelic: white-headed
KEOKUK	North American Indian: watchful fox
KERMIT	Celtic: the dark and free
KERR	Celtic: the dark Anglo-Saxon: a leader KEIR, KEIRAN, KEIRON, KERRIN, KIER, KERRIE, KEARY
KERWIN	Irish Gaelic: little jet-black one KERWYN, KERWEN
KESTER	Old English: from the Roman Army camp
KEVIN	Irish Gaelic: gentle, lovable
KIDD	Old Norse: a child KYD, KIDDE
KILDARE	Teutonic: in battle array KEELDARE
KILLIAN	Irish Gaelic: little warlike one
KIM	Old English: chief, ruler
KIMBALL	Old Welsh: warrior-chief KIMBLE, KIMBELL, KIMBALD, KIMBEL

KING	Old English: ruler KAI, KAISAR, CZAR, KEIZER, KONGE
KINGDON	Old English: from the king's hill
KINGSLEY	Old English: from the king's meadow
KINGSTON	Old English: from the king's town
KIP	German: from the pointed hill KIPP, KIPPE, KIBBE
KIRBY	Teutonic: from the church by the byre
KIRK	Old Norse: a church
KIRKWOOD	Old English: from the church wood
KNIGHT	Middle English: a military follower
KNOX	Teutonic: from the hill
KYLE	Irish: a chapel CUYLER, KILE
KYNE	Anglo-Saxon: the bold KYRAN

L

LABAN	Hebrew: the white
LACHLAN	Celtic: the warlike Scottish: from the water LAUGHLAN, LOUGHLAN
LADD	Middle English: a boy LADDIE, LADDOCK, LADAKIE, LADKIN
LAIRD	Scottish: a land owner
LAMBERT	Old German: land-brilliant
LANCE	Latin: one who serves LANCELOT, LANCELOTT, LANZO, LOT, LOTT, LANCELET, LAUNCLET, LAUNCELOT
LANDER	Middle English: from the long island
LANE	Old English: a country road
LANNY	Celtic: a sword
LARS	Etruscan: lord
LAURENCE	Latin: the laurel-crowned one LAWRENCE, LORENZO, LAURAN, LORIN, LOREN, LAWRIE, LAW, LARRY, LONNIE, LARKIN, LORRY, RENZO, LAURITZ, LAWS
LEANDER	Greek: lion man LEE, ANDY, LEANDROS

LEE	Old English: from the pasture meadow
	LEIGH
LEIF	Old Norse: beloved one
LEIGHTON	Old English: from the meadow farm
	LAYTON, LEYTON
LEITH	Scotch Gaelic: the wide river
LELAND	Old English: from the lea (meadow) land
	LEYLAND, LEIGHLAND
LENNOX	Gaelic: chieftain
LEO	French/Latin: lionlike
	LEON, LIONEL, LYONEL, LION, LIONELLO, LIN, LI, LENNY, LEONARD, LEONARDO, LENARD, LEONIDAS
LEOPOLD	Old High German: bold for the people
LEROY	Old French: king
	LEE, ROY, LE ROY
LESLIE	Scotch Gaelic: from the gray stronghold
LESTER	Anglo-Saxon: the shining camp
LEVI	Hebrew: joined
	LEV, LEVY
LEWIS	Old High German: famous warrior
	LOUIS, LEWES, LOU, LU, LUKIN, LUDWIG, LUIS, LUIGI
LINCOLN	Celtic-Latin: from the colony by the pool
	LINC
LINDALL	Old English: from the dale of the waterfall
	LYNDALL
LINK	Old English: from the bank or ridge
LINUS	Latin: flaxen-haired
LIVINGSTON	Teutonic: from Lief's place
LLOYD	Celtic: the gray
LOGAN	Scottish: from the still meadow
LOMBARD	Teutonic: the long-bearded
LONDON	Anglo-Saxon: a "place" name
LONGFELLOW	Old English: a tall fellow
LOREN	Latin: the lost
LORN	Irish and Scottish: the bereft
LOT	Hebrew: the veiled
LOYAL	Old French: the faithful
LUCIUS	Latin: light
	LUCIAN, LUCIEN, LUKE, LUCA, LUCCA, LUCE, LUKAS, LUCAS, LUCK

LUTHER Old High German: illustrious warrior
LUTHA, LOTHAR, LOTHAIRE, LOTHARIO

LYULF Danish: fierce wolf
LIOLF

M

MAC Irish-Scotch: son, son of
MacADAM, MacDONALD, MacDOUGAL,
MacFLYNN, MacBETH, MACK

MADDOCK Old Welsh: good, beneficient
MADOC, MADOCK, MADOG

MAGEE Irish Gaelic: son of the fiery one

MAGNUS Latin: great one
MANUS, MANASSES, MANASSEH, MANNAS

MAHON Celtic: a bear
MAHONEY

MAJOR Latin: greater

MAKEPEACE Middle English: to make peace (English
Puritan "virtue" name)

MALACHI Hebrew: messenger

MALCOLM Celtic: worker for COLIN

MALONE Greek: the dark

MANCHU Chinese: the pure

MANDEL German: the almond

MANFRED Teutonic: man of peace

MANLEY Teutonic: virile, manly
MANNY

MANVILLE Latin: from the main town

MARK Latin: warlike one
MARTIN, MARTIAL, MARTEL, MARS, MARCUS,
MARCOS, MARCO, MARTINI, MARC, MAREK,
MARKUS, MARCH, MARCEL

MARLOW Old English: from the water by the hill

MARSDEN Old English: dweller at the marshy valley

MARSHALL Middle English: steward
MARSHAL

MASON Latin: a stone worker

MATTHEW Hebrew: gift of Jehovah
MATTHIAS, MATHIAS, MATT, MAT, MACE

MAURICE	Late Latin: dark MORRIS, MORREL, MORICE, MORITZ, MAURIE
MAXIMILIAN	Latin "maximus": the greatest MAXIM, MAX, MAXY, MAXIMILIANO, MAXWELL
MAYER	Latin: greater one
MAYHEW	Old French: gift of Jehovah
MEIKLEJOHN	Scottish and North English: big JOHN
MELBOURNE	Old English: from the millstream
MELCHIOR	Spanish/German: a king
MERCER	French: a merchant MERCIER, MARCHAND
MERLIN	Middle English: a falcon
MICAH	Hebrew: like unto the Lord
MICHAEL	Hebrew: who is like God? MITCH, MITCHEL, MICKEL, MICKEY, MICKIE, MIKE, MICKY, MIKHAEL, MISCHAEL, MICHEL, MICHON, MICHAU, MIGUEL, MISHA, MIKEL, MIKAEL, MICHAIL, MISKA, MISCHA
MILAN	Latin: the loveable MILANO
MILES	Latin: soldier, warrior MYLES, MILO
MINER	English: "occupational" name Latin: young person MINOR, MYNOR
MODRED	Old English: brave counsel
MOGAN	Danish: the mighty
MOHILL	Old English: from the hill on the moor
MONROE	Celtic: from the red marsh MONRO, MUNROI, MUNRO
MONTAGUE	French: dweller at the pointed hill
MONTE	Latin: from the mountain MONTY
MONTGOMERY	Latin: mountain hunter
MOODY	Anglo-Saxon: of the mind
MORELAND	Old English: from the moor-land
MORGAN	Celtic: from the sea
MORTIMER	Old French: from the still water
MOSES	Hebrew: taken out of the water MOSE, MOSIE, MOE, MOSS, MOSHEH
MUNGO	Celtic: loveable MUNGHU, MUNGER
MURDOCK	Scotch Gaelic: prosperous from the sea

MURPHY   Celtic: sea warrior
MORAN, MURF

MYRON   Greek: the fragrant
MERYL, MERRIL

N

NAPOLEON   Greek: forest lion
NAP, POLEON

NARCISSUS   Greek: to put to sleep (Greek mythology: the beautiful boy who fell in love with his own image in a pool)
NARCISSCO, NARKISS

NATHAN   Hebrew: the given
NAT, NATE, NATHANIEL, NATTY, NATHON

NEAL   Irish Gaelic: champion
NEIL, NIEL, NEALE, NIELS, NILES, NELS

NEHAMIAS   Hebrew: comforted by Jehovah
NEHAMIAH

NELSON   English: champion's son

NEMO   Greek: from the glade   Latin: no one

NERO   Italian: the black

NESTOR   Greek: he remembers

NEVILLE   Old French: from the new estate

NEVIN   Latin: of the snow

NEWCASTLE   Old English: from the new castle

NEWELL   Latin: a fruit stone

NEWLAND   Old English: from the new land

NEWLIN   Old Welsh: dweller at the new pool
NEWLYN

NICHOLAS   Greek: victorious
NICOLAS, NICOLAY, NICHOL, NICOL, NICKLAS, CLAUS, NICKY, NICK, NICCOLO, NICCOLINI, COLA, NIKOLAUS, NIKLAS, KLAUS, NIKOLAI, NIKKA, NICKIE, NIK, NIKKI

NICODEMUS   Greek: victory over the people
DEMAS, NICK, NICKY

NIGEL   Latin: the black

NINIAN   Celtic: the sky

NISSEN   Scandinavian: of the wee folk or elves

NOAH Hebrew: rest, comfort
NOE, NOAK, NOEY

NOBLE Latin: the well known, famous
NOBEL, NOLAN, NOLAND

NOEL Latin: birthday, born at Christmas

NORBERT Teutonic: Njord's brightness (Njord was the Norse diety of the winds)

NORMAN Old French: a northman
NORM, NORMIE, NORMIN, NORMAND

NORVAL Teutonic: from the north valley

NUMA Latin: of divine force

NYE Old English: the near, neighbor

O

OAKES Middle English: the oak

OAKLEY Old English: from the oak meadow

OATES Anglo-Saxon: the oat grass

OBADIAH Hebrew: servant of the Lord
OBIE, OBADIAS

OBED Hebrew: the serving

OBERON Frankish: the obedient

O'BRIEN Celtic: son of Brian

ODELL Anglo-French: little wealthy one
WODIN, ODIN

ODOLF Old German: rich and brave wolf

ODGEN Old English: from the oak valley

OLAF Old Norse: peace

OLIVER Old Norse: kind affectionate one
OLLIE, OLLEY, OLLY

OLYMPIOS Greek: of Olympus
OLYMPIO

OMAR Arabic: the better

ORAN Irish Gaelic: pale-complexioned one
OREN, ORIN, ORRIN

ORSON Old English: spearman's son
ORRY, ORSINO, ORSINI, URSELLO, OURS, URSUS

ORVAL Old French: from the gold town
ORVILLE

OSBERT	Old English: divinely brilliant
	OS, OSSIE, OZZIE
OSCAR	Anglo-Saxon: power of godliness
	OSGAR, OS, OZZIE
OSGOOD	Old Norse: divine goth
OSRED	Teutonic: divine counsel
OSRIC	Teutonic: divine king
OSSIAN	Gaelic: a fawn
	USHEEN
OTIS	Greek: keen of hearing
OTTO	German: the rich
	OTHELLO, OTTORINO, ODON
OZIAS	Hebrew: strength of the Lord
	UZZIAS
OZIEL	Hebrew: a shadow

P

PADGETT	French: young attendant
	PADGET
PAGE	Greek: a child or serving boy
	PAIGE, PAGET
PAINE	Latin: a rustic, pagan
	PAYNE
PALMER	Latin: a palm bearer
	PALMA
PARK	Old English: of the enclosed woods
	PARKE, PARKER
PARNELL	Old French: little Peter
PARRISH	Old English: of the parish
	PARIS
PARRY	Old Welsh: son of Harry
PARTRIDGE	Middle English: the partridge (an English "bird" name)
PASCAL	Hebrew: of the passover
	PACE, PASE, PASCH, PASCHA, PASCHAL, PASQUALE
PASTOR	Latin: a pastor or quardian
PATRICK	Latin: noble one
	PAT, PADDY, PADRICK, RICKY, RICK, PAYTON, PEYTON

PAUL	Latin: the little
	PAOLO, PABLO, PAULEY, PAWLEY, PAVA, PAVAL, PABLOCITO, PAVEL, PAVLIN, PAVEK
PAXTON	Old English: peace town
	PAX
PEAKE	Norse: from the pointed mountain top
	PIKE
PENROD	Old German: famous commander
PEPIN	Old German: perseverant one
	PEPI, PEPPI
PERCIVAL	French: the perceptive
	PERCE, PERCY, PERC, PURSEY, PARZIVAL
PEREGRINE	Latin: a wanderer
PERTH	Pictish-Celtic: thorn-bush thicket
PERRY	Anglo-Saxon: the pear tree
PETER	Latin: a stone
	PETE, PETIE, PETEY, PIETRO, PEDRO, PIERRE, PIERS, PETERKIN, PETROS, PIERCE, PEERS, PETRUSCHA, PIERROT, PETRUCCIO, FERRIS
PHAON	Greek: the brilliant
PHAROAH	Egyptian: king
	FARO
PHELAN	Celtic: wolf
PHILANDER	Greek: loving man
	PHIL, ANDY
PHILIP	Greek: lover of horses
	PHIL, PHYL, PHIP, PIP, FLIP, PIPPO, FELLEEP, PHIPPS, PHILLIPS, PHILIPPE, FLIPPO
PHILO	Greek: love
	PHILLY, PHIL, PHILADELPHIA
PHINEAS	Greek: mouth of brass
PIERPONT	French/Latin: from the stone bridge
PIPER	Anglo-Saxon: one who pipes
PITT	Anglo-Saxon: from the quarry
POLLUX	Greek: a crown
POMEROY	Latin: the apple of the king
POMPEY	Latin: of Pompey
POWER	Latin: power
	PODESTA, STARK
PREWITT	Old French: little valiant one
	PRUITT

PRIDE	Anglo-Saxon: to be proud
PRIMUS	Latin: the first
	PRIMO, PRINCE
PROSPER	Latin: the prosperous
	PROSPERO
PURVIS	Old French: a provider
PYE	Middle English: the spotted
PYNE	English: a pine tree
	PINE, PINEY

Q

QUAIN	Old French: the clever
QUENEL	Old French: dweller at the little oak tree
	QUENNEL
QUENTIN	Latin: the fifth
	QUINTILIAN, QUINTO, QUINTIN, QUENT, QUINT, QUINTEN
QUERON	Celtic: the dark
QUILLAN	Irish Gaelic: cub
QUILLER	Middle English: a writer
QUILLON	Latin: a sword
QUIMBY	Scandinavian: from the woman's cottage
QUINCY	French/Latin: from the place of the fifth son
QUINN	Irish Gaelic: wise

R

RAD	Old English: counselor
RADLEY	Old English: red pasture meadow
RADNOR	Old Enlgish: at the red shore
RADOLF	Old English: swift wolf
RAFFERTY	Irish Gaelic: prosperous and rich

RALEIGH	Old English: dweller at the roe-deer meadow
	RAWLEY
RALPH	Anglo-Saxon: wolf counsel
	RANDOLPH, RANDOLF, RANDO, RANDALL, RANDAL, RANDLE, RANDY, RAND, RANNIE, RANNY, RAN, ROLFE, ROLF, RALF, RAFE, RAOUL
RALSTON	Old English: from Ralph's farm
RAMSEY	Teutonic: from Raven's island
RANCE	French: the bitter
RANGER	Teutonic: a forest ranger
	RAINGER
RANSOM	Old English: son of shield
RAPHAEL	Hebrew: healed by God
	RAFF, RAFE, RAFAELLE
RAY	Old French: the radiant
RAYMOND	Old German: mighty
	RAMON, RAYMUND, RAIMOND, RAYMENT
REDMAN	Old English: counsel man
	REDMOND, REDMUND
REECE	Welsh: a chief
	RACE, REESE, RICE, REES
REEVE	Middle English: steward
	REEVES, REAVE
REGAN	Latin: regal
	REGIS, REX, REGGIE, REGEN
REGINALD	Old High German: strong ruler
	RENAULT, REYNOLDS, REGGIE, RANNIE, RAYNOLD, RENAUD
REINOLF	Teutonic: wolf brave
REMINGTON	Old English: from the raven-family estate
REMUS	Latin: speedy motion
	REMY
REUBEN	Hebrew: behold a son
	RUBEN, RUBE
REUEL	Hebrew: God is his friend
REX	Latin: king
REYNARD	Old High German: strong counsel
	RAYNARD, RAYNOR, RAINER, REYNOR, NARDO, REGGIE, REINEKE, RENKE
RICHARD	Old German: powerful ruler
	RITCH, RICH, RICK, DICKEN, DICK, DICKIE, RIIKARD, RITCHIE, DICKS, RIX, RICKER
RIDER	Anglo-Saxon: horseman
	RYDER

RILEY	Old English: warlike one RYLEY, REILLY
RING	Danish: to sound clearly RINGE, RINGO
RIPLEY	Anglo-Saxon: dweller at the shouter's meadow
ROAN	North English: dweller by the rowan-tree Spanish: reddish-brown ROANER
ROARKE	Teutonic: of strong fame ROARK, RUARK
ROBERT	Old High German: bright in fame BOB, BOBBY, ROB, ROBB, ROBBY, ROBIN, RUPERT, ROBINET, ROBSON, ROBBINS, HOBBS, DOBBS, RABBIE, ROBERS, ROBERTO, RUPRECHT, POP, POPKIN, DOBBIN, NOBBY, NOB, NODDY, NOD, ROD
RODERICK	Old German: rich in fame BRODERICK, RODRICK, ROD
ROGER	Old High German: famous spearman RODGER, HODGES, HODGKIN, RODGE
ROLAND	German: fame of the land ROLLAN, ROLLIN, ROLLO, ROLLY
ROLPH	(Contraction of Ralph, Rudolph, etc.) ROLFE, ROLF
ROLT	Old German: famous power
ROMEO	Latin: a Roman ROMER, ROMULUS, ROMANY
RONAN	Irish Gaelic: little seal
RONSON	Old English: son of mighty power
ROONEY	Irish Gaelic: red one
ROPER	Old English: rope maker
RORY	Irish Gaelic: red king RORIE
ROSCOE	Teutonic: swift horse
ROXBURY	Old English: from Rook's fortress
ROY	Latin: king
ROYAL	French/Latin: the kingly RYLE, RYALL, ROYLE
ROYCE	Old English: son of the king
ROYD	Scandinavian: from the forest
ROYDEN	Latin-English: from the king's valley
RUCK	Old English: rook-bird

RUDOLPH	Old High German: glory wolf RUDOLF, ROLFE, DOLPH, RUDIE, RUDY
RUFUS	Latin: the red-haired RUFE, RUFF
RUSSELL	Latin: rusty-haired RUSS, RUSTY, RUSKIN, RUSH
RUTLEDGE	Old English: from the red pool
RYAN	Irish Gaelic: little king
RYLAN	Old English: dweller at the rye land
RYLE	Old English: from the rye hill

S

SABAS	Hebrew: rest, Sunday SABBA
SABER	French: sword SABRE, SABE
SACHEVERELL	French: a true saxon SACH, SACHA, SACHIE, SASCHA
SADLER	English: a harness maker
SAMPSON	Hebrew: sun's man SAMSON, SHIM, SIMPSON, SIM, SIMPKIN, SAM, SAMMIE
SAMUEL	Hebrew: His name is God SAMMEL, SHEM, SAM, SAMMY
SANDERS	Middle English: son of Alexander SANDIE, SANDY, SAUNDERS, SANDERSON
SANTO	Latin: saintly
SARGENT	Old French: officer SARGE, SARGIE, SERGEANT
SAUL	Hebrew: the longed for SOL, SOLLY
SAVILLE	French/Latin: from the place of the willows
SAWNEY	(Scottish diminutives of Alexander) SAWNIE, SAWNY
SAWYER	Middle English: a sawer of wood
SAXON	Teutonic: of the sword-people SAX, SAXE, SAXTON, SAXO
SAYER	Welsh/Cornish: carpenter SAYERS, SAYRES, SAYRE

SCANLON	Irish Gaelic: a little scandal
SCIPIO	Latin: a staff
	SKIP, SKIPPY, SKIPPER
SCOTT	Old English: from Scotland
	SCOTTIE, SCOTTY, SCOT
SCULLY	Irish Gaelic: town crier
SEABERT	Old English: sea glorious
	SEABRIGHT, SEAVER
SEBASTIAN	Latin: the reverenced
	BASTIAN, BASS, BASTO, SEB
SEDGWICK	Old English: from the village by the sedge
SEELEY	Old English: happy, blessed
SEGER	Old English: sea warrior
	SEAGER
SEIF	Arabic: sacred sword
SELDEN	Teutonic: from the manor valley
	SELDON
SERGE	Latin: to serve
SETH	Hebrew: the appointed
SHADWELL	Old English: from the arbor-spring
SHANAHAN	Irish Gaelic: wise one
SHANDY	Anglo-Saxon: the boisterous
SHANNON	Irish Gaelic: little old wise one
SHATTUCK	Middle English: little shad-fish
SHEEHAN	Irish Gaelic: little peaceful one
SHEPHERD	Old English: a tender of sheep
	SHEP, SHEPP, SHEPPY
SHERIDAN	Irish Gaelic: wild man
SHERLOCK	Old English: fair-haired
SHERRIFF	Middle English: a sheriff
SHERWOOD	Old English: bright forest
SHIELD	Middle English: a shield
SHOLTO	Celtic: the dark
SIDNEY	Phoenician: the enchanter
	SYDNEY, SID
SIGFRID	German: victory peace
	SIEGFRIED
SIGMUND	Old German: victorious protector
	SIGISMUND, ZIGMOND, ZIGMON, ZIGGY, SIGGY
SIGRID	Teutonic: war counsel
SIGURD	Old Norse: victorious guardian

SILAS	English: of the forest (form of the Latin Silvester)
	SILVANUS, SILVESTER, SYLVANUS, SYLVESTER, SILVERIUS, SYLVAN, SIL, VEST, SILVIO, SILVAIN, SILVESTRO
SIMON	Hebrew: the hearing
SINCLAIR	French: the sanctified (contraction of Saint Claire)
SKEET	Middle English: swift one
	SKEETS, SKEETER
SKIPP	Old Norse: ship owner
	SKIP, SKIPPY, SKIPPER
SLADE	Old English: dweller in the valley
SLAVIN	Irish Gaelic: mountaineer
	SLAVEN
SLOAN	Celtic: a warrior
	SLOANE
SMEDLEY	Old English: from the flat meadow
SNOWDEN	Old English: from the snowy hill
SOLOMON	Hebrew: peaceful
	SOL, SOLLIE, SOLLY
SOLON	Greek: wisdom
SOLVAR	Teutonic: well warrior
SOMERSET	Old French: to leap over
SOMERTON	Old English: from the summer estate
SOMMERVILLE	Old Franco-German: from the summer estate
SORRELL	Old French: reddish-brown
SPANGLER	Old French: one who glitters
SPARK	Middle English: gay, gallant one
	SPARKY, SPARKLER, SPARKIE
SPEED	Anglo-Saxon: success, swiftness
SPENSER	Old French: storekeeper
	SPENCE, SPENCER
SQUIRE	Latin: a shield bearer
ST. JOHN	Latin: Saint John
	SINJUN, SINJON, SAINT JOHN
STACEY	Middle Latin: stable, prosperous
	STACY, STACIE
STAFFORD	Old English: from the landing ford
STANDISH	Old English: from the stony pen
STANHOPE	Old English: from the stony marshland

STANISLAUS	Slavonic: glory of the Slavs
	STAN, STANISLAV, STANISLAS
STANLEY	Old English: from the stony meadow
	STANLY, STANLEIGH, STAN, STANNIE
STARLING	Latin: a "bird" name
STARR	Middle English: star
STEPHEN	Greek: crowned one
	STEVE, STEVIE, STEVEN, STEFFEN, STEFANO, STEFFEL, STEFAN, STEPKA
STERLING	Teutonic: the genuine
	STIRLING
STEWART	Old English: steward of the estate
	STU, STEW, STUART
STOKE	Middle English: village
STORM	Old English: the tempest
	STURM, STORMR
STORR	Old Norse: great one
STRAHAN	Irish Gaelic: poet, wise man
SUMNER	Old French/Latin: one who summons
SWAIN	Middle English: herdsman
	SWAYN, SWAYNE, SWALES, SWALEY, SWALE
SWEENEY	Irish Gaelic: little hero
SWINTON	Old English: dweller at the swine farm
SYNGE	Anglo-Saxon: a song

T

TABB	Gaelic: a well-spring
	TAB, TABBY
TABER	Middle English: drum beater
	TABOR
TADD	Old Welsh: father
	TAD
TAGGART	Irish Gaelic: the shaggy haired
	TAGGARD
TALBOT	Old French: pillager
TALLY	Persian: the learned and wise
TAMMANY	Aramaic: a twin (through Thomas)
TANCRED	Middle French: a tankard bearer
	TANKRED

TARLETON	Old English: thunder ruler's estate
TARRANT	Old Welsh: thunder
TATE	Anglo-Saxon: the cheerful
TAVIS	Celtic: David's son TAVIDS, TAVES, TAVISH
TAYLOR	French/Latin: a tailor
TEAGUE	Celtic: a poet
TED	(diminutive of Edward/Theodore) TEDDIE, TEDDY
TEMPLE	Anglo-Saxon: a temple
TEMPLETON	Old English: temple town
TENNANT	Old English: one who lives on the land
TENNYSON	Middle English: son of Dennis
TERENCE	Latin: the smooth, tender TERRY, TERRENCE, TORRANCE, TORREY, TOREY, TERRISS, TERRIS
TERRELL	Old English: thunder ruler TERREL, TERRY, TERRYL
TEVIS	Scottish: the quick tempered
THADDEUS	Hebrew: praising God THAD, TADDY, TAD, THADDY
THANE	Old English: warrior attendant THAINE, THAYNE
THATCHER	Middle English: a roofer THACHER, THAXTER, THACKERAY, THATCH
THAYER	Teutonic: animated
THEODORE	Greek: gift of God TEODOR, TUDOR, TEDDY, TEDDIE
THEODORIC	Old German: ruler of the people TED, TEDDIE, RICK, DEREK, DERK, DERRICK, DIETRICH, TEDRIC, DIDRIK, DIRK
THERON	Greek: godly or hunter
THOMAS	Aramaic: a twin TOM, TOMMIE, TOMMY, TAMMEN, TAMMANY, THOMKIN, MAZO
THOR	Old Norse: thunder TOR, THORR, THORD
THORN	Anglo-Saxon: the hawthorn THORNE, THORNY
THORNDYKE	Old English: from the thorny dike
THORNHILL	Old English: from the thorny hill
THRALL	Middle English: one held in bondage
TIMON	Greek: honor, reward

TIMOTHY	Greek: honoring god
	TIM, TIMMIE, TIMMY, TIMPKIN, TIMOTH, TIMEEN
TIREY	Anglo-Saxon: the weary
TITUS	Greek: of the giants
TOBIAS	Hebrew: the Lord is God
	TOBE, TOBY, TOBIE, TOBIT, TOBIAH
TODD	North English: a fox
TOLER	Middle English: a toll taker
TOMKIN	Old English: little Tom
TONA	Nahuatl (Aztec Indian): sun god
TORBERT	Teutonic: Thor bright
TOREY	Anglo-Saxon: the towering
	TORREY, TORRY, TORR, TORRANCE
TOWNSEND	Middle English: from the town's end
TRACY	Latin: bold, courageous
	TRACE, TRACEY
TRAHERN	Latin: iron strong
TRAVERS	Old French: from the crossroad
	TRAVIS
TREMAYNE	Celtic: from the town of the stone
	TREMAIN
TRENT	Welsh: torrent, rapid stream
TREVELYAN	Latin: a horseman
	TREV, CAVALIER
TREVOR	Celtic: the prudent
	TREV, TREFOR
TRIGG	Old Norse: true, trusty one
TRIPP	Middle English: a traveler
TRISTAN	Latin: the sorrowing
	TRISTRAM, TRISTREM, TRYSTAN
TROWBRIDGE	Old English: dweller by the tree bridge
TRUESDALE	Old English: from the beloved one's farmstead
	TRUE
TUCKER	Middle English: a tucker of cloth
TUDOR	Old Welsh: (diminutive of Theodore)
TULLY	Irish Gaelic: people mighty
	TULLIUS, TULLIO, TULIE
TUPPER	Old English: a ram (sheep) raiser
TYBALT	Old German: people's prince
	TYBALD, TEDDY, TY

TYE   Anglo-Saxon: a tie or binding
       TIGHE

TYRONE   Greek: Lord
       TYRRELL

TYRUS   Greek: of Tyre (Lord)

u

UDOLPH   Teutonic: fortunate, noble wolf

ULAND   Teutonic: from the noble land

ULF   German: wolf

ULFRED   Old English: wolf peace

ULICK   Teutonic: mind reward

ULRIC   Old German: wolf ruler

ULYSSES   Greek: I hate
       ULIX, ULISSE

UNO   Latin: the˙one

URIAH   Hebrew: my light is Jehovah
       URIAS

URIAN   Greek: the heavenly
       URANUS, URIEN, URE, UREY

UZZIAH   Hebrew: might of the Lord

v

VAIL   Middle English: valley dweller
       VALE

VAL   Teutonic: power
       VALD

VALDEMAR   Old German: famous ruler

VALDIS   Old Norse: destructive in battle

VALENTINE   Latin: strong, valorous, healthy
       VALIANT, VALENTE, VALENTINE, VALENTINO,
       VALENTINUS, VALENS, VALENCIA, VALENCE

VALERIAN   Latin: to be strong
       VALERIUS, VALERIO, VALERIOS, VALERY

VAN	Dutch: of the
	VAN, VANNY
VANCE	Dutch: Van's son
VARDEN	French-Celtic: from the green valley
	VARDON
VARIAN	Latin: the changeable
VARICK	Icelandic: sea drifter
	VARECK
VARLEY	Old French: a young knight or valet
VARNE	Old French: bringer of victory (masculine of Veronica)
	VARNEY
VAUGHN	Celtic: the little
VERRILL	Old French: true one
	VERRALL
VICTOR	Latin: a conqueror
	VIC, VICK, VITTORIO
VINCENT	Latin: to conquer
	VINCE, VINN, VIN, VINT, VINCENS, VINCENZ, VINCENTE
VIRGIL	Latin: the unbloomed, virginal
VITO	Latin: life
	VITUS, VITALIS
VLADIMIR	Slavic: world prince, glory of princes
VLADISLAV	Slavic: glory of the slavs
VOLNEY	Teutonic: of the people

WACE	Anglo-Saxon: the watchful
	WAKE
WADE	Teutonic: one who moves forward
WAINWRIGHT	Teutonic: a maker of wagons
	WAINE, WAYNE
WAKEFIELD	Old English: from the field of Wace
WALDEMAR	Teutonic: the powerful and famed
	VALDEMAR
WALDO	Old High German: to wield
WALKER	Anglo-Saxon: a fuller of cloth

WALLACE	German: a man from Wales
	WALLIE, WALLY, WALSH, WELSH, WELCH
WALTER	Old High German: ruling the host
	WALT, WATKINS, WATSON
WARBURTON	Teutonic: bright in war
WARD	Old English: watchman, guardian
WARFIELD	Old English: from the war field
WASHBURN	Old English: dweller at the flooding-brook
	WASH
WASHINGTON	Old English: from the washing place
WENZEL	Czech: to know
WESLEY	Old English: from the West meadow
	WESTLEIGH, WESTLEY, WEST, WES
WHEELER	Old English: wheel-maker
WHISTLER	Old English: one who whistles
WHITELAW	Old English: from the white hill
WICKHAM	Middle English: from the willow hamlet
WICKWARE	Anglo-Saxon: village guard
WILBERFORCE	Teutonic: of bright reserve
WILE	Teutonic: beguiling
	WYLE, WYLIE, WYLEY, WILEY
WILKES	Middle English: the welkin (sky)
	WILKE, WELKIE
WILLIAM	Old High German: resolute protector
	WILLET, WILL, WILLY, WILLIE, BILL, BILLY, BILLIE, WILKIN, WILHELM, WILLETS, WYLLIS, WILLANS, WILEY
WILLOUGHBY	Old English: from the willow farm
WILMOT	Teutonic: dear heart
WINCHESTER	Celtic: from the friendly camp
WINDSOR	Teutonic: from the river bend
WINFIELD	Teutonic: from the friendly field
WINGATE	Teutonic: friendly, guard
	WINGARD
WINSTON	Old English: friend's town
WINTHROP	Teutonic: from the friendly village
WITT	Anglo-Saxon: action of mind
	WYTE
WOLFE	Teutonic: wolf
	WOLF, WOOLF, WOLFF, WOULFF
WOLFGANG	Teutonic: wolf gone
WOLFRAM	Teutonic: wolf raven